17.—
HI

SEP - 2004

Hooker, Virginia Matheson, 1946-
A short history of Malaysia
959.5 HOO

A SHORT HISTORY OF

MALAYSIA

Short History of Asia Series

Series Editor: Milton Osborne

Milton Osborne has had an association with the Asian region for over 40 years as an academic, public servant and independent writer. He is the author of eight books on Asian topics, including *Southeast Asia: An Introductory History*, first published in 1979 and now in its eighth edition, and, most recently, *The Mekong: Turbulent Past, Uncertain Future*, published in 2000.

A SHORT HISTORY OF

MALAYSIA

LINKING EAST AND WEST

Virginia Matheson Hooker

ALLEN&UNWIN

First published in 2003 by Allen & Unwin

Copyright © Virginia Matheson Hooker 2003
Maps by Ian Faulkner

All rights reserved. No part of this book may be reproduced or transmitted in any form or by any means, electronic or mechanical, including photocopying, recording or by any information storage and retrieval system, without prior permission in writing from the publisher. The *Australian Copyright Act 1968* (the Act) allows a maximum of one chapter or 10 per cent of this book, whichever is the greater, to be photocopied by any educational institution for its educational purposes provided that the educational institution (or body that administers it) has given a remuneration notice to Copyright Agency Limited (CAL) under the Act.

Allen & Unwin
83 Alexander Street
Crows Nest NSW 2065
Australia
Phone: (61 2) 8425 0100
Fax: (61 2) 9906 2218
Email: info@allenandunwin.com
Web: www.allenandunwin.com

National Library of Australia
Cataloguing-in-Publication entry:

   Hooker, Virginia Matheson, 1946- .
   Short History of Malaysia : linking east and west.

   Includes index.
   ISBN 1 86448 955 3

   1. Malaysia – History. I. Title.

   959.5

Set in 11/14 pt Goudy by Midland Typesetters, Maryborough, Victoria
Printed by South Wind Production, Singapore

10 9 8 7 6 5 4 3 2 1

FRANKLIN TOWNSHIP PU   LIBRARY
        485 De MOTT LANE
      SOMERSET, NJ 08873
          732-873-8700

*For Max, Elizabeth and Jamie
And in memory of John Iremonger*

CONTENTS

Acknowledgments

In writing this book I have turned to a number of colleagues for advice and assistance. They have been generous with their time and knowledge in suggesting references and checking details. Particular thanks are due to Professor Geoffrey Benjamin, Professor Peter Bellwood, Dr John Funston, Dr David Bulbeck and Professor Clive Kessler. I alone bear responsibility for the narrative in the text.

Other colleagues have contributed a great deal and I extend warm thanks to each of the following: Diana Carroll, Hugh Hickling, M.B. Hooker, Deborah Johnson, Amrita Malhi and Anthony Milner. The Malaysian High Commission in Canberra supplied recent data and statistics, the National Archives of Malaysia allowed me to consult their photographic collection and the staff of the National Library of Australia and of the Menzies Library, the Australian National University were most helpful. Rebecca Kaiser and Claire Murdoch of Allen & Unwin were exemplary publishing colleagues with whom it was indeed a pleasure to work.

Some financial support towards realisation of this project was provided by the Australian Research Council's Small Grants Scheme (1999) and by the Faculty of Asian Studies, the Australian National University. Their contribution is gratefully acknowledged.

It remains to extend my special appreciation to the Series Editor, Milton Osborne, and John Iremonger, whose informed and intelligent comments shaped the book's final form.

Preface

As a modern nation state, Malaysia is not very old, but some of the oldest known human remains and artefacts have been found within its present borders. It is a multiracial federation formed without revolution and, although its territory is divided by the South China Sea and organised into 13 states and two federal territories, it has remained intact and weathered the economic upheavals of the late 20th century better than many of its neighbours. Among its successes may be counted the construction of a national history developed by successive governments to teach Malysian citizens and others about the formation of their modern nation state.

This book acknowledges the official version but it includes other histories as well. Each of Malaysia's constituent states has its own rich local traditions and celebrates individuals who have influenced the course of events in their own time and place. The national history and the local histories together are crucial for an understanding of the nature of modern Malaysia. A short history is necessarily selective and this one has the perspective of hindsight (knowing the outcome of critical events) and emphasises the contribution a variety of individuals have made to their societies and peoples. In this way it is hoped to give the general reader a real taste of the flavour of the Malaysian experience.

A 'short' history might suggest that it is possible to present a survey of events from 40 000 BCE to the early 21st century as a compact and neat package. To do so would be misleading because history is never neat and the federation which is now known as Malaysia was, until 1963, a fluid and bureaucratically untidy conglomeration of disparate and very varied parts. This book does not pretend Malaysia's past was neat but tries to describe the essential characteristics of its component parts and the experiences which have produced its present shape.

Experts will note how much detail has had to be omitted. Selection has been the most challenging task in writing this book. Hopefully the **bibliographic essay** on page 299 will encourage and stimulate readers to go on to more detailed and specialised works, of which there are now, thankfully, many.

Some of the complexity of Malaysia's past is reflected in the various changes of name which, like its neighbour Indonesia, it has borne. In this account, the phrase 'the Malaysian territories' is used to refer to Sabah, Sarawak, Singapore, the Riau islands and the Malay Peninsula before 1965. Thereafter, the practice followed by the Malaysian government since 1971 will apply; that is, peninsular Malaysia, Sabah and Sarawak.

Note to readers

Readers may find the **Time chart** helpful to establish the dates of 'significant moments' in Malaysia's past.

The skeleton of the time chart is fleshed out by the **Fact file**, which is organised alphabetically by subject or event (Independence, political parties, currency, etc) followed by a brief factual description. It is here that one would look for details of Malaysia's constituent states or the date of the National Day, for example. Translations of Malay words are contained in the **Glossary**. Acronyms and abbreviations have a separate listing under **Abbreviations**.

A series of maps, ranging over time as well as space, gives a graphic impression of locations as well as indicating how outsiders perceived the seas and coasts of the region. They also show vividly that the mapping of the interior and inland regions was slow, gradual, inaccurate and, until last century, incomplete. For this reason, it was only relatively recently that Europeans gained a composite picture of the complexity of the terrain and interior of the Peninsula and Borneo.

Sources

A short history is not a work of new research but draws on existing, published material. The full **bibliography** at the end of the book includes all works consulted during the preparation of the history. Notes for each chapter at the end of the book indicate the sources of direct quotations. A **bibliographic essay** lists the main sources for individual chapters and suggests some futher reading for those wishing to follow up particular areas or topics. Many primary sources (Malay manuscripts, official colonial records, travellers' accounts, court records, Malaysian government records, memoirs of Malaysians and non-Malaysians) have been either published or integrated into published analyses and translated into English, and so are available to non-Malay speakers. Malaysians themselves have been actively writing about their past since the days of the Melaka sultanate (15th and 16th centuries CE) and wherever possible I have drawn on those invaluable resources.

It is easy to overlook the fact that not all records about the past are in the form of 'official' documents. Evidence comes also from archaeology, reconstructing older forms of languages to try and establish core vocabularies to learn what they reveal about lifestyles, anthropology and so on. Each of these sources has something to contribute to the picture of Malaysia's past. And there are further sources which have not yet been fully exploited. All cultures in the Malaysian territories are rich in oral traditions. Customs, laws, wise sayings, prayers, agricultural practices, forest lore, navigational methods and guides, origin stories and cautionary tales used to be an integral part of daily life. Only a fraction of this material has been recorded and published. One of the casualties of modernity is the loss of communal memory and individual knowledge of oral traditions. Some attempts, both within and outside Malaysia, are being made to preserve this specialist knowledge. Much of it is recognised as 'scientifically' accurate, but a great deal has already been lost. The renewed interest by young Malaysians in their heritage provides hope for the future.

Abbreviations

ABIM	*Angkatan Belia Islam Malaysia* (Islamic Youth Movement Malaysia)
ASEAN	Association of Southeast Asian Nations
BA	*Barisan Alternatif* (Alternative Front)
BN	*Barisan Nasional* (National Front)
BCE	Before Common Era, used in preference to BC (Before Christ)
Berjaya	*Bersatu Rakyat Jelata Sabah* (Sabah United People's Party)
CE	Common Era, used in preference to AD (Anno Domini)
CPM	Communist Party of Malaya
DAP	Democratic Action Party
DO	District Officer
EIC	East India Company (British)
ESI	English Speaking Intellectuals
FELDA	Federal Land Development Authority
FMS	Federated Malay States
Gerakan	*Gerakan Rakyat Malaysia* (Malaysian People's Movement)
IMP	Independence of Malaya Party
ISA	Internal Security Act
JHEOA	*Jabatan Hal Ehwal Orang Asli* (Department of Orang Asli Affairs)
keADILan	Parti keADILan Nasional (National Justice Party)
KMM	*Kesatuan Melayu Muda* (Union of Malay Youth)
KMT	Kuomintang
MAS	Malay Administrative Service (for Malays only)
MCA	Malayan Chinese Association
MCP	Malayan Communist Party
MCS	Malayan Civil Service (for British cadets only)
MIC	Malayan Indian Congress

MNP	Malay Nationalist Party
MRLA	Malayan Races Liberation Army
MPAJA	Malayan People's Anti-Japanese Army
MSC	Multimedia Super Corridor
NCC	National Consultative Committee
NDP	National Development Policy
NEP	New Economic Policy
NOC	National Operations Council
PAP	People's Action Party
PAS	Malay acronym for *Persatuan Islam SaTanah Melayu* which changed its name in 1973 to *Parti Islam Se Malaysia* (Pan-Malayan Islamic Party) but retained PAS as its abbreviated form.
PBS	*Parti Bersatu Sabah* (United Sabah Party)
PERNAS	*Pertubuhan Nasional*, National Development Corporation
PESAKA	*Party Pesaka Anak Sarawak* (Party of native born Sarawakians)
PKI	*Partai Komunis Indonesia*, Indonesian Communist Party
PMIP	See PAS
POASM	*Persatuan Orang Asli Semenanjung Malaysia* (Malay Peninsula *Orang Asli* Association)
PRM	*Parti Rakyat Malaysia* (Malaysian People's Party)
PTA	*Pembela Tanah Air* (Defenders of the Homeland)
SCO	Sarawak Communist Organisation
SEMARAK	*Setia Bersama Rakyat*, Loyalty with the People
SNAP	Sarawak National Party
SUPP	Sarawak United People's Party
UMNO	United Malays National Organisation
UMS	Unfederated Malay States
USNO	United Sabah National Organisation
VOC	Vereenigde Oostindische Compagnie (United Netherlands Chartered East India Company)

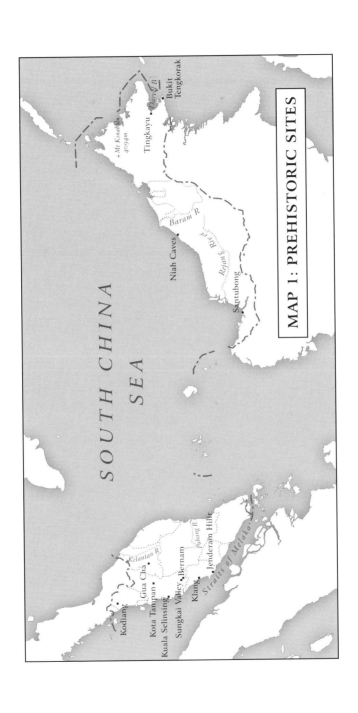

MAP 1: PREHISTORIC SITES

SOUTH CHINA SEA

+ Mt Kinabalu 4094m

Tingkayu

Bukit B.

Bukit Tengkorak

Baram R

Rejan River

Niah Caves

Santubong

Kelantan R

Gua Cha

Pahang R

Bernam

Kota Tampan

Sungkai Valley

Klang

Jenderam Hilir

Kuala Selinsing

Straits of Melaka

Kodiang

MAP 2: EARLY TRADE NETWORKS

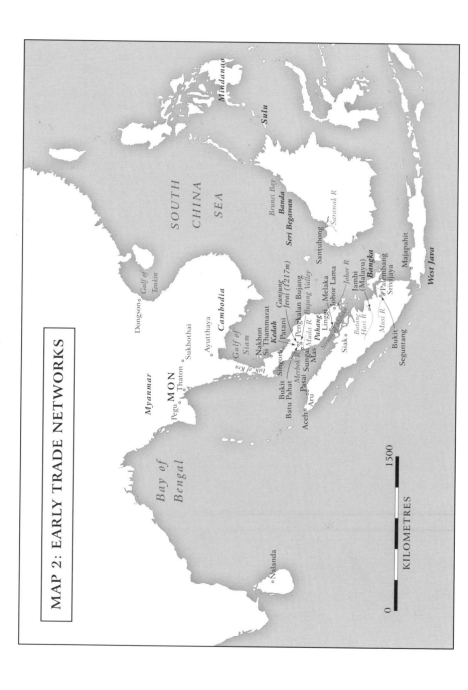

Nalanda

Bay of Bengal

Myanmar

Pegu
Thaton
MON

Sukhothai
Ayutthaya

Cambodia

Dongson

Gulf of Tonkin

SOUTH CHINA SEA

Mindanao

Sulu

Brunei Bay
Banda
Seri Begawan

Santubong

Sarawak R

Gulf of Siam

Isth. of Kra

Nakhon Si Thammarat
Kedah
Singora/Patani
Gunung Jerai (1217m)
Pengkalan Bujang
Bukit
Merbok
Batu Pahat
Pasai
Sungai Muda R
Bujang Valley
Pahang
Mas
Aceh
Aru
Slining R
Lingga
Melaka
Johor Lama
Johor R

Siak
Jambi
(Malayu)
Batang Hari R

Bangka

Musi R
Palembang
Srivijaya
Majapahit

Bukit Seguntang

West Java

KILOMETRES
0   1500

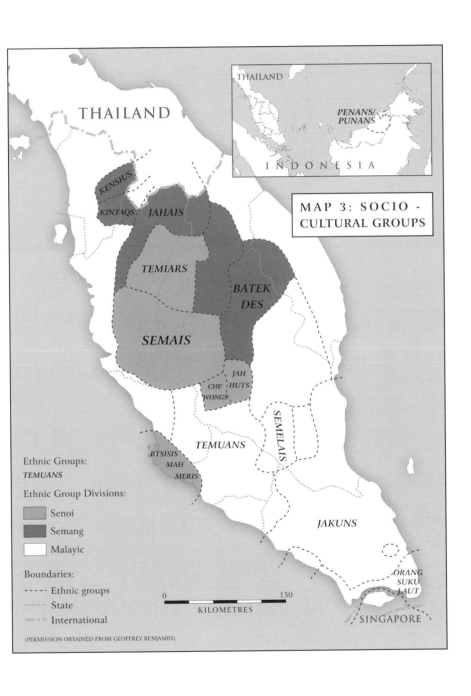

THAILAND

THAILAND

PENANS/
PUNANS

I N D O N E S I A

MAP 3: SOCIO -
CULTURAL GROUPS

KENSIUS

KINTAQS

JAHAIS

TEMIARS

BATEK
DES

SEMAIS

JAH
CHE HUTS
WONGS

SEMELAIS

TEMUANS

BTSISIS
MAH
MERIS

JAKUNS

ORANG
SUKU
LAUT

SINGAPORE

Ethnic Groups:
TEMUANS

Ethnic Group Divisions:

Senoi

Semang

Malayic

Boundaries:
- - - - Ethnic groups
· · · · · · State
— · — · International

0   150
KILOMETRES

(PERMISSION OBTAINED FROM GEOFFREY BENJAMIN)

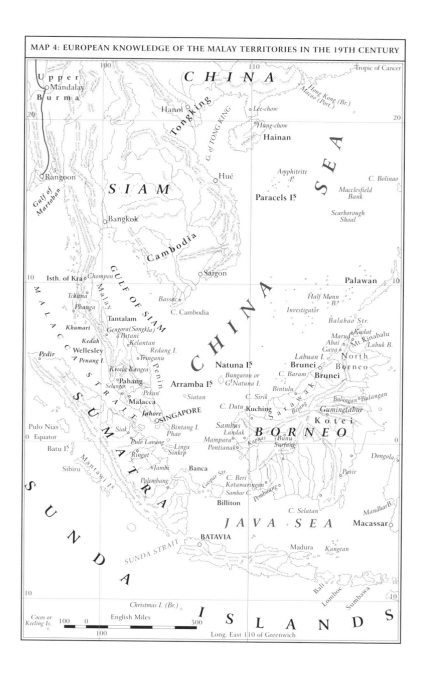

MAP 4: EUROPEAN KNOWLEDGE OF THE MALAY TERRITORIES IN THE 19TH CENTURY

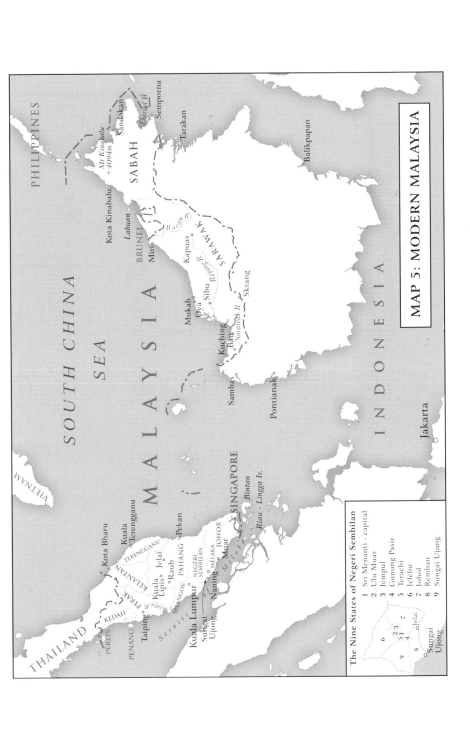

MAP 5: MODERN MALAYSIA

The Nine States of Negeri Sembilan

1 Sri Menanti - capital
2 Ulu Muar
3 Jempul
4 Gunung Pasir
5 Terachi
6 Jelebu
7 Johol
8 Rembau
9 Sungai Ujung

1
MALAYSIA AS HISTORY

History is the root of nationalism.
Guide to the Museums of Melaka[1]

Malaysia has a new image. The sleepy tropical backwater stereotyped in the novels of Anthony Burgess and Somerset Maugham's short stories has been superseded by Malaysia the high-tech urbanised regional powerbroker. The world began to notice when, in September 1998, Malaysia hosted the XVI Commonwealth Games, the first Asian country to do so. The government of Malaysia used the event to focus international attention on the small nation and chose carefully the image it wished to project to the world. In the decade leading up to the Games, Malaysia had experienced boom conditions and its prime minister, Dr Mahathir Mohamad, had propelled the nation into the forefront of technological development by completing the tallest buildings in the world (the 451.9-metre Petronas Twin Towers in the federal capital, Kuala Lumpur), initiating a Multimedia Super Corridor, a futuristic satellite capital, a state of the art international airport and a

Light Rail Transit (LRT) system designed to alleviate traffic congestion on the new super highways and toll roads built during the 1980s. In the midst of this technological upgrading, the government was also attending to the presentation of the past and a new-look Museum of National History was opened in time for the Games.

It is important to note that this new museum was part of the Games build-up because it is an indication of the importance the government attaches to the role of history in its depiction of Malaysia as an Asian nation which is modern and technologically advanced. The purpose of this public presentation of history is to emphasise the glorious achievements of the past in order to inspire today's Malaysians to re-establish that glory in the present. Significantly, the Museum of National History is located in an old colonial building at the northern end of Dataran Merdeka (Independence Square), in the heart of Kuala Lumpur and near the site of the Declaration of Independence in 1957, to emphasise its central role in national culture.

In its presentation of history in the museum, the Malaysian government wants to reach as many people as possible—its own citizens as well as visitors—so captions are in both English and Malay. The selection of the events and people of the past for inclusion in the museum and the subtle emphasis given to some periods is revealing about the kind of history the government wants to promote. It is this version of the nation's past which shapes school curricula, tourist brochures and postcards and is evident also in the choice of street names, buildings and public monuments. This is the 'official' version of Malaysian history and it provides the framework for the way most Malaysians understand their own history. For that reason this book begins with a summary of the main points in the display of the Museum of National History to try and understand the view of the past that Malaysians themselves learn. But there is one important issue which is not addressed in the official version of history in the museum—the idea of change. We might ask, for example, how were diverse populations of specialised traders, rice-growing peasants and fisher-people, experienced entrepreneurs and the aristocratic members of extended royal courts persuaded to give their allegiance to a new over-arching entity called 'Malaysia'? Why were the present political boundaries established when there are a number of alternative possibilities? Another interesting question is why Islam is so influential in contemporary Malaysian politics when it is the religion of little more than half the population (unlike Indonesia, where it is clearly the predominant religion). Although these questions are not answered by the 'official' version of history they will be addressed in this short history.

The official version

For the purposes of its national history, the government has defined Malaysia as the territory occupied by its modern component states; that is, the Peninsula and Sabah and Sarawak, with Singapore being included in events which occurred before 1965. 'History' in the Museum of National History, is interpreted as any event, person, or artefact which provides evidence of Malay or Malaysian achievement and 'progress'. For the period of British government, the museum focuses on individuals or movements which resisted this colonial 'intrusion' into Malaya.

The ground floor of the museum is devoted to the pre-history of the territories of modern Malaysia. Exhibits begin with the 'Natural Environment and Prehistoric Era' which show the geological formation of the Peninsula, Sabah and Sarawak to emphasise that the territory now called Malaysia is one of great antiquity. There are displays also of human bones from the Niah caves near Kuching in Sarawak, stone tools from Kota Tampan in Perak and Tingkayu in Sabah, whose dates range from 38 000 to 18 000 years ago. They provide evidence for human occupation of the Malaysian territories during the Palaeolithic period (see map 1, page xv).

The Neolithic period (2800 to 500 BCE) is represented in the museum by exhibits of pottery and stone objects from both the Peninsula and Borneo. At that time earthenware vessels were used for food and drink and also as burial items in graves. Relatively few iron and bronze artefacts have been found in Malaysia but most have been linked with the most famous Bronze Age culture in Southeast Asia, known as the 'Dongson'. Named after a site in North Vietnam, the culture flourished around 500 to 300 BCE and produced intricately ornate bronze objects, including large drums, produced by the 'lost wax' method of casting. The museum has five of these drums on display, some dating back to the second century BCE, to indicate that the territories of Malaysia participated in this highly regarded and advanced metal-age culture.

Evidence of contact between Malaysia and centres of other major world civilisations is provided by the next set of displays which use first century Chinese sources to show that during that period there were settlements in the Bujang Valley (Kedah) and in Santubong (Sarawak) (see map 2, page xvi). Captions inform visitors that trade relations existed also between Malaysia and India and that the traders were Chinese, Indians and Arabs. There is also a special section devoted to 'Megalithic Culture' which refers to locations of megaliths (giant carved stones) in the Peninsula, Sabah and Sarawak. Visitors are told that although these sites seem to have been contemporary with the early settlements in the Bujang Valley where Hindu–Buddhist temples have been found, the people associated with the megaliths must have practised a different religion. The display notes: 'The situation shows the existence of a diversity of concurrent ways of life in Malaysia'—a theme the Malaysian government emphasises continually in its domestic policies.

The Hindu–Buddhist period is represented by models of the 7th or 8th century temple-remains in the Bujang Valley. The captions stress that the area was a centre for international trade and shipping passing through the Straits of Melaka. Considerable attention is devoted to the next phase of history which is called 'Srivijayan Culture' from the name of a Sumatran-based maritime kingdom active between the 7th and 12th centuries. Srivijaya had close links with both China and India and was a centre of Buddhist learning. Captions note that the temple-remains in Kedah resemble structures and objects found in Sumatra, southern Siam and Sarawak (Santubong) which were once under the influence of Srivijaya. This kingdom was a focus, it is explained, for traders from Egypt, Persia and China, thus emphasising that settlements in Malaysia during this period were part of a very wide network. It is significant to note that neither the Peninsula nor Sarawak is said to have been *ruled* by Srivijaya, rather that there are historical remains which show Srivijaya's 'influence'.

'The Spread of Islam' is the title of the next series of displays and a map with flashing lights tracks the course of Islam through and across the Southeast Asian region. Associated with the map is a replica of the famous 'Terengganu Stone', an inscribed pillar which bears a date equivalent to 1303 CE. The pillar's inscription is in Malay written with the Arabic script and describes Islam as the local religion. The Terengganu Stone is the earliest record of the presence of Islam on the Peninsula and is cited as evidence that Malaysia has one of the oldest links with Islam in Southeast Asia.

The arrival of Islam completes the displays on the ground floor and the next stage of Malaysia's history, the period of the famous 15th century kingdom of Melaka, begins upstairs on the first floor of the building. On the wall of the verandah which leads into the display rooms on this floor is a massive bronze statue of the legendary Melakan hero, the warrior Hang Tuah. Above him is the often quoted Malay motto: 'Malays will never vanish from the earth.' The first display on this second level of the museum is 'The History of Early Melaka 1403–1511' and there are no further references to Sabah and Sarawak until the 20th century displays. The caption for medieval Melaka establishes the ideological foundation for the multi-ethnic modern Malaysian state as follows:

> Through the determined efforts of its early rulers Melaka became a dominant power and created a Malay Empire. Melaka became an international port city and a magnet for traders from around the world. Some of these adapted to local conditions, settled down and served the government which thus evolved into a cosmopolitan society. Government, power and the right to rule were the preserve of Malays . . . Foreigners in Melaka included Arabs, Gujeratis, Indians, Siamese, Chinese, Japanese, Cambodians, Persians, and Malay communities from throughout the archipelago.

The displays illustrate different aspects of the Melaka sultanate: as a vital point for the spread of Islam, as a cultural centre (listing works of Malay literature including the *Sejarah Melayu* [*Malay Annals*] which were compiled there) and as a model for administration and trading practices. The impression produced is that Melaka was the hub of political, cultural and commercial life for the whole archipelago.

The Portuguese conquest of Melaka in 1511 is represented by several paintings of European armour-clad figures firing guns at Malay warriors who are armed only with swords and spears in a contest that is clearly unequal. Melaka's 'fall' is not given the same attention as its rise. The arrival of Europeans in the region is described by three displays entitled respectively, 'The Portuguese Era', 'The Dutch Era' and 'The English Era'. They are concerned with the occupation of Melaka after the defeat of the Malay sultanate in 1511 by a series of European trading and administrative regimes and information is not very detailed. However, the section entitled, 'The British in the Malay States 1786–1941' is a more expansive examination of the colonial presence. It is explained as follows:

> In the beginning the British came merely for trade without any intention of interfering in matters of local

politics or administration. However, the unstable political situation in the Malay states, the wealth of economic resources and certain socio-economic and socio-political changes in Europe pushed the British to interfere after all in the politics and administration of the Malay states. As a consequence in 1826 Penang, Melaka, Singapore and the Dindings were brought together as the Straits Settlements headed by a government. Administration in Malaya began in 1874 with the Treaty of Pangkor. As a result a British Resident was appointed to help to manage the state's administration. British interference continued to expand to Selangor, Negeri Sembilan and Pahang under the pretext of maintaining order in these states which were ultimately united under one administration of the Federal Malay States. A British Resident was appointed to administer finances and other matters with the exception of Malay customs and the Islamic religion.

Here, the British presence is referred to as 'interference', yet it is also described as being brought about by the 'unstable' political situation of the Malay states. The visitor is left with the impression that if the Malay states had been better governed by their sultans the British may not have 'interfered'.

In a display entitled 'The Unfederated Malay States' one of the consequences of British interference is depicted. This is in the form of a diorama showing Malay leaders of the state of Perak discussing what action they should take against the British resident J.W.W. Birch, who 'introduced a new administrative system which was in conflict with the traditional Malay system of values and administration'. As a result, the caption states, he was murdered. It concludes with a note of warning: 'This incident served as an eye-opener to the British to be more sensitive and tolerant in handling Malay affairs.'

Two final sections conclude the displays on the colonial presence. Entitled 'Foreign Powers in Sarawak' and 'Foreign Powers in Sabah', they note briefly that the northwest coast of Borneo was ceded in perpetuity in 1876 by its nominal overlord, the Sultan of Sulu (in the Philippines) to Baron von Overbeck and Alfred Dent for an annual payment of $5000 and that Sarawak 'was given over to James Brooke in 1841'. There is no mention of the sultan of Brunei's role in this transfer.

The third and last section of the museum begins with displays which illustrate the growth of nationalism. Captions explain that Malaysia lost its independence in 1511 when the Portuguese took Melaka but that there are many examples of Malaysians who resisted foreign authority including individuals in Sabah and Sarawak. Examples are given of people struggling against British rule from the mid-19th century up to the late 1940s. One display in the rise of nationalism is called 'The Rise of Islam'. This explains that the Islamic reform movement in the Middle East, particularly Cairo, influenced events in Malaya through returning students who then established journals and magazines and led campaigns in religious schools. According to the captions, the pan-Islamic ideals of these individuals led to a more comprehensive nationalist spirit which in turn led to the formation of Malay associations in every state and prepared the way for later political action.

'The Japanese Occupation 1942–1945' is the theme of the next section which is described as a period of depression in economic terms but in political terms as giving many nationalist activists a new sense of confidence. They realised that the power of the British was not unassailable and the Japanese slogan 'Asia for the Asians' inspired Malays to take the destiny of their homeland into their own hands. Anti-Japanese action is described in one of the captions which notes that 'the people and nationalist fighters formed an underground movement to oppose the power of the Japanese military and to help the Allied Forces'. The violent post-war clashes between Malays and Chinese in some parts of the Peninsula are not mentioned.

The Malayan Union proposal (1946), promoted by the British after the war, is also described as a focus for nationalism. 'For the first time in history,' the caption reads, 'the Malays rose in one movement to fight against the formation, putting aside parochial sentiments relating to individual states, districts or clans.' The First Malay Congress, held in 1946, is described as the impetus which led to the formation of the United Malays National Organisation (UMNO) in May of that year.

Attention then shifts to 'The Federation of Malaya' and 'The Emergency' and continues on to the 'Proclamation of Independence' in 1957 which is marked by an impressive bronze bas-relief of the first prime minister, Tunku Abdul Rahman, shouting 'Merdeka!' (Independence). Next comes 'The Formation of Malaysia—Sarawak' and 'The Formation of Malaysia—Sabah' with a further display entitled 'Confrontation', covering the 1963–66 period of hostilities between Indonesia and Malaysia.

The post-Independence period is divided into the terms of the four prime ministers who have governed Malaya/Malaysia since Independence. They are named according to the characteristic features of their terms in office. Thus Tunku Abdul Rahman (1957–70) is known as Bapak Kemerdekaan (Father of Independence), Tun Abdul Razak (1970–76) as Bapak Pembangunan (Father of Development) and Tun Hussein Onn (1976–81) as Bapak Perpaduan (Father of Consolidation).

It is obvious that in comparative terms the most recent period has been given the most space. It is devoted to displaying achievements during the term of Dr Mahathir as prime minister (beginning 1981) and is a detailed representation of Malaysia's progress under his leadership. The displays are entitled 'The Magnificent Decade: The Vision of a Leader' and they depict industrial and technological progress. One of the captions reads: 'Dr Mahathir Mohamad . . . will be remembered as the person who cares for the nation and the people—Malaysia in an era of political stability and rapid economic growth.'

Before leaving the Museum of National History it is useful to summarise the main periods and themes which the displays have been emphasising. First, although spread over a geographically fragmented area, even from prehistoric times 'Malaysia' is depicted as a real entity based on evidence of a shared history and shared nationalistic activities. Second, despite its recent political formation (1963) there is evidence of human habitation extending back 40 000 years, so that Malaysia's history can be said to begin in the prehistoric period. Third, both the Peninsula and the Borneo territories have been engaged in international trade since the early centuries of the Common Era. The focus for this trade is the Straits of Melaka where Kedah and then the port of Melaka attracted foreign traders in large numbers. This engagement with international trade, visitors are told, resulted in the acceptance of diversity and the development of skills in diplomacy. Fourth, the displays depicting the rise of nationalism emphasise that the history of nationalism in Malaysia extends back beyond the 20th century and has its roots in the Portuguese conquest of Melaka which stimulated Malays to want to regain their independence. The subtle sub-text associated with this theme is that sultans are not always reliable or capable rulers.

The need for a national history

In 1969, violent riots broke out in Kuala Lumpur, an event not recorded in the Museum of National History. Although they have not been given a place in the official version of national history the tensions which led to them have shaped the government's political, economic and social policies to this day. A direct result of the riots was a major program to devise a national ideology of unity. It was believed that if the citizens of Malaysia felt they had a common past and a stake in a better future together, then the ethnic tensions which had fuelled the riots would be lessened. The project of the Museum of National History was designed to give Malaysian citizens a sense of past achievements and to inspire them to work together for a common national purpose.

A second factor influencing the depiction of national history is the colonial experience of British rule and the emphasis on nationalism. The territory of present day Malaysia is based on colonial boundaries so although Malaysia rules as a sovereign power, its sovereignty is based on colonial foundations. While recognising the colonial past, a nation wishing to emphasise its independence had to develop its own distinctive style. To explain the 1963 inclusion of Sabah and Sarawak in a nation-state they had previously not been associated with, the national history displays include evidence of ancient human habitation which show links between Borneo and the Peninsula.

The themes emphasised in the National History Museum are carried into the education system and are reflected in the way history is taught to Malaysian school children and university students. Their understanding of the nation's past is based on concepts of unity and nationalism. Even the history matriculation examination papers reflect this concern and questions on nationalism are always set.

A national history has its own purpose—to interpret the nation to itself in the mould determined by the government of the day. It must necessarily be selective and it is important to recognise this and to look for what has not been included. We have noted already that the official history does not include consideration of the processes of change because its purpose is to emphasise achievements and the formation of Malaysia in its present form. This focus on the formation of the nation state has a number of consequences for the presentation of Malaysian history: first, it tilts the balance towards the more recent history of the 19th and 20th centuries; second, it favours urban events rather than developments outside major centres; and third, it emphasises the activities of Malays rather than non-Malays (although this imbalance is being partially redressed in the most recent versions of national history). This selectivity in the official version of history means also that little attention has been paid to Malaysia's original, tribal peoples, on the Peninsula and in Borneo. They are depicted as 'minorities' who have made relatively insignificant contributions to the formation of Malaysia.

To understand Malaysia's past in a context which is more broad than the political interests of the modern nation-state, it is necessary to go beyond the official version and to embrace wider themes.

2
PEOPLING MALAYSIA

Great streams of history, and of peoples, had for centuries met
at that spit of land at Asia's south-eastern extremity.

Rehman Rashid[1]

The 'official' version of Malaysia's history can be deepened and expanded through five broad themes.

These are:

- the influence of terrain, climate and environment on lifestyles and occupations
- the character of indigenous social and religious systems
- the strategic position of Malaysia
- concepts of power
- Malay political culture (traditional Malay statecraft).

These themes are ongoing features in Malaysia's past and future. They influence how the peoples of the region live and contribute to the way they interact with each other. They apply equally to events at the local as well as the national level and help explain why some features of Malaysian sociopolitical culture continue to have significance and have been maintained. Through these themes, the tensions which exist in Malaysian society and are expressed in events such as the 1969 riots, are exposed and seen in a broader context of social change and local interests. In essence, the themes provide a series of reference points which, singly or in combination, suggest the why's and how's of change over time in the region now called Malaysia.

Physical features and geographic location inevitably affect the way societies live and interact with each other. Similarly, social organisation and the concept of power are features which characterise individual cultures and underlie their distinctive forms. The fifth theme, Malay political culture, is included because all modern Malaysian leaders have incorporated stories, symbols and legendary figures into their political rhetoric and acknowledge a political system which draws on traditional Malay statecraft.

Geography, climate and environment

At the macro or regional level, the Malaysian territories of the Peninsula, Sabah and Sarawak lie to the south and the southeast respectively of the landmass of continental Asia. The natural divisions, formed by southward-flowing rivers, mountain ranges and seas, shape the cultural and commercial orientations of the inhabitants in the following ways:

1. From the earliest times of human habitation the inhabitants of the northern areas of the Peninsula had contact with the peoples of what are now Burma and Thailand.

2. Those living in the southern parts of the Peninsula had contact with peoples on the nearby coasts of east Sumatra and probably west Java and west Borneo.
3. Dwellers in the coastal areas of Sabah and Sarawak were in contact with peoples in the nearby islands of what are now the southern Philippines and Sulawesi as well as with those across the South China Sea in southern Vietnam and Cambodia. The inhabitants of Sarawak probably also had contact with settlers in areas of Sumatra.

At the macro-level then, the peoples of what is now Malaysia had a variety of opportunities for external contact depending on their location at a given time. The significance of these contacts and cultural orientations will be discussed as part of the third major theme, the strategic position of Malaysia.

Geologically, all the Malaysian territories belong to the Sunda shelf or Sundaland, an extension of the Asian landmass. During periods of low sea-levels in the prehistoric period (the Pleistocene) much of Sundaland was joined as dry land to Asia. The distinguishing feature of Sundaland is that it is geologically stable and not subject to volcanic action. Although safer for human habitation, the soils of Sundaland were not renewed with volcanic lava and therefore are not as fertile as those of the volcanically active areas of Sumatra, Java and Bali. However, what Sundaland lacked in soil fertility it made up for with rich mineral deposits—tin, gold, copper, zinc, silver and lead, iron, manganese, chromium, cobalt, molybdenum and tungsten. The extraction of these minerals, in the distant and not so distant past, has created commercial networks which have had long-term consequences for the history of Malaysia. In fact, it was the easily accessible alluvial tin in several areas of the west coast of the Peninsula and the gold deposits in the interior mountain ranges which enabled a highly productive interaction to occur with 'foreign' traders, from at least as early as 500 BCE.

The climatic features of the region are influenced by proximity to the equator. Most of the territory of modern Malaysia lies within 5 degrees of the equator (most of Peninsula Malaysia, Sabah and Sarawak but not the northern Peninsula states). The climate in this zone is termed 'equatorial' and is characterised by heavy, frequent rainfall all year which leaches natural nutrients from the soil resulting in conditions of low fertility. As if to compensate, much of the zone is rich in tin and aluminium. There is no strong differentiation between wet and dry seasons. These conditions are perfect for dense rainforest formation but are not good for intensive rice agriculture.

The northern areas of the Peninsula lie in the so-called 'intertropical' zone which has a clearly differentiated wet and dry season, with most rain falling between November and January. In the intertropical zone, the soils are less leached than those in the equatorial zone and, equally importantly, the dry period allows grain crops to ripen. In neither zone, however, was soil fertility replenished from natural sources such as volcanic ash.

Besides the humidity and uniformly high temperatures (the mean is 26°C), perhaps the best known climatic feature of Southeast Asia is the seasonal winds known as the monsoons. The effect of the monsoons will be discussed in more detail below but the regularity and strength of these wind patterns make them an important feature of the pre-modern period when wind-powered boats were the main method of transport for goods and people.

Four distinct types of environment characterise the Malaysian territories.

1. The sea
   This is the most obvious, but it is easily overlooked by outsiders. From prehistoric times up to the present, the

sea has provided communication, high protein food, opportunities for raiding (piracy) and marine products suitable for trade and exchange. In fact, it has been recently established that the seas of the Sunda shelf are the 'single primary centre of world diversity' for marine fauna. This is partly because these seas contain two ecosystems unique to the tropics—coral reefs and mangrove systems. Some groups of people spent their whole lives either living on the sea in boats or living above it in stilted dwellings, such as still exist in parts of southeast Sabah and Bandar Seri Begawan, capital of Brunei. The South China Sea, which lies between the Peninsula and Borneo, has rich deposits of oil and gas.

2. The coastal estuaries
   Mangroves are the key component of a rich ecosystem of marine life which has long supported human populations. Professional fisher-people still live here as they have always done and grow coconuts, palms from which sago can be extracted, bananas and kitchen vegetables.

3. The inland river valleys
   Travelling up the many rivers from the coast, at locations where the water changes from salt to fresh, is a third kind of environment characterised by a range of agricultural activities. Here, small villages exist along the rivers in areas between the coast and the hills and mountain ranges which form the interior (of both the Peninsula and the Borneo states). In patches of land along the small valleys, as well as on swampy river flats, grain crops are grown, cattle and buffalo are grazed and fruit trees are cultivated.

4. The mountainous areas

These are heavily covered with evergreen rainforest in the equatorial zone ('the jungle') and less densely so in the intertropical zones of the north of the Peninsula. Mount Kinabalu (4104 metres), is the highest mountain in Southeast Asia and lies in Sabah but because of its height and lowered temperatures (ground frosts occur) has tropical alpine scrub to about 3000 metres and above that only very sparse and specialised grasses and algae, giving a very bleak and spectacular appearance. Elsewhere in Malaysia at lower altitudes in the equatorial zone (to about 1000 metres) the ever green rainforest thrives with a canopy 30–50 metres above ground and supports a complex undergrowth of saplings, vines and canes. In its primal or uncleared state, these forests can exhibit an enormous natural variation of species. In northern Sarawak, for example, one 10-hectare plot yielded 780 different species of trees. Equatorial forests provide very little that humans can eat (except in Borneo where wild sago palms grow and are harvested by Penans) but the primal forests are the only source for trade items such as rare resins, waxes, camphor, fragrant timbers and high quality canes.

A few points should be made about the influence of topography and climate. The soils and climate of much of Malaysia are not suitable for long-term, intensive irrigated rice production of the kind which developed in Java and Bali. It is believed that in the prehistoric period, carbohydrate needs were readily met by tubers (yams), foxtail millet, seeds and fruit. These foods have the advantage of requiring less land than rice, less labour to grow and harvest them, and they do not require storage and complex preparation. Evidence of rice grains in pottery and pestles and mortars show that from as early as the second millennium BCE, rice was available in coastal Sarawak and in the northernmost parts of the Peninsula but the rice may not have been grown where it was found. However, it is believed that during the first millennium BCE, rice began to be cultivated in swampy areas using a system of lengthy fallow periods which enabled soil nutrients to regenerate. It would be fair to generalise that before the 19th century, only in the coastal areas of Kedah and Kelantan was wet-rice grown on any considerable scale.

Protein needs in prehistoric times were provided by domesticated animals (pigs, poultry), fish and molluscs, and the capture of reptiles, birds and wild animals (deer, wild boar, ox). Although modern observers might realise that such a system was in harmony with the environment and ecologically balanced, to almost any pre-20th century European such a lifestyle would have appeared primitive and in need of 'development'. Population numbers were small and evidence of 'industry' or organised labour were not apparent to foreign eyes. For Europeans, accustomed to measuring levels of civilisation by monumental architecture and orderly fields of grain crops, before the 19th century the evidence in Malaysia for civilisation is scanty. It is only with the West's recent preoccupation with sustainable development that systems such as those practised by the 'undeveloped' inhabitants of Malaysia have been recognised as meriting further investigation. It has now become a race against time to recover much of this indigenous knowledge as increasing areas of natural environment are leased or sold to developers particularly in areas of primal rainforest.

Indigenous social and religious systems

In pre-modern times, environment and mode of lifestyle had a great deal of influence on the kind of social organisation that shaped the way individuals related to each other. For example, small populations dependent on mobility (foragers in upland forest areas, or boat-dwelling peoples) might be expected to have different conventions concerning marriage, child-rearing, inheritance and organisation of labour from people who chose a more settled way of life. Sedentary groups, such as peasant farmers, who relied on land for food production and passed the 'rights' to that land to their close relatives, would probably have quite different forms of social organisation.

It is possible to see a set of shared beliefs common to the religious systems of many of the groups indigenous to the Malaysian territories. Among these is the understanding that all matter has its own spiritual essence and that well-being and harmony results from their correct matching whereas misfortune and disaster result from their mismatching or separation. The general term for this system is animism and the specialists who can deal with the spiritual powers of the non-material world are generally termed shamans. While other beliefs can (and usually were) borrowed and added to this system, there was often a process of adaptation in which the borrowed elements underwent change to fit in with the existing body of beliefs.

Social systems were perhaps less prone to adaptation but individuals could withdraw and move to other systems if there were mechanisms for acceptance in the new system, say through adoption or marriage. So although distinct social systems and religious beliefs are evident in the territories which now make up Malaysia they were not rigid or unchanging over time and space. A degree of flexibility is particularly necessary in a region like Southeast Asia where high degrees of cooperation are necessary between groups so that trade and exchange can occur. Nevertheless, some groups, such as the Malays, developed systems which could include non-Malays if they adopted Malay customs. Others, such as some upland swidden (fell and burn) and foraging groups, seem to have consciously remained exclusive in their social systems in order to maintain their highly adapted and ecologically specific lifestyle.

It should be noted that it is no longer scientifically acceptable, when describing the various groups of people in Malaysia, to talk about 'waves' of migrations. The 'wave' theory does not reflect the complexity of interactions nor does it explain the considerable archaeological, genetic and linguistic data now assembled. On the basis of genetic and biological evidence (including craniometric studies and dental morphology), it has been established that people recognisably the same as modern humans have occupied Borneo and the Malay Peninsula from about 40 000 years ago. Beyond that, to date there is no single theory which can convincingly explain the prehistoric situation of all the peoples in the Malaysian territories. The relationship between the prehistoric populations and modern populations is a topic of hot debate among the experts with considerable differences of opinion still remaining. As one of the leading researchers of prehistoric Malaysia expresses it: 'If the results from the Malay Peninsula are to be generalised at all, it would be to suggest that Holocene [prehistoric] human evolution in Southeast Asia should be understood not in terms of broad generalisations but in relation to the specific historical circumstances of each study area.'[2]

One useful way of trying to understand the relationship between the diverse groups of indigenous peoples of the Malay Peninsula is to compare types of social organisation and lifestyle. When this is done, four broad socio-cultural patterns can be recognised. They have been termed: Malay, Senoi, Semang and Malayic.

The Malay pattern

This has been the dominant socio-religious pattern on the Malay Peninsula only since approximately the 18th century. It should be understood, however, that the category 'Malay' is a very fluid one, *not* defined by physical characteristics, but by language, dress, customs and, most importantly, by the profession of Islam. None of these characteristics is innate, in the sense that an individual is born with them. Each can be adopted and it is now recognised that it is possible to 'become' a Malay by assuming these characteristics. It is therefore, to some extent, a matter of choice as to whether groups and individuals wish to identify themselves as 'Malays' and to accept the consequences of being seen as 'Malay'. In contemporary Malaysia, there are some social and financial benefits from being thus categorised and some individuals have 'become' Malay to gain access to them.

The Malay language is part of the very large group known as Austronesian, whose speakers stretch from the Pacific to Madagascar. Speakers of Austronesian languages also have many sociocultural features in common, one of them being social ranking based on relative age. Seniority is accorded status and respect. In marriage it is considered that the husband should be older than the wife who should ideally be of the same blood line (consanguine). Marriages with first or second cousins are the neatest way of implementing these principles. Associated with this kind of society is a sedentary mode of livelihood in a village context, where women's labour is given high value and the husband and wife form the basic labour unit. Descent is described in terms of both father and mother and men give gifts or money to the bride on marriage and these remain her property. It is expected that men will travel beyond the village to extend the agricultural income by fishing, trade or raiding. One of the results of the close-knit social pattern is that each local community is a strong inter-related group, which discourages loosely connected or 'fringe' members. As noted above, however, if 'outsiders' choose to follow Malay customs and Islam, they can become part of the Malay community and non-Malay children are often adopted and regarded as Malays.

Over the past two centuries, the terms 'Malay' and 'Islam' have become so closely linked that the Malaysian Constitution uses profession of Islam as one of the legal definitions of a Malay. The religion of Islam originated in the Middle East in the 7th century CE and its spread to Southeast Asia will be described in the following chapter. It is important to note that Islam is a religion which was imported and that local peoples in Southeast Asia accepted it for a variety of reasons and at different periods in their history. Because it is not a religion which originated in the region, it is perhaps surprising that it has become one of the defining characteristics of a major group such as the Malays. Some of the anomalies this can cause are illustrated in Sarawak and Sabah, all of whose indigenous populations are considered by anthropologists to be Austronesian (and therefore in linguistic and sociocultural terms belonging to the same group as Malays). However, only those Sarawak peoples who profess Islam, or convert to Islam (for example, some Melanaus and Kedayans) are called 'Malays'. The Ibans, the dominant indigenous group in Sarawak, have not converted in large numbers, and are therefore classified as 'non-Malay'. In Sabah, for blatantly political reasons many recent Muslim migrants from the southern Philippines have been classified as 'Malay', while non-Muslim, native Sabahans have not.

Putting aside issues of ethnic classification, the religion of Islam is followed by more than half Malaysia's present population. Being a religion of adoption, it has developed in the Malaysian territories, as elsewhere outside its heartland, in the presence of earlier belief systems. Traces of these older beliefs and practices survive in traditional agricultural rites and at celebrations to mark specific life-stages as well as at times of misfortune (such as disasters and illness). They usually take the form of acts of propitiation to spirits and ancestors conducted by experts who are skilled in dealing with the supernatural.

Turning to the remaining three sociocultural patterns, the peoples who were already living in parts of the Peninsula before the Austronesian speakers settled there in large numbers are known by the generic name of *Orang Asli*, the 'Original Peoples'. They have long attracted scholarly interest, but it is only since the 1960s that they have been studied with scientific rigour. Enough is now known about their society and culture to recognise the three broad patterns of Senoi, Semang and Malayic. These patterns are linked also with dominant modes of environmental use: Senoi with semi-sedentary horticulture; Semang with nomadic hunting and gathering; Malayic with collecting forest and marine products for trade.

The Senoi pattern

Peoples who follow this pattern mainly depend on swidden (fell and burn) farming supplemented by trading. This way of life is found mainly in the mountain areas of the central parts of the Peninsula. Peoples following this sociocultural pattern include the Temiars, Semais, Jah Huts and Btsisis (or Mah Meris) (see map 3, page xvii). Because swidden farming depends on allowing the land to lie fallow after several seasons it is necessary to move regularly, even if the group returns after many years to lands worked previously. While there are many variations in religious systems among these peoples, the common practice of swidden farming makes it possible to make some very general points about their social systems. They respect individual autonomy and the nuclear family is the basic unit of society, but household units often consist of extended families who live together, work together and share child raising. Care is taken not to offend, coerce or frustrate others and decisions are reached through consensus and discussion and even then, an individual is not necessarily bound by the group decision. Individuals are, however, expected to practise self-restraint and failure to do so is believed to lead to supernatural retribution. Religious beliefs centre round the strength of cosmic forces which can be unleashed by improper behaviour. In this system it is thought that spirits inhabit natural sites and have to be appeased before entering their domains. Shamans can be asked to ward off evil spirits and to find lost souls by seeking aid from their spirit familiars.

The Semang pattern

This is based largely on a foraging (hunting and gathering) lifestyle. It is rare in the 21st century that any people can live entirely off the natural resources of the land, constantly on the move and without cultivating crops. However, this was possible in the lowland forests of the northern Malay Peninsula and in upland areas of Sabah and Sarawak until the early 20th century. Today, the only true hunter-gatherer people in

Borneo are the Penans (also known as Punans) who live in isolated areas in Sarawak, but who are physically unrelated to the Semang groups of the Peninsula. Social organisation is characterised by low population density of small groups—individuals and married couples—who maintain a wide network of acquaintances so that they can come and go from other groups as they need to. Dispersal, not concentration, of population is their key to survival. On the Peninsula, the following small populations still follow this pattern to some degree: the Kintaqs, Kensius, Jahais, Batek Des and Che Wongs (see map 3, page xvii). Religious beliefs are, in general, similar to those of the Senoi pattern, discussed above, with particular attention being given to protection from calamities and cosmic disasters, as well as augury using signs from birds.

The Malayic pattern

This is followed by people who combine subsistence farming or fishing with the collecting of forest or marine products for trade. Peoples following this kind of lifestyle (which combines elements of both the Senoi and Semang patterns) include Temuans, Semelais, Jakuns and *Orang Suku Laut* the 'Sea Peoples'. They are found in lowland areas of the Peninsula (particularly in the south) in lowland areas of east and south Sumatra, and the islands in the Straits of Melaka. They seem to have adopted some of the cultural and linguistic features of early Austronesian settlers—suggesting they found it advantageous (probably for reasons of trade) to establish regular contact with them.

Chinese and Indians

Most descriptions of the population of Malaysia include accounts of Chinese and Indian groups as if they were not settlers of long-standing in the region. This is based on the misapprehension that the majority of the forebears of Chinese and Indians, now living in Malaysia, migrated there in the mid or late 19th century. On these grounds, they are not considered as 'native' as others. This is misleading in the sense that during that same period there were also many migrants arriving from Java, Sumatra and other parts of Indonesia (at that time the Netherlands East Indies), but because their socioreligious organisation was recognisably similar to that of the Malays, they are regarded as 'Malays'. However, it is the customs and lifestyle of the Chinese and Indians which distinguish them from other groups rather than their date of arrival.

Chinese and Malay accounts, of the 15th century and earlier, describe commercial and diplomatic contacts being established informally (between individuals) and more formally (through court officials). Similar contact between merchants from southern Indian ports, particularly traders in textiles, existed during this early period and the commercial advisers to the Malay rulers of local kingdoms were often from the Indian subcontinent. Although there is evidence of permanent Chinese settlement from as early as the 14th century, large-scale migration from China and India did not occur until the 19th century. Forced by dire conditions in their own country to seek their livelihood elsewhere, Chinese from the maritime provinces of southeastern China migrated to the Peninsula and Borneo. From their work as labourers in tin-mines and the building industry, many prospered and invested their savings in enterprises such as mines, plantations, factories, shops and banks, forming institutional networks now regarded as characteristic of the overseas Chinese.

In Malaysia, the Chinese established a system of mutual help through associations and societies for labour, trade, hospitals, schools and funerals. These were strengthened by strong clan links at local levels. Their commercial operations were similarly independent of outside assistance and were based on a small number of leading financiers at major commercial centres (Kuala Lumpur, Ipoh, Singapore) who dealt directly with Chinese firms in smaller centres. These, in turn, traded with much smaller Chinese enterprises, often at the level of village shopkeeper. Through this kind of networking and control of capital, the Chinese succeeded in dominating the commercial sector of the Malaysian economy. Today, some Chinese are Christians but the majority follow Buddhist, Confucian or Taoist practices combined with reverence for the ancestors.

Links between the Malaysian territories and south India go back to at least the first millennium CE, but substantial migration began only with British interest in plantation agriculture (particularly rubber from about 1900) and the colonial need for labour to develop public works and railways. The British administration of India facilitated linkages with British interests in the Malaysian region and workers were mainly from Tamil, Malayalee and Telugu areas with some Sikhs from the north. The majority worked on the west coast of the Peninsula where most development was occurring and people of Indian descent in Sabah and Sarawak are much less numerous. In contemporary Malaysia visitors may note that the majority of money changers are of Indian descent. They are probably Chettiars (moneylenders) whose links with commercial life in Malaya are long-standing. Through their hands flows much of the Indian investment in property in Malaysia. Some Malaysian Indians are Christians or Muslims but the majority are Hindus or Sikhs.

The strategic position of Malaysia

For as long as the Middle East and China have been at the heart of the world's trading networks, the Malaysian territories have played a crucial and pivotal role in global trade. In the early 19th century, one of the first British administrators described the Peninsula as 'centrically situated with respect to all the great and civilized nations of Asia' with its eastern extremity 'within three days sail of China and its western not above three weeks sail from Arabia'. The British observer then notes that from the Malay Peninsula it was only 15 days sail to Hindustan and 90 days sail to Europe.[3] He writes as if this information is his own discovery but others had been travelling through the region for millennia before he arrived. His words emphasise the point that 19th century European accounts of Southeast Asia—and it was those accounts which shaped the European image and understanding of the region—rarely acknowledged that Europeans were the last peoples to make contact with this part of Asia. Not only were they newcomers, but they viewed the region in terms of their own interests rather than as part of much wider patterns and sub-patterns which had been in process since at least the first centuries of the Common Era.

The map shows that the Malaysian territories lie across the sea routes which connect West and East and a voyage from one hemisphere to another required two different wind patterns or monsoons. Ships from the West needed the southwest monsoon winds which blew from that direction between mid-May to September to cross the Bay of Bengal and reach Southeast Asia. Vessels sought safe harbour in the Melaka Straits to await the reverse cycle of the northeast monsoon (mid-October to March) to take them back. Vessels from China travelling to the southern seas needed the northeast monsoon. The safe harbours were not only places of transit, they became 'entrepôts' or ports where goods were trans-shipped for an onward journey. When shipping was no longer dependent on wind-power, the Malay Peninsula area remained a pivotal navigational zone. Today, its strategic importance is undiminished—it is estimated that 40 per cent of the world's trade still passes through here.

The accessibility of the region meant that Peninsula and Borneo peoples were especially vulnerable to hostile and to predatory powers. Perhaps as a result of this, one of the characteristics of successful leaders in the pre-modern period was skill in diplomacy and an ability to establish diplomatic links and alliances with a wide range of other leaders. Most commonly these were marriage alliances with close neighbours (such as those in Sumatra and Java), or 'tributary' relationships with more distant leaders whereby symbolic gestures of allegiance were initiated in return for protection. In this manner connections were established and maintained with China and Siam (now Thailand), and from the 18th and 19th century, with Turkey and Japan as well as with European powers.

Concepts of power

The peoples of the Malay Peninsula and the west coast of Borneo were ideally situated to participate in the international trade which flowed between East and West. Leaders had much to gain, in terms of power and influence as well as material prosperity, if they were able to control points of exchange in the trading networks which spanned the region. Not all peoples, however, were interested in full engagement with commercial life, nor were they willing to exchange a lifestyle with a high degree of autonomy (such as foraging and hunting and gathering) for a more controlled and autocratic system. For groups who did not need to be fully engaged in trade, concepts of leadership and power were very different from those societies which relied on a hierarchically organised system to direct labour and support a ruling elite.

As noted above, the Peninsula and Borneo had, and still have, a relatively low population density with little shortage of land and no shortage of sea. The necessity to control large amounts of territory in order to have power and influence was therefore not a major concern. However, access to people—to provide labour and services—was crucial to those who wanted to engage in full-time and centralised commercial activities. In the Malaysian territities, therefore, in those contexts where organised labour was necessary for the maintenance of the socio-economic pattern, power was understood as the ability to attract obedient and willing followers. Conversely, in contexts such as self-sufficient small groups (of foragers, swidden farmers, collectors and boat-dwelling people), the concept of power and authority was more diffuse and was not necessarily associated with only one member of the group.

In the section describing patterns of sociocultural organisation, it was noted that those groups following a fairly self-sufficient lifestyle (for example, the Semang and Senoi patterns) had a high degree of personal autonomy, used consensus to reach decisions and worked in very small groups (sometimes only two or three people) to accomplish tasks. In this kind of group, power was linked with mastery of special skills in those areas that were useful to the group. Such skills could be specialisation in certain crafts or tools, skills in spiritual matters (interpreting dreams, for example), hunting, climbing, singing, or child-raising (particularly for women). Other individuals might be recognised for their skills in representing the interests of the group to outsiders and acting as intermediaries between them and others in situations such as the exchange of goods. To outsiders, these individuals may have appeared to be 'headmen' whereas in fact they had 'power' in just one area in their community and may not have been leaders in other contexts.

In contrast to the concept of power as specialised skill which was manifest in a number of members of a group is the understanding of power which was restricted to just one member of a group. Power believed to be from a supernatural source invested in one individual set them apart. In the context of traditional Malay statecraft this power was believed to be a sign of sovereignty and was restricted to the ruler. 'Ordinary' (non-royal) individuals were unable to withstand the force of this power (known as *daulat*) and if mishandled it was believed to cause death. The Malay ruler, the focus of power for the Malay community, was also seen as the source of power and able to bestow some of it on loyal followers. Such a system cannot function unless there are lower-ranked individuals who recognise and acknowledge the power. A greater degree of social differentiation and hierarchy is required in this kind of system. This may all seem rather theoretical but, in practical terms, if labour is in short supply and must be mobilised to achieve particular purposes, there must be a leader who can activate those workers and the workers must believe there is some reward or incentive for following the leader. This, in crude terms, was the concept of power in most traditional Malay societies.

These are just two ways of expressing and understanding power in the territories that now comprise Malaysia. The only commonality is that neither involves possession of territory. The distinguishing feature is focus. One system acknowledges that a number of individuals in the one community can have 'power' (in the sense of special skills) while the other system can exist only if members of the community acknowledge the possession of power by one individual, who becomes a revered figure. It also seems that over time, the concept of power as emanating from only one person—sometimes termed the 'great man' or 'man of prowess' theory of power—transformed that individual (and their descendants) into sources of spiritual energy. The allegiances that power generates provide the basis of the political organisation for that community. The very personal nature of power in that kind of system has implications for the understanding of power in contemporary Malaysia.

Finally, it should be noted that the diversity of the natural environment of Malaysia encouraged a corresponding diversity of social and power systems to suit the physical context. If commercial networks of trade and exchange were developed around these different environments (collecting from forests, growing food or extracting metals in more open terrains, sea and strand collecting) success would depend on the ability to respond to and adapt quickly to changes in market demand. Tastes may change radically or greater quantities of particular items may be needed. Thus, it was important to encourage diversity in order to meet all eventualities and for middlemen and leaders to be in regular contact with their suppliers. In difficult terrains with sparse populations the most effective way to achieve this would have been through individual contact and ties of personal loyalty to key individuals. If leaders failed to maintain a diversity of links, or encouraged and protected a small group of favourites at the expense of a broader network of alliances, they ran the risk of restricting their options and decreasing their flexibility to respond quickly to new situations.

Diversity decreased these risks and successful leaders needed the skills and incentives to encourage and exploit the advantages of variety.

Malay political culture

The politics of Malaysia today draws on these concepts of power and leadership. Political culture (the way political concepts and experiences are expressed) implies the existence of politics and the state—concepts whose origins lie in Western culture. Nevertheless, Malaysia is a modern nation-state which has chosen a Western-style democracy as its form of government. The pre-Independence nationalist movements had to develop symbols and rhetoric which would inspire support and would stimulate the peoples of Malaysia to combine to work for national (rather than local) aims. The majority of nationalist leaders were Malays (rather than Chinese or Indians). During the course of their colonial education from the period of the late 19th century, these Malays had been introduced to selected works of traditional Malay literature, sections of which were used in schools as set-texts for Malay history. Chief among these were the *Sejarah Melayu* (*Malay Annals*) and *Hikayat Hang Tuah* (*Story of Hang Tuah*) both of which describe the sultanate of Melaka in its heyday before the Portuguese conquest in 1511. Each of these works, formerly read aloud in the Malay royal courts and later adapted for use in Malay schools, had an enduring influence on Malay political life because the nationalist leaders drew on their stories and value-system to express their visions for an independent nation. The traditional Malay works focus heavily on Malays and Malay concerns with little attention given to non-Malays. This was one of the reasons why Prime Minister Mahathir's 'Vision 2020' policy, elaborated in the early 1990s and now the blueprint for development in the foreseeable future, specifically includes all Malaysians in its aims.

3
NETWORKS OF POWER AND EXCHANGE

*Merchants from distant places congregate there. This country
is therefore considered to be very prosperous.*
Extract from the *P'ing-chou k'o-t'an*, referring to
the port of Srivijaya in the early 12th century[1]

This quotation, from a Chinese source of the early 12th century,
reveals three things: that a place called Srivijaya was well-known to
Chinese merchants, that it attracted traders from beyond the immediate region and that it was regarded as commercially very successful.
Srivijaya was, in fact, merely one of a number of commercial centres
in the Malaysian territories that were visited by foreign merchants in
the first millennium CE. Another port which was well-known to international traders as a major entrepôt was in Kedah, a kingdom at the
northern end of the Straits. It flourished for several centuries but then
lost some of its influence to competitors. The reputation of Srivijaya,
in southeastern Sumatra at the other end of the Straits, outstripped
that of Kedah and other successful ports. In fact, Srivijaya was clearly

a model for the even more famous entrepôt of Melaka, which in many ways was its successor. Srivijaya, Kedah and Melaka were major centres of Malay power.

Austronesians on the move: navigating the first millennium BCE

The Austronesians are people who spoke (and still speak) languages belonging to the Austronesian language family. This very large language family is thought to have originated in Taiwan but its speakers spread south through the Philippines, Borneo and Sulawesi and then branched south and west into Java, Sumatra and the Indian Ocean. Others spread further east into Oceania. This extraordinarily wide distribution 'reflects one of the most phenomenal records of colonization and dispersal in the history of humanity'.[2]

Researchers are agreed that although the details of the Austronesian movements cannot be known with certainty, they were very complex. Based on linguistic reconstructions, for example, scholars postulate that some Austronesian groups settled in southwestern Borneo before others settled in Sumatra, while, later in time, other Austronesians sailed from Sumatra to coastal areas of Borneo. This demonstrates that the Austronesians were highly mobile and used their sailing and navigational skills to specialise in collecting a wide range of marine items for trade. They established networks of exchange throughout island Southeast Asia and at points along the coasts of the mainland. Those groups who found it useful to trade with Austronesian speakers found it similarly useful to adopt some or all of their language in order to negotiate with them. The Malay branch of Austronesian seems to have developed comparatively late and there is considerable speculation about the pre-Malay forms of Austronesian spoken in the territories which later became Malaysia.

Early archaeological evidence for the presence of Austronesian influence in southeastern Sabah has been found in a rock shelter at Bukit Tengkorak where fragments of pottery, shell beads, agate tools and obsidian flakes have been dated at between 1000 to 300 years BCE (see map 1, page xv). It is particularly significant that the obsidian flakes used as tools originated thousands of kilometres away in New Britain, western Melanesia. New Britain and its export of obsidian has been associated with an Austronesian culture known as the 'Lapita' culture. The most likely explanation is that the people in southeastern Sabah were part of a trading network which involved both places and doubtless other points in-between. During the first millennium BCE, the Sabahans collected items from the beaches and seas and exchanged them for the obsidian items. The archaeological evidence includes remains of portable pottery hearths, suitable for use on boats. The same hearths are associated with groups of maritime nomads, like the Bajaus who still operate in Sabah waters, and it is not impossible that the Bajaus have ancient connections with the prehistoric groups who lived in the Bukit Tengkorak area.

Gold from the interior

The finds in Sabah indicate the existence of a network of marine trade operating in an easterly direction towards eastern Indonesia and Melanesia. Archaeological finds on the Malay Peninsula indicate that there were also other networks, using different items of exchange but still associated with Austronesian cultures. Dated at between 500 BCE and 500 CE, a number of stone slab graves similar to those found in other Austronesian areas, have been identified in southern Perak (see map 1, Bernam and Sungkai, page xv). Experts interpret this as an indication that Austronesians were active on the Peninsula from this time.

The location of the graves provides a clue about the kind of networks the Austronesians were utilising on the Peninsula. They are all near major sources of tin on the west coast and also close to the routes which were used to reach gold deposits in the upper reaches of rivers. These routes have been traced from the east and from the west coasts of the Peninsula along the Kelantan River and its main tributaries across to Perak (Bernam) and also along the Pahang River (see map 1, page xv). Traces of old water-supply canals in remote parts of the jungle along these rivers and primitive tools bear witness to ancient mining activities which must have produced the gold that found its way down the network of tracks through the interior to exchange points leading to the coast. Researchers have reconstructed some of these routes, which older reports say were still being used before roads were built in the interior. The reconstructed routes link up points on both sides of the Peninsula, as well as running north–south almost the entire length of the Peninsula. This complex series of coastal–interior routes seems to have linked the sea-going Austronesian traders working their way round the coasts with the peoples skilled at collecting forest products and finding gold in the difficult inland terrain, peoples who were probably the ancestors of the present-day populations of *Orang Asli*.

Tin and Indian beads: the Klang valley sites (Selangor)

Fairly rich archaeological evidence, dated between 500–200 BCE, has been discovered at sites in a riverine area of the west coast of the Peninsula, near the modern city of Klang (See map 1, page xv). Whereas the Perak and Pahang finds from this period seem associated with the extraction and exchange of gold, the coastal sites are in a very rich tin-bearing region and a demand for tin probably stimulated the prehistoric activity here. Six of the Dongson drums located on the

Peninsula were found in this region, together with a large number of beads of Indian or Indian influenced manufacture, bronze bowls, iron tools and resin-coated pottery.

The demand for tin at this particular time was not fortuitous. Research has linked the increase in extraction of tin along a string of ports on the eastern coasts of the Bay of Bengal (extending from Myanmar to the southern parts of the west coast of the Malay Peninsula), with events on the Indian subcontinent. From about the middle of the first millennium BCE, linked with the expansion of Buddhism and Jainism, a series of urban coastal centres on the eastern seaboard of India were established and began issuing coinage which included bronze coins with a high tin content. Deposits of tin in India are rare and the metal had to be imported. Tin-bearing regions across the Bay of Bengal, on the Malay Peninsula, provided a ready supply. It was at this time that the terms 'Suvarnabhumi' and 'Suvarnadvipa' were being used in Sanskrit literature to refer to eastern lands (that is, in Southeast Asia) which were rich in gold and tin. The finds of beads of Indian origin at the Klang sites suggest that the region was a major exchange point for incoming foreign goods and outgoing local items, particularly tin and also gold, from the uplands of the interior with other luxury items such as fragrant woods and resins.

The Dongson drums found in this area have been associated with burial sites (as mentioned above) marked by megaliths in the form of stone slab graves and standing stones. The drums provide evidence about trade patterns and about some features of the society which used them. Researchers have plotted the location of these drums in relation to the reconstructed trade routes. Each of the drums has been found close to the end-points of the routes, suggesting a close association with the old networks. From the drums and their locations, it has been suggested that first, the west coast of the Peninsula was linked into a network which reached at least to the northern regions of Vietnam. Second, the association of drums with megaliths which required organised labour for their installation implies 'some degree of group effort'.[3]

Third, because not many stone graves have been found, it is thought that only people of status were entitled to, or could afford, these items. This suggests that wealth was concentrated in a small social group who must have acquired it by gaining control over important sectors of the trading network. We know this is what occurred in later societies, such as those of Srivijaya and Melaka. The Klang Valley sites, therefore, provide us with very early evidence that elite groups were organising significant parts of the trade in some (if not all) of these major exchange points.

Two language families

Linguistic evidence provides further clues about the interactions occurring on the Malay Peninsula. The existence of two quite distinct language families—Austroasiatic and Austronesian (see glossary) in close association but in fairly distinct territories suggests that their speakers had distinct lifestyles and cultures. The archaeological evidence supports this. Many artefacts from northern areas of the Peninsula, in territory now occupied by *Orang Asli* (Austroasiatic speakers), are similar to artefacts from surrounding regions of modern Thailand, Myanmar and Cambodia/Vietnam. In the southern and western parts of the Peninsula, however, the archaeological evidence suggests contact with Austronesian-based cultures.

The languages of some *Orang Asli* groups in the south of the Peninsula (those which follow the Malayic sociocultural pattern) support this theory because they show evidence of extended contact with Austronesian speakers. The evidence of the old inland tracks and upland routes linking coastal points on each side of the Peninsula strongly suggests that trade was the stimulus for contact. Thus, both the linguistic and archaeological evidence from the first millennium BCE points to a diverse range of cultures and ethnic groups living in the Malaysian territories who interacted with each other and with neighbouring regions through commercial networks which operated on land and around the coasts.

These descriptions of prehistoric trade and exchange patterns reveal that distance was not an obstacle to the establishment of extensive networks. Obsidian from Melanesia reached Sabah and large bronze drums, most manufactured far from the locations where they were found, travelled long distances to reach their exchange points. Boats must have provided the primary means of transportation and marine archaeology, still a relatively new science, has yielded good results in Southeast Asian waters.

All the vessels so far discovered dating from the prehistoric and early historic periods (up to about 6th century CE) have been of Southeast Asian construction, providing very strong evidence that maritime transport was in local (that is, Austronesian) hands. The networks were even more extensive because many of the items originating in the Malaysian territories were destined for delivery to markets in China, India, the Middle East and from there, ultimately, to the Mediterranean and Europe. Centres, such as those in the Klang region (see map 1, page xv), used local shipping networks to bring in luxury items from the northern ports and items from Indian centres (to the West), and then circulated these items into the local systems in return for exportable items. Clearly, the networks were extensive and well developed even in the period before the Common Era and to understand why, we need to examine what was fuelling the larger networks which operated to link Southeast Asia with other continental systems.

An international system

The complex ethnic and cultural mix of peoples who were amalgamated into the Chinese empire produced powerful political and economic forces which influenced the nearby regions and beyond. In about 100 BCE, for example, the northern part of Vietnam which had been producing the ceremonial bronzes (including the Dongson drums) was absorbed into the Han empire and the export of the bronzes through the southern-linked trading networks seems to have stopped. The southwards expansion of the Han drew them into the exchange networks operating with Southeast Asia and they became part of the increasingly dynamic flow of goods and people. Bronze items were still in demand in Southeast Asia and, when bronze goods from Vietnam were no longer available, the exchange points on the Malay Peninsula increased their contact with their closer northern neighbours, particularly the Mons of Southern Burma, who were also producing good bronze work. As well, the peninsular exchange points strengthened links with the burgeoning ports of India.

South Indian ports were enjoying the increased demand for exotic and luxury goods coming from the markets of the Roman empire, at its zenith in the first century BCE and through the following two centuries. It is believed that at this time the centres in south India dominated the trade between the Roman West and the East—a trade which drew goods from nodes in Southeast Asia and was carried through and beyond that region by Austronesian vessels and sailors. The two points to note are first, the skill of the Austronesians in navigation and long-distance travel, and second, the demand for particular items which made hazardous voyages attractive and worth-while. Although we do not know the full list of merchandise being traded between Southeast Asia and other parts of the world in the early centuries CE, reports from the 15th century indicate a mixture of foodstuffs (bananas, grains, fish), spices, cloth, precious metals and specialist luxury items such as birds' nests, resins and aromatic woods. A network linking China and the Mediterranean through the Straits of Melaka was thus well established by the 1st century CE.

Even when empires, such as those of Rome and China, changed their configurations, the trading networks did not disappear but adapted and re-linked to respond to the ever-changing, but always hungry, markets for specialist products. As Roman trade decreased in the third century CE, some Indian ports suffered but others intensified their links with the ports on the opposite side of the Bay of Bengal. Through this period, Buddhism travelled with the merchants as their favoured religion and played an important part in strengthening links between traders.

By the fourth century CE, the southern states of the Chinese empire were able to exert some independence and engaged more actively in trade with various Southeast Asian ports. From this period come references in Chinese records to places in the Southeast Asian region which were visited by Chinese merchants, travellers and pilgrims wanting to visit the holy sites of Buddhism in India. Travel was not exclusively by sea and reports mention some routes which involved portions of travel overland or took shortcuts using river links between coasts. The landmass that was most often traversed by these methods was, of course, the Malay Peninsula. As we have already seen, inland tracks and river routes linking east and west coasts of the Peninsula date back to at least the first millennium BCE and were well established and often used. Evidence of how these exchange points functioned comes from a series of archaeological sites in the southern river valleys of the Malay state of Kedah.

Sea and land: Kedah and Buddhism

In geopolitical terms, the southern rivers of Kedah offer great potential for tapping into local and international trade networks. Situated at the southern end of the Isthmus of Kra (see map 2, page xvi), and at the northern end of the Straits of Melaka, this region was also the beginning of the overland route to important ports on the Gulf of Siam, notably Nakhon Si Thammarat, Singora and Patani. The overland routes passed through the territory of the Austroasiatic speaking *Orang Asli* groups, who actively participated in the networks as porters, guides and collectors of specialist jungle products for exchange. Before the 12th century BCE (when peoples later called the Thai were moving into Thailand), this region was influenced by Mon culture and civilisation.

A number of Mon characteristics and Mon words are still evident in the northern parts of the Peninsula. We will see that in the 18th century, control of the isthmus region was a vital aspect in the relationship between Burma, Siam and the northern Malay Peninsula.

Because it is sufficiently north of the equator to experience seasonal variation and because it has areas of fertile soil, Kedah has long history of sustained agricultural activity and was known for rice, pepper, cattle and poultry production. It is also within the tin-belt which runs down the eastern coast of the Bay of Bengal and into the Malay Peninsula. It is not surprising that archaeologists have found Kedah very rich in early settlement sites.

The earliest evidence (at the time of writing) of this region's links with ocean-going trade is a series of prehistoric cave paintings at Kodiang in northern Kedah (see map 1, page xv). The paintings show processions of human figures with buffalos, other animals and ocean-going vessels with masts. Animal domestication and sea-voyaging were obviously known to the inhabitants at that time. By the 6th century CE, archaeological finds indicate that the southern rivers of Kedah were the focus of activity and there is substantial evidence of wide-ranging foreign contact. Sites excavated in the Sungai Mas area (a tributary of the much larger Sungai Muda) have yielded a large quantity of Chinese ceramic fragments (7th to 13th centuries) and fragments from pottery which originated in the Middle East (dated 8th to 10th centuries). There are also many beads—of pottery, glass, bone, gold and semi-precious stones—as well as some of local manufacture. This adds substance to the theory that coastal sites, such as these, used locally manufactured products as trade items with interior groups in exchange for jungle products, or raw metals, which would then be fed into the international trading networks. It also implies that there were local artisans who specialised in producing items for exchange and who must have been supported (paid in some way) to enable them to work and produce goods in quantity.

After Independence, there was strong support for restoring evidence of past achievements such as these Hindu–Buddhist shrines in Kedah's Bujang Valley.
(*Source:* Straits Times Annual, 1968)

A number of items associated with Buddhism have also been found at these sites, including Sanskrit inscriptions using local stone, dating from the 5th and 6th centuries CE. One of the sites has a Buddhist inscription about ignorance and rebirth, as well as the head of Buddha statue and a Buddhist votive tablet with the picture of a seated Buddha. From these we deduce that Buddhism, the networking religion of Indian merchants and artisans, was also being practised on the Peninsula from the 5th and 6th centuries. It is not clear, however, from these remains whether Indian visitors or settlers were involved, or whether local people were actively following Buddhist rites and beliefs.

Further evidence comes from about 5 kilometres north of Sungai Mas, from the next major river system, Sungai Merbok and its tributaries in the Bujang Valley (see map 2, page xvi). This region is near Gunung Jerai, or Kedah Peak, a striking mountain clearly visible from the sea and which is believed to have served as a navigational aid for ships making for the port upstream, on the Sungai Merbok. On the mountain are the remains of many small stone structures associated with Buddhism and it has been suggested they may have marked a route to the top of the mountain where there was a substantial temple. A considerable Buddhist community lived here which constructed and then maintained the temples served by monks and nuns.

South of Gunung Jerai, 16 temple structures dating from the first millennium CE have been identified. At least six were Buddhist and two Hindu. One of the Hindu temples, which has been partially restored, is the famous Candi Bukit Batu Pahat (Temple on the Hill of Cut Stone), probably dating from the 9th or 10th century CE. It is approached by an extended flight of steps and has a base of 30 × 80 feet (9 × 24 metres), with 100 000 brick-sized pieces of stone being used for its construction. On the basis of multichambered reliquaries found here and at other candis close-by, it has been suggested that they were built to commemorate a dead ruler or member of the elite and to enshrine their ashes. These remains provide evidence of a high degree of social organisation and leadership.

There is another important site which adds further information about more mundane aspects of life in the region at this time. At the village currently known as Pengkalan Bujang (Bujang Quay), which is situated at the confluence (always an auspicious site for exchange centres) of the Merbok and Bujang rivers, extensive finds of pottery, glass and other objects dating from between the 9th to the 13th centuries have been uncovered. They provide evidence that:

> . . . a prosperous trade conducted through the river included Chinese ceramics, Caliphate coins (one dated 234 of the Hijrah, the [Islamic] equivalent of 848 CE), pearls, gold, diamonds, beads, sapphires, moulded glass, Chinese bronze mirrors and bronze temple hanging lamps of the type used in South India, bronze images, ritual objects and glass bottles of near Eastern origin. The gemstones came from Burma, the beads and glassware from West Asia, clay votive tablets from India and porcelain

from China. Vivianite, a rare blue crystalline mineral known only in Selangor and Borneo, was also in use. Pengkalan Bujang therefore, had early trade contacts with many parts of Asia.[4]

The provenances of these items prove that ships from a variety of international ports collected, deposited and transferred cargoes at a point or points near the Kedah coast. The Kedah sites must also have been able to provide two important services for visitors. First, they would have been able to repair and supply ocean-faring vessels as well as provide accommodation while crews waited for the monsoon winds to change for return voyages. Second, they would have warehouses with supplies and stockpiles of local items for exchange (tin, gold, forest products) ready as cargo for ongoing vessels. These coastal sites were probably also points where arrangements were made to transport goods from the west coast to the east, so that shipment could be continued from ports on the Gulf of Siam. Adding further weight to this picture is Kedah's long history of shipbuilding and supplying food for provisioning. The large numbers of Buddhist votive tablets found along the river valleys in northern Kedah confirms that these were the routes used by carriers to tranship goods from coast to coast.

A major work of traditional Malay literature, *Hikayat Merong Mahawangsa* (named after one of Kedah's legendary early rulers) recounts the origins of the royal dynasty and the deeds of some of the rulers. As a written document, it has existed since at least the late 18th century but oral versions have been circulating much longer. Of particular interest here are its references to close links between the earliest Kedah rulers and other lands: Siam, Perak and Patani, as well as less formal ties with China and the Middle East. In *The Story of Merong Mahawangsa*, Kedah is presented as a kingdom with a wide range of contacts, and each is seen a centre of commercial and strategic interest to the well-being of the kingdom. It has also been suggested that one of

45

the themes which runs through the work is the ongoing tension in Kedah history between the attractions of the sea (trade) and the demands of the land which requires governance and a degree of control. The problems of governance seem to refer not only to the coastal inhabitants but also to inland groups such as the *Orang Asli*, and possibly later, the Thais. In general circulation, then, are very old stories about Kedah's place in the wider world and its dual function as seaward-looking node for international trade and an inland-oriented collection centre for local products.

This brief description of Kedah has hinted at its ambiguous position in the Malay sphere. Location and geopolitics incline it towards contact with its northern neighbours and with the further coast of the Bay of Bengal, while to the east, the overland routes across the Isthmus of Kra connect it with ports on the Gulf of Siam. Archaeological evidence reveals its links with Mon culture and with Buddhism. However, from about the 15th century, its links with the traditional Malay courts to the south (Perak and Melaka) and the adoption of Islam by the elite in the following centuries, show that culturally it was also strongly aligned with the Malay world. The range of orientations available to Kedah, and the tensions this caused, are expressed as major themes in *The Story of Merong Mahawangsa*, its most important literary text.

The advantages of Kedah's geographical position and its terrain, which yielded tin and could support mixed agriculture, attracted the attention of its neighbours. From the 13th century after the Thai occupied Siam, they became interested in Kedah as a gateway to Burma and the Bay of Bengal. From the 16th century, a range of peoples from the Indonesian archipelago established power bases in the kingdom. But even earlier, in 1025, the Cola rulers of south India were so disturbed by Kedah's success as a commercial competitor that they attacked and destroyed Pengkalan Bujang in 1025. During this period, they also attacked Srivijaya in southeast Sumatra, a well-known centre for trade passing through the Melaka Straits. Although Srivijaya is now part of

Indonesia, its prestige was so great that all later Peninsula Malay kingdoms claimed connections with it.

Srivijaya: federation and the mystique of power

Srivijaya has left more traces of its existence than the early ports of Kedah. The main sources are Chinese and Arab records, travellers' accounts and stone inscriptions. Using these, archaeologists and historians have worked together to try and locate the exact site of this ancient kingdom. The following account is based on the results of many years' research by scholars who have been dedicated to trying to understand the mystique of Srivijaya.

The earliest evidence about Srivijaya comes from a number of 7th century stone inscriptions from southeast Sumatra which mention the name 'Srivijaya' and from references in 7th century Chinese records to a place called Shih-li-fo-shih—the Chinese rendering of Srivijaya. The indications are that the centre of Srivijaya was near modern Palembang (see map 2, page xvi) but it was not until the early 1990s that archaeologists were able to confirm this. They uncovered over 55 000 artefacts from sites in the heart of Palembang, most of local manufacture, but also more than 10 000 pottery sherds from imported wares. Such a dense amount of material from one site indicates a significant concentration of people and these finds together with the inscriptions found in the vicinity of Palembang have convinced most scholars that this was the site of the main port of the kingdom of Srivijaya.

The references to Srivijaya in the Chinese records, and then from the 9th century in Arab sources as well, describe it as a place of significance and status in the region so that it attracted a great deal of trade. It was also renowned as a centre of Buddhist learning where Chinese pilgrims could go to study and prepare for visits to the holy sites of Buddhism in India. That such a large centre could have developed in southeast Sumatra surprised many modern researchers. It was believed that large centres needed a strong agricultural base and a rich and controllable hinterland. Like the coastal regions of the southern areas of the Malay Peninsula (separated only by the narrow Straits of Melaka), the southeast of Sumatra does not have volcanically enriched soils and links with the many groups inhabiting the uplands had to be established with diplomacy and maintained by mutual agreement. As one scholar has pointed out, 'in spite of the lack both of an agrarian base capable of producing substantial surpluses and of large concentrations of population, Srivijaya was one of the first, not one of the last, large polities to appear in the maritime region'.[5] In other words, the patterns of government and commerce which were established in Srivijaya were repeated in later Malay-dominated centres such as Melaka, Perak and Johor-Riau. Many of the same characteristics can still be found in the most successful modern port of the region, Singapore.

During this period both Srivijaya and Kedah were able to exploit the strategic advantages of their positions as commanding points at the crossroads of intersecting trade networks. Kedah had access to the Bay of Bengal, the Isthmus of Kra and thereby to the east coast of the Peninsula and the Gulf of Siam, as well as the northern entrance to the Straits of Melaka. Srivijaya was on the China–India sea route which hugged the coasts of the Gulf of Tonkin south to the Gulf of Siam, through the South China Sea, then to the island of Bangka. From there, ships could enter the Musi River of southeast Sumatra and sail up it to reach Srivijaya where cargoes were waiting and facilities were available to prepare for further travel: either to the east and Java and the Spice Islands or, via the Melaka Straits, to India.

I-Ching

We are fortunate to have the detailed account of a Chinese pilgrim, I-Ching (635–713 CE), who visited Srivijaya three times between 671 and 695. His perspective is of a foreign visitor who was attracted to

Srivijaya by its facilities for scholars of Buddhism. His first visit took 20 days by ship from Canton and he stayed six months to improve his knowledge of Sanskrit so that he could study effectively at Buddhist centre of Nalanda in India. The vessel he took to India was owned by the ruler of Srivijaya. He spent ten years in India, returning to Srivijaya to translate Buddhist texts (from Sanskrit into Chinese). He went briefly to Canton in 689 and returned with four assistants to continue with the translation work. I-Ching's notes are invaluable sources of information about how Srivijaya was viewed by Chinese Buddhists (*the* place to prepare for pilgrimage to India and a rich source of sacred Buddhist scriptures), and for information about the sea links between southern China and Southeast Asia. I-Ching describes the voyage which could take as little as three weeks and notes that there was a steady and regular stream of merchant vessels making the trip. He refers also to the large number of Buddhist monks (he gives the figure of 1000) living in the 'suburbs' of Srivijaya, and having among them very famous Indian teachers. A number of Buddhist images, very old bricks and the remains of a stupa have been found on or near Bukit Seguntang (the small Hill of Seguntang near Palembang—mentioned as a special site in the *Malay Annals*) and this evidence, together with the fact that the land around the hill is suitable for vegetable and fruit cultivation, has led some scholars to suggest that this was the region of Buddhist 'suburbs' which I-Ching referred to in his account of Srivijaya.

I-Ching presents a picture of a substantial concentration of people in the Palembang region and also records the expansion of Srivijaya's influence during the period of his visits (and this must have been only one of many additions to its influence). In his account, he notes that by the time of his last visit in 690, the region of Malayu had become a dependency of Srivijaya. It is fairly certain that 'Malayu' refers to an area north of Palembang, near modern Jambi, on the Batang Hari River (see map 2, page xvi) and indicates that Srivijaya's power was growing. Inscriptions from the same period add to this information. In one found to the east of Palembang (known as the Sabokingking Inscription), the ruler of Srivijaya refers to 'the large number of mandala under my system of datus'. Although this may appear to be rather cryptic, the terms 'mandala' and 'datu' are known to mean 'circle of power' and an office of leadership which could be rendered 'chief' or 'headman'. (As the modern word *Dato*, it is still awarded as a title for outstanding public service in Malaysia.) From I-Ching and the inscription, we learn that during the 7th century CE, the rulers based at Palembang, then known as Srivijaya, were expanding their influence and that they did not totally absorb these new additions, but administered them through leaders called *Datus*. The word 'mandala', with its circle associations, suggests that the modern concept of a federation of allies is more appropriate than that of an empire to describe the organisation of Srivijaya. The heartland of Srivijaya does not seem to have enforced tight control over its 'subject' areas but rather, worked in cooperation with them.

Further information about how the mandala/*datu* relationship probably worked in practice comes from Srivijaya's inscriptions. These inscriptions are so important it is worth describing them briefly. They begin to appear in the late 7th century CE, using Old Malay and Sanskrit language, written in a script originating from south India. They are the oldest evidence of a language which is recognisably similar to modern Malay. To date, they have been discovered in the vicinity of Palembang, on the nearby island of Bangka, and at locations much further away, including upper reaches of rivers in Sumatra. Inscriptions and artefacts linked with Srivijaya and dated from between the 10th and 12th centuries have been discovered in west Java, islands in the Straits of Melaka and on the Malay Peninsula, suggesting a wide sphere of influence. The inscriptions found near Palembang can be divided into three kinds: a prayer or mantra asking for success in an enterprise (the same formula as the Kedah Buddhist inscription mentioned above), announcements of royal gifts or royal victories and oaths of loyalty apparently administered to chiefs who were affiliated with Srivijaya. It is from the latter two types of inscription that we can gain some idea of the system of trade and exchange on which Srivijaya's standing as a port, and its system of administration depended.

The 'oath' inscriptions start with a short, non-Buddhist invocation to local spirits and continue with a list of curses and punishments which will befall those who break this oath of loyalty to their leader. One of these inscriptions is presumed to have been from near the royal residence of the ruler because it was directed to the ruler's family, household, military chiefs, palace officials, port officials and the *datu*. The other oath stones follow the same pattern but define loyalty to the *datu* and are presumed to have been for allegiance to the *datu* by lesser chiefs. From this we can reconstruct the levels of authority: lesser chiefs were bound by oaths to datu, who were bound in a similar way to the ruler of Srivijaya.

The location of the inscriptions and the pattern of trade, follow the type of exchange mechanisms which operated in prehistoric times on the Malay Peninsula—that is, a network of upland groups collecting products for trade and, by overland routes and/or river tributaries, bringing them to particular points where they would be exchanged for other items (from the coastal regions). The inland goods were taken, in stages and by various modes of transport, to coastal nodes where they were fed into the international system. This model applies equally to maritime trade networks where sea products were delivered to agreed points along coastlines and exchanged with the other goods which had been assembled there.

The advantages of this system were its capacity to respond quickly to changes in market demands and its cost effectiveness in terms of complex bureaucracy and long distances. The weaknesses were always that the affiliated groups would not cooperate or would transfer or shift their allegiance and deal exclusively with other nodes. The options for coercion and active enforcement by those in control of the central collection points were limited. They relied primarily on the supernatural power of their reputations and the dreadful threats of punishment contained in the oath inscription curses. Labour was a precious resource in these fragile terrains and punitive military action was avoided if at all possible. Although the Srivijayan inscriptions mention military personnel as part of the ruler's following, and give two accounts of large military expeditions (one to an interior area and the other to Java), later evidence of Malay political behaviour suggests that it is more likely that these expeditionary forces *looked* as if they would use military means to gain their ends. In reality, they were probably intent on achieving an outcome through negotiation and gifts or inducements.

One inducement that was both attractive and effective was to offer potential allies relationships with elite families through marriage. There are many instances of chiefs marrying the daughters (monogamy may not have been the rule then) of leaders of groups with whom they regularly traded. The ruler and his relatives likewise married the daughters of chiefs and neighbouring rulers with whom they needed firm alliances. The children of these unions would find it in their own interests to maintain the effectiveness of the system which sustained them and would in turn make their own marital alliances.

The viability of the Srivijaya commercial system—a network of collection and exchange points linked into a loose confederation of groups under *datus* giving their loyalty to a ruler—rested on the ruler's ability to reward that loyalty and on his personal charisma. One historian has examined the relationship between the Malay ruler and the acquisition of wealth. Using examples from the 18th and 19th century, he argues that the rulers were motivated 'not by avarice but by a desire to acquire and retain subjects, and it is clear that wealth was one condition for gaining supporters'.[6] Although the reference is to a later period, it is very likely that the same principle was operating in earlier times. The rulers of Srivijaya would have used their profits from trade to reward loyal allies and to support their personal retinues and perhaps some military personnel. In the sense that wealth was used to attract and retain supporters, it became a key factor in attaining and retaining power although it had a significant disadvantage. 'Rich

Malays became powerful Malays and the Raja therefore sought not only to enhance his own fortune but to prevent the accumulation of wealth on the part of his Malay subjects.[7] In other words, the ruler was always wary of those members of the elite who, through their own trading success, were acquiring wealth and were therefore potential threats to his power.

Wealth was a necessary part of the ruler's power of attraction but it was not the only aspect. Personal charisma associated with some kind of supernatural aura was also essential, especially in a primus inter pares system of confederation. One leader had to be different from the others to serve as the focal point. The inscriptions of Srivijaya again provide evidence about the aura, or mystique, of the late 7th century ruler. In 684, one of the inscriptions announced that the ruler was a Bodhisvatta—a being who has attained enlightenment but postponed nirvana, or eternal bliss, in order to assist others to attain it. The same ruler offered his 'loyal' subjects an 'immaculate tantra' and 'eternal peace', indicating that he was the source of rewards not only in this life but in the next. Those who maintained their oaths of allegiance to him would prosper and also gain eternal peace; those who betrayed him would be damned in this world and in the next.

Any ruler who made such extravagant claims and succeeded in attracting the notice of a wide range of foreign merchants would attract also the attention of competitors. The inscriptions mention several military expeditions which were sent to nearby regions but there must also have been threats to the major nodes in Srivijaya's network of exchange. Chinese records mention Javanese invasions of Srivijaya between 988 and 992 and Srivijaya did not escape raids from the Cola kings of southern India in about 1025, which Kedah also experienced. There were probably other attacks but the geopolitical advantages of Srivijaya, together with its reputation as major node for international trade, ensured that it remained on the global map for many centuries. From the Chinese point of view, Srivijaya was a reliable source of frankincense brought there from the Middle East and in the early 12th century Chinese sources describe the number of ships which congregated at Palembang and comment on its prosperity. In the 1390s, however, the ruler's residence in Palembang was destroyed by Javanese forces from the kingdom of Majapahit and the focus of Malay commercial activity moved elsewhere—further north on the Sumatran coast, and across the Straits to the rapidly growing centre of Melaka. Such was Srivijaya's reputation, that Melaka's royal chroniclers established a pedigree for their rulers which linked them directly with Palembang and presented them as heirs to Srivijaya's mystique. Palembang was not completely abandoned and some of its trade was maintained by the community of overseas Chinese who had settled there during the centuries that Srivijaya dominated the intricate system of exchange and international trade.

The legacy of language: an ancient pedigree for Malay

The inscriptions from the late 7th century located in the region of Palembang describing Srivijaya and its ruler, are the earliest surviving evidence of the Malay language. The script is Indian and terms for geographical concepts are borrowed from Sanskrit, but the terms for political relations and authority are Old Malay. Some of those Sanskrit terms have remained in usage and appear in contemporary Malay and Indonesian—terms such as desa (village) and istana (palace).

It has been shown recently that these Srivijaya inscriptions are the earliest surviving examples of the graphic representation of the sign for zero with its current function.[8] Although the system of mathematics based on the power of ten and using the void to indicate zero had its origin in India in the early centuries CE (or earlier), there has not yet been any evidence of its graphic representation which pre-dates the Srivijayan inscriptions. The significance of this 'find' lies not only in the very early evidence of a written sign for the zero but also in the fact that the Srivijayan inscriptions used Indian script, but not Indian *conventions*, for recording dates. Inscriptions in India from the same period record dates with words, not figures, and use a different dating system. The Srivijayan/Old Malay inscriptions reveal a confident local culture which expressed itself in terms familiar to foreign visitors while retaining its own identity.

The Old Malay of the Srivijayan inscriptions is formal in style and tone and restricted to official royal business yet it is recognisably related to standard modern Malay. If we compare Chaucer's English with modern English and Old Malay with modern Malay, the latter is recognisably closer than the former. Inscriptions using Old Malay have been found beyond Sumatra—seven in Java and one in the southern Philippines—and date from between the 8th and the early 10th centuries. Their distribution, near coastal centres, suggests they were associated with trading contacts but it is significant that their language and style is similar to those from Srivijaya and is evidence of the status which Old Malay had achieved. The existence of these inscriptions outside southeast Sumatra reminds us also that trading networks were extensive and that points along the network were in communication with each other.

Regional trade

The local networks which supplied Srivijaya with products for exchange had counterparts throughout the region wherever coastal nodes were linked into the patterns of international trade. Srivijaya was a major centre, and we know some of the details of its organisation because of archaeological evidence and travellers' reports. This kind of evidence has been harder to find for other centres. A small breakthrough came with the discovery of remnants of a characteristic type of locally made pottery distributed in areas around the Brunei Bay, the Sarawak River delta and at Johor Lama (in the southern part of the

Malay Peninsula). The pottery has been dated to between 700 CE and 1500 CE and its pattern of distribution overlaps with areas where coastal Malays now live. The researchers responsible for making these finds suggest that the pottery reveals a trading pattern linking southern China with northern and western Borneo, the southern areas of the Malay Peninsula and probably areas in between.

Marine archaeology conducted in the Brunei Bay in 1998 recovered 13 500 artefacts from the wreck of a 15th century vessel trading in the South China maritime network. This find has added further detail to our knowledge of the regional trade systems. First, the quantity and range of goods is greater than has hitherto been suspected and second, the diversity of geographical origins of the cargo. The pottery and porcelain came from southern China and various places in Thailand and ranges from high-quality decorative pieces and domestic ware to everyday utilitarian ware and mass-produced small pots. The latter appear to have been shipped to Borneo ports to be filled there with expensive products (perfumes, medicines) for re-export to other markets.

The Brunei Bay shipwreck cargo includes many items of Chinese origin and is from a period which saw increasing numbers of Chinese vessels trading directly with Southeast Asian ports. This suggests that from about the 12th century, there were sufficient numbers of Chinese vessels to enable a number of centres outside southeast Sumatra to develop. Srivijaya was no longer the only major entrepôt offering goods from the West and local produce. It now had rivals. The Javanese kingdom of Majapahit was one, and, from the 13th century onwards, the increasingly confident and powerful Thai at Sukhothai and later Ayutthaya, demanded allegiance from regional centres in Indochina and on the Malay Peninsula.

Regional geopolitics were complex and shaped around centres whose military capability added muscle to their claims to local loyalties. During the 11th and 12th centuries Burmese influence was strong in the northern parts of the Malay Peninsula but this was overshadowed in the following century by the Thais, who considered areas on the Malay Peninsula as part of their sphere of influence. Nodes in northern Borneo had links with the southern Philippines, southern Vietnam and Cambodia, and with other ports on the Borneo coast, in Brunei and Sarawak and possibly also with parts of the Malay Peninsula. The intricacies of diplomacy were based on acceptance of the fact that the imperial officials of China were the most powerful foreigners and required regular missions of tribute to invoke imperial protection and attract fleets of trading junks (boats). It is in this context of quite fierce rivalry and a growing number of attractive entrepôt options, that Srivijaya's hold on international trade was loosened and opportunities opened for new initiatives.

Although big power politics influenced the most-favoured nation policy of China, the major player in the region, the flow of trade through the established regional networks was sustained wherever collection points were maintained. So although the royal centre of Srivijaya was destroyed by a Javanese attack in the 1390s, there were sufficient numbers of Chinese merchants still living there to enable it to continue to function as an entrepôt. By this time, the presence of Chinese traders at active exchange points would have been widespread through Southeast Asia and the stability and contacts they provided enhanced the efficient operation of those ports. The movement of Chinese overseas and the permanent settlement of many of them dates back to at least this period. Henceforth, they would form a characteristic part of every major trading centre in Southeast Asia, occupying an economic and social niche in the cosmopolitan milieu of a port city by providing entrepreneurial and financial skills.

4
MELAKA: A TRADITIONAL MALAY KINGDOM

. . . and Melaka became a great city. Strangers flocked thither . . . and from below the wind to above the wind Melaka became famous as a very great city . . . so much so that princes from all countries came to present themselves before [the] sultan who treated them with due respect bestowing upon them robes of honour and of the highest distinction together with rich presents of jewels, gold and silver.

From the *Sejarah Melayu* (*Malay Annals*)[1]

The quotation above, from the famous 17th century Malay account of the Sultanate of Melaka, was chosen by Prime Minister Dr Mahathir to introduce the final section of his book *The Way Forward*, which was launched in 1998 by Britain's Baroness Thatcher. The prime minister was using the passage, which describes the success and fame of Melaka, to try to 'show the way forward' to contemporary Malaysians and prove to them (and the world) that Melaka had been a great commercial centre. It is a good example of the use of *Malay Annals* as an essential part of modern political culture but it also illustrates Melaka's reputation for being the greatest port in 15th century Southeast Asia. From very early times, the demands of international trade and the strategic situation of ports in the region of the Straits of Melaka contributed to the working of a system of collection and exchange points which circulated through the region and fed into longer-distance trade routes. Unlike most of the other ports in the region, however, visitors to Melaka left written accounts describing its royal court, commercial success and power politics. A Portuguese traveller, Tome Pires, in the early 16th century wrote to persuade the Portuguese that Melaka was of crucial importance to Europe: 'Whoever is lord of Malacca has his hand on the throat of Venice. As far as from Malacca, and from Malacca to China, and from China to the Moluccas, and from the Moluccas to Java, and from Java to Malacca and Sumatra, [all] is in our power.'[2]

The *Malay Annals* is an invaluable source for trying to understand the priorities and values of a Malay sultanate and it will be a primary source for this discussion. The system of governance and the royal ceremonial developed at Melaka during the 15th century were maintained by later Malay kingdoms, such as Kedah and Johor which will be described in the following chapter.

International commerce

During the 12th and 13th centuries regional and international trading activity was booming. One analysis of global trade patterns for this period has identified three major interlocking systems: a European subsystem with Genoa and Venice as commercial centres; a Middle Eastern network incorporating routes in and out of Mongol Asia using the Persian Gulf and the Red Sea; and the Indian Ocean–East Asia system, incorporating Southeast Asia and the China–India networks. Venice and Genoa owed their wealth to their roles as intermediaries between Asian goods and European markets.

The sea route for any of the cargoes from Eastern Indonesia and Java, and from China, Indochina and Borneo, lay through the Straits of Melaka. Any ports along the route had the potential to attract vessels engaged in this trade and ports in west Java as well as others on the east coast of Sumatra tried to do so. One such attempt was made by a person known as Paramesvara from Palembang, who in the 1390s is credited with establishing a settlement on the modern island of Singapore, then called Temasek.

Archaeological evidence from Singapore and the nearby islands of the Riau archipelago provides confirmation of substantial trading activity in this region during the 14th century but it was not sustained. Malay, Javanese and, later, European accounts record attacks on Paramesvara's settlement by Javanese and also by Siamese fleets, forcing him to abandon Singapore and move further north. Chinese records of the *Ming Imperial Annals* pick up his story in 1403 at Melaka, where he had settled and made contact with Chinese ships, sent south by the newly installed Ming dynasty. Chinese officials found it in their interests to recognise Paramesvara's settlement and in return for his offers of tribute, gave him gifts of costly silks and parasols and granted him their protection. This meant that Chinese trade flowed to Melaka and Chinese imperial protection shielded it from Siamese and Javanese attacks, providing it with a special status in the region—a favoured Chinese port. The early rulers of Melaka personally visited China on a number of missions (each recorded in official Ming records) to ensure continued Chinese protection for their port.

The influence of Islam

Paramesvara led Melaka until his death in 1414 when he was succeeded by his son Megat Iskandar Shah, who is also mentioned in Chinese records. He ruled for the next decade. As noted earlier, one of the early Srivijaya inscriptions linked the ruler with Buddhism by presenting him as a Bodhisvatta and it is thought that Paramesvara continued this concept. But his son and successor is credited with being the first Malay ruler to convert to Islam. Why would it have been advantageous for him to present himself as a sultan as well as a raja?

To understand some of the reasons for adding Islam to the Melaka ruler's attributes, we need to understand the status of Islam in the 15th century. The Abbasid rulers of Baghdad (8th to 13th century) had created a splendid image of Muslim kingship in which the ruler was God's shadow on earth. This Persianised expression of sovereignty was attractive to many rulers in the Middle East and India. They embraced Islam and the culture of kingship which the Abbasids had developed. There was thus a growing number of medieval Muslim sultanates and this news would have quickly reached Southeast Asian centres.

Islam was attractive not only to the ruling elite but also to those participating in the international trade network, whose feeders into the Mediterranean and the European markets were through the heartlands of Islam. In the 8th and 9th centuries, Buddhism had been the religion of southern Indian merchants and artisans as recorded in the inscriptions of Kedah as well as Srivijaya. However, as the influence of Islam spread, the merchant guilds and trading cooperatives in Gujerat and Bengal began adopting the outward symbols of Islam and benefiting from the solidarity and recognition this provided. There were also small communities of Chinese converts, some of who were involved with regional trade. Although these traders had been in contact with Southeast Asian networks since the 9th century, it was not until the Persian expressions of Muslim kingship were circulating in India and then Southeast Asia, that Malay and other local elites began to adopt Islam. The reasons probably varied according to local contexts, but it has been emphasised that the political cultures of the Malayo–Indonesian archipelago at this time were 'compatible in important respects with the prevailing political culture of medieval Islam', and that local rulers 'came to see their functions and objectives in Muslim terms'.[3]

Paramesvara protected his new settlement at Melaka through alliances with imperial China while his son and successor ensured its commercial position and enhanced his own status by adopting Islam as the official court religion. There were other advantages. As a patron of Islam, the ruler of Melaka was able to assume the title of sultan, placing himself on the same level as other sultans in the Middle East and India and exploiting the rich traditions of Persian leadership which included claiming descent from Alexander the Great.

Once Islam had become the court religion of Melaka, no time was lost in making this widely known. Coins from 15th century Melaka bore the new titles of sultan and shah and used Arabic phrases to describe the ruler as 'Helper of the World and of the Religion'. Visitors to Melaka from other Muslim regions would have recognised these formulae of authority and perhaps felt reassured that they were dealing with a ruler who upheld Muslim values, respected Muslim law and protected fellow Muslims.

Commercial life

The Ming dynasty's need for pepper and sappanwood (for making dyes) from Southeast Asia in the early 15th century provided the sympathetic context for Melaka's establishment, but the spice merchants of Cairo, intent on dominating the trade into the Mediterranean, also added new momentum to the demand for nutmegs and cloves from Eastern Indonesia. Both these factors guaranteed a continuing strategic role for entrepôts along both sides of the Straits of Melaka, so that ports on Sumatra's east coast (such as Aru, Pasai and Aceh) also attracted considerable trade. The centres in the Straits were in competition but each also had their own special attractions. Melaka, for example, became the main centre for textiles from Gujerat and Coromandel, which were traded for spices from the Moluccas, silk and porcelain from China, gold, pepper and forest products from Sumatra, camphor from Borneo, sandalwood from Timor and tin from the Malay Peninsula.

Melaka, like Srivijaya before it, became a major stapling centre, distinguishing it from smaller ports and collection points where goods were collected and exchanged during only brief interactions between local traders. At Melaka, foreign merchants stayed for several months trading, refitting and provisioning their vessels. The most numerous of these long-term visitors were the Gujeratis, whose numbers grew to about 1000 by the late 15th century. Other major groups of permanent residents included Tamils, Javanese, Chinese, Bengalis, with smaller communities of Chams (from southern Vietnam), Parsees, Arabs, Burmese and Siamese.

The supervision of the day-to-day business of running a complex entrepôt like Melaka was delegated by the Malay ruler to officials termed *shahbandars*. This was a position of power and was used by incumbents to gain their own share of taxes and dues and grant favours. In the early 16th century, when the volume of trade being handled at Melaka was at its height, four *shahbandars* were appointed, each working with a particular trading community. In this way the Gujeratis and Chinese, for example, would have a *shahbandar* to oversee their needs and collect taxes on behalf of the ruler. In a cosmopolitan port such as Melaka, those best-placed to liaise with foreign merchants were themselves foreigners and the records indicate that the *shahbandars* were usually not Malays.

The *shahbandars* were responsible for providing transport to unload cargoes, collecting dues from ships' captains and ensuring the accuracy of weights and measures. Goods were sold by barter, or for gold and coinage. Detailed regulations for all aspects of maritime trade, at sea and in port, were set out in a special Melaka Maritime Code (*Undang-Undang Laut Melaka*) which gives a vivid picture of contemporary commercial and shipboard life. From it, and other sources, we learn that women played an active role in commercial life, in the local markets as well as in international trade. For this reason, foreign merchants found it a great advantage to marry a local woman who could engage in trade on his behalf and supervise his business interests.

The available records for details of the types of goods being traded through Melaka show that the port attracted large-scale, high-return goods as well as lower-return, but necessary local trade. The high-return trade was focused on long-distance markets (China, the Middle East and Europe) and specialised in whatever luxury goods were in fashion. It returned high profits, took little space, but required a considerable investment to make the original purchase. The Malay elite engaged in this kind of trade as well as foreign merchants. The smaller-scale trade did not require vessels capable of making long-distance voyages and consisted of items needed for daily life: for example, food (Melaka had to import most of its rice from Java and Siam), spices and textiles for ordinary wear.

The *Orang Suku Laut*

Some of the small-scale trade was carried in local boats and many of these would have been manned by members of the various sea-peoples known as the *Orang Suku Laut*. The islands, atolls and sea-strands were their habitat, particularly in the southern parts of the Straits throughout the Riau-Lingga archipelago (see map 5, page xix). They collected marine products for exchange and were masters of the complex currents, hidden straits and treacherous waters of the South China Sea between southwest Borneo, the southern tip of the Malay Peninsula and the east coast of Sumatra. They were recognised as the expert seamen of the region and seem to have established working relationships with those local chiefs who had contact with them. There is evidence that during the Srivijaya period some of the groups had a special and direct relationship with the rulers of Srivijaya. The rulers protected the Sea People in return for services, such as acting as pilots and providing manpower for Srivijaya's vessels. It is also thought that the Sea People did not raid vessels which traded with Srivijaya and that they may even have actively diverted passing trade to enter Srivijaya-linked ports and conduct their business there.

The *Orang Suku Laut* who operated in this area were known by the names of the islands around whose coasts they operated. They had then, and still lay claim to, specific locations where they came ashore to take fresh water, collect firewood and food from the sea strand, and settle for short periods. Any coastal trading centre in the vicinity of *Orang Suku Laut* groups had to establish working relationships with them or their independent trading and raiding activities would deter larger commercial vessels from entering the Straits. In the 15th century, when the Malay sultans of Melaka claimed that they were descended from the old rulers of Srivijaya, the court was able to call on some groups of the *Orang Suku Laut* to assist with special court duties. The relationship between powerful Malays and the Sea People was symbiotic and endured into the 20th century with groups in the Riau-Lingga archipelago claiming that their ranks and titles dated back to descendants of the Melaka rulers.

Political culture

The second half of the 15th century was a boom time for Melaka. Actual population figures for Melaka at its peak vary greatly. It was in the interests of both the Malay rulers and the Portuguese conquerors to exaggerate them. The Portuguese Admiral Alfonso de Albuquerque, gives 100 000 but the figure of 10 000 dwellings, or 40–50 000 individuals, the estimate of a Portuguese captured by the Malays in around 1510, has been accepted as realistic, bearing in mind that Melaka was heavily dependent on rice imports from Siam and Java for food supplies.

Ruled by a Malay sultan whose court had diplomatic links with the major centres of the time and whose ceremonial impressed foreign missions, Melaka was well-organised and welcoming for foreign traders. Foreigners were also reassured that orderly procedure and fair practice was guaranteed in a framework of Islamic laws combined with indigenous codes, implemented by senior officials who were close to the sultan himself. The four most senior ministers were the *bendahara*, chief executive for the sultan, the *temenggung* whose duties included law enforcement, the *laksamana* or admiral of the fleet, and the *penghulu bendahari*, or treasurer.

Malaysians are taught at school that the Malay court of Melaka embodied the earliest expression of Malay ideals for governance and correct behaviour. These are explicitly stated in the *Malay Annals* which record a covenant made between the first Malay ruler and the local chief, who became his chief minister and entered into the agreement on behalf of the ruler's subjects. The covenant was initiated by the local chief to protect all subjects from being humiliated or maltreated without just cause by the ruler. The ruler agreed, but added the stipulation that all subjects, present and future, should never be disloyal to the ruler, even if maltreated. If ever the ruler broke the covenant by humiliating or publicly shaming even one of his subjects, he would be punished by losing his kingdom. Thus, loyalty and public humiliation were made the cornerstones of the relationship between the ruler and his subjects. Throughout the *Malay Annals*, the symbiotic link between ruler and subject is emphasised, expressed in sayings such as, 'There would be no tree if there were no roots and no ruler if there were no subjects.'

The code for Malay subjects was unswerving loyalty to the sultan. In return, the sultan, who was believed to be invested with supernaturally-given powers of sovereignty (*daulat*) at the time of his coronation, had to treat his subjects with generosity, fairness and compassion. As leader of his subjects, the sultan had to show qualities of courage and bravery. The literary conventions of the traditional texts always describe the sultan as being handsome beyond compare, dressed in the finest garments and surrounded by exquisite women, the most beautiful of whom was his consort, and attended by brave and intelligent young men.

One of the traditional stories set at the court of Melaka in its heyday, *Hikayat Hang Tuah* (*The Story of Hang Tuah*), concerns the relationship between Melaka's greatest sultan and five of his bravest young warriors led by one called Hang Tuah. The story is well-known in modern Malaysia from school texts, comic books, films and videos and describes the rise of Hang Tuah and his four comrades to high positions at the court of Melaka. The jealousy this arouses in other courtiers leads to slander against Hang Tuah and the sultan orders him to be put to death. The sultan's wise chief minister (the *bendahara*) does not carry out the order but hides Hang Tuah. His comrades believe he has been executed, and one avenges this injustice by occupying the royal palace and sleeping with the sultan's women attendants. This behaviour breaks all rules and is considered an act of the highest treason (*derhaka*) but the sultan does not have any warriors brave enough to confront the perpetrator. The wise chief minister is able to summon Hang Tuah who places loyalty to his sovereign above loyalty to his comrade, fights a gruelling duel and kills him. Hang Tuah's example of unswerving devotion to the sultan has traditionally been regarded as the model for all Malay subjects to follow. During the 20th century, however, some modern Malays have questioned the appropriateness of Hang Tuah's almost blind obedience to his ruler. They championed instead the comrade who lost his own life trying to avenge an injustice to his friend. Both Hang Tuah and his comrade live on in contemporary Malaysian consciousness as symbols of the strengths and weaknesses of the traditional sultanate.

The unsung hero of the Hang Tuah story is the wise *bendahara*. He disobeys the sultan's order to execute Hang Tuah on the grounds that it is not only unjust but unwise, because he knows that Melaka cannot afford to lose one of its most intelligent and courageous men.

The position of the *bendahara* in the traditional sultanate is second only to the ruler. The *bendahara* did not have the *daulat* (sacred power of sovereignty) invested in the sultan but he was the highest ranking courtier and was usually closely related to the sultan by blood or marriage. It was appropriate for the daughter of the *bendahara* to become consort for the sultan, thus maintaining the genealogical links between the two senior levels of government. Besides serving as senior adviser to the sultan, the *bendahara* was also responsible for the defence of the kingdom and the implementation of its laws. The *Malay Annals* devotes almost as much attention to descriptions of the *bendahara* as it does to the sultan, thus emphasising his crucial role in the sultanate.

Questions of status

An important aspect of Malay political culture was the distinction between elite and non-elite Malays.

The elite

Those who were close to the sultan through blood-ties or position were accorded the highest status in Melaka. The elite were differentiated from others by a strict code of dress and ornamentation reserved for them alone and by degrees of physical propinquity to the sultan. Within the elite, status was graded. The *bendahara* and the other three senior officials mentioned above took precedence.

The ruler and his family, his retinue and attendants and the senior ministers were physically separated from the non-elite with residences around the top of the small hill which dominates the rather flat area of Melaka. The *Malay Annals* describe the palace built by the *bendahara* for Sultan Mansur (1459–77), sixth sultan of Melaka. The *bendahara* brought people from Bentan, his domain in the *Orang Suku Laut* region of the Riau-Lingga archipelago, to construct the palace. The description of its seven-tiered roof, pillars, bays, cupolas, gilded spires, inset panels of Chinese mirrors and roof of copper and zinc shingles, is so detailed that the palace was able to be reconstructed in modern Melaka and is now used as the Cultural Museum. The residences of lesser officials were on the lower slopes, while the non-elite lived in settlements along the Melaka River.

The non-elite

Details of daily life in and around Melaka are available from sections of the Melaka Law Code which mention the growing of rice, sugarcane, bananas, fruit trees, betel nut, buffalo, cattle and goats. The fertile areas lay inland and rice may have been obtained from the hill crops of *Orang Asli* groups living upriver and referred to in early Portuguese reports as 'Benuas'.

Slaves

Slaves were used for labour in agriculture, to man vessels and to perform household tasks. People were enslaved for debt or because they were regarded as non-Malays, culturally inferior and available for exploitation. Debt slaves could repay their debt and have their free status restored. Other slaves were regarded as permanently in bondage and many in this category were the children of *Orang Asli* who were taken in raids and sold or exchanged in much the same way as natural products from the interior.

The number of provisions in the Melaka Law Code concerning slaves reflects their economic and social importance as the major source of labour. The low population density of the Malaysian territories meant that manpower was a precious resource. Wealth was measured not only in terms of material possessions but also in terms of the number of slaves a leader controlled.

Foreign residents

Although the sultan and the highest ranking Malay officials directly engaged in trade, they worked also with foreign merchants. These merchants were divided into those who settled permanently in Melaka and worked as intermediaries between other foreigners and local merchants, and those who merely used Melaka as a staging post on a return or a longer voyage. Those foreigners who resided permanently in Melaka were in a position to gain the trust of the Malay elite. Several married into leading Malay families and founded lines which became famous in Melaka's history.

As well as large merchant groups from south India, there were significant communities of Chinese and Javanese who had their own districts, or *kampungs*, near the waterfront and along the river and who lived from trading or worked as labourers (including small-scale tin-mining), artisans and mercenaries. Other foreigners, including Persians, Arabs, Burmese, Siamese and Cham (from southern Vietnam) also chose to live permanently in Melaka, thus making it a very diverse and no doubt volatile society. Many had local wives and their children formed the beginning of the *mestizo* communities which became a characteristic and essential part of the major cities of Southeast Asia. The majority of these people must have remained in Melaka after the Portuguese assumed control in 1511 because population estimates for the mid-16th century do not vary greatly from those of the late 15th century.

Diplomacy

Several factors contributed to the value placed on diplomatic skills as an essential quality for a Malay leader. Chief among these was the need to avoid warfare or any direct conflict which would lead to extensive loss of life. As well, trade and commerce relied on contact with people from different backgrounds, who would take their business elsewhere if they did not feel secure and respected. The strategic position of the Malaysian territories also exposed them to the influence and designs of powerful neighbours like Siam and China.

A careful reading of the *Malay Annals* suggests a range of strategies were employed to establish and maintain good relations with neighbours near and far. For areas beyond Melaka, the ruler delegated authority to trusted chiefs in a way that may have resembled the *Datu* system of Srivijaya. The *bendahara*, for example, had authority over the regions of Muar and Bentan (see Map 5, page xix), while other chiefs were granted areas on the east coast of Sumatra, a region whose access to the jungle products of upland Sumatra and to the gold of the interior made it of crucial importance to Melaka, as it had been to Srivijaya.

Other territories and centres were presided over by a close relative of the ruling sultan of Melaka and there they established the ceremonial of the Melaka court. In this way, Pahang and Kampar (on Sumatra's east coast) became linked with Melaka and, after 1511, the ruler and *bendahara* of Perak came from the Melaka ruling line.

Alliance by marriage is referred to often in the *Annals*, and the bride usually brought her husband the rights to particular territories. Thus, when one of the Melaka sultans married a Javanese princess, he was given the important centre of Inderagiri on Sumatra's east coast and later, in the 19th century, Inderagiri historians proudly emphasised these links with Melaka. When Kelantan surrendered to a delegation sent from Melaka, a Kelantan princess was chosen to become the wife of the Melaka ruler.

Very different strategies were adopted towards non-Malay centres such as those in Siam and China. It was the protection of the fleets of Ming China which enabled Melaka to become established in the Straits region, and Chinese records note that the early rulers of Melaka made regular visits to the Imperial Court. The Thais were consistently interested in the areas to the south of their heartland (as they were in all their neighbouring regions). The *Malay Annals* contains accounts of several attacks on Melaka which were repelled, in one instance, by tricking the Thais into believing the Malay forces outnumbered their own. The ruler of Melaka then decided to use diplomacy and formal relations were established. At the time Melaka was settled, the centre of the Thai kingdom was at Ayutthaya which established its own direct relationships with Malay centres in the northern parts of the Malay Peninsula. A custom introduced by the rulers of Ayutthaya, and accepted by Malay rulers wanting to remain on friendly terms, was the sending of ornamental trees made from gold and silver. These were recognised by both sides as a symbol of submission which did not cost the sender more than token obeisance.

In these ways—diplomacy, marriage, alliance, delegation of authority and symbolic gestures of submission, as well as negotiation and bluff—Melaka established its position in the region and maintained a prolonged relationship with Siam and China. These strategies, however, did not work with the Portuguese who first made contact with Melaka in the early 16th century.

Spices for Europe: the Portuguese attacks

By the late 15th century, the ruling powers of Portugal were determined to break the Muslim monopoly of the spice trade to Europe. The Papal Bull of 1493, *Insulae Novi Orbis*, divided the world between Spain and Portugal and gave each the task of propagating the faith wherever they went. The Portuguese pursued their commercial mission with zeal and after establishing posts along the west coast of Africa, then winning naval supremacy of its east coast, they reached the west coast of India and gained a foothold in Cochin (1503). After several years of intermittent naval battles against Egyptian and Gujerati fleets, on St Catherine's Day (10 November) 1510, Afonso de Albuquerque took Goa from the sultan of Bijapur and made it the centre of Portuguese influence in the East.

Albuquerque implemented a policy of commercial contact rather than military commitment. However, a Portuguese mission under Diogo Lopes de Sequeira, despatched to open trade with Melaka in

1509, had ended in disaster with some of the mission being imprisoned. Malay accounts suggest that the Portuguese offended Malay officials, while the Portuguese believe they were slandered by Gujerati merchants. In July 1511, Albuquerque himself came to rescue his men and also sought compensation and permission to build a fortified trading centre. The Malays declined and Albuquerque attacked and took the Melaka bridge but was beaten back. A month later the Portuguese again attacked and gained a foothold which they were able to exploit in a later attack and take the town. The battle scenes are described graphically in the *Malay Annals*, in Portuguese paintings and in later representations. Although the forces of Melaka are often romantically depicted as being overwhelmed by Europeans armed with superior weaponry, contemporary accounts note that the local forces had good supplies of firearms, possibly manufactured at Pegu and Ayutthaya, and that their heavy cannon caused considerable loss of life to the Portuguese. One contemporary European account describes the Malays as 'most valiant men, well trained in war, and copiously supplied with every type of very good weapon.'[4] This suggests that the battle was by no means one-sided but the Malay elite decided to retreat from the town. For the next few years although they regularly sent small fleets to harass Portuguese ships they did not succeed in dislodging them from Melaka.

Albuquerque stayed to oversee the construction of A Famosa, the stone fortress whose remains are still a symbol of Melaka, and, on the site of the Malay royal palace, built the church of St Paul's. A wall was built to encircle the main Portuguese buildings and the locals forced to live outside, a separation started by the Malay elite. It was Albuquerque's aim to maintain Melaka as it had been under the Malays and to this end he kept as closely as possible to the existing system of customs dues and continued the administration of foreign merchants under their own representative *shahbandars*. When they first occupied Melaka, the Portuguese were in a much weaker position than the Malay rulers had been, because they controlled only the town and a small

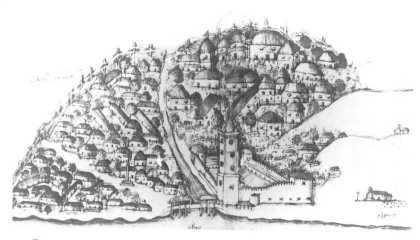

Portuguese impression of Melaka from the sea in 1515 showing clearly the division between the fortified elite quarters on the right and the suburbs of the merchants and non-elite on the left of the Melaka river. (Source: National Archives of Malaysia)

amount of surrounding territory. They did not have the support of neighbouring chiefs and local rulers and one of their first moves was to try to establish friendly relations with neighbouring states.

Albuquerque also believed that Portuguese long-term interests would be well served by a permanent community of Eurasians working in Melaka and he encouraged Portuguese men to marry local women. As a gesture of good faith to those women who accepted Portuguese offers of marriage, he gave dowries of the cultivated land which had been left by the retreating Malay elite. Working with Indian merchants, the Portuguese traded Indian textiles for spices from the centres in Sumatra and eastern Indonesia.

The move from Melaka

Some Malays remained in small settlements around Melaka exchanging produce with the merchants of the entrepôt as they had done under Malay rule. The Portuguese did not impose their laws or religion on them. The Malay elite, however, repeated the strategy of Paramesvara, Melaka's founder who, when driven from Singapore by Javanese attacks, simply withdrew and resettled elsewhere.

The Malay sultans and the Malay elite of Melaka had benefited greatly from the profits of trade. In fact, so great were the profits during this very active 15th century, that it was not possible for the sultan to monopolise all the wealth which flowed from dues and taxes. Foreigners, particularly Indians, and senior members of the Malay elite, like the *bendahara*, the *temenggung* and the *laksamana*, became extremely wealthy in gold and money, as well as substantial numbers of followers. The sultan was no longer the sole source of advancement and, although several sultans did have rivals executed or banished, this did not eliminate the problem of competitors. Only one royal prince could succeed as ruler and many disappointed princes either left Melaka voluntarily or married into ruling families at other centres, especially in east Sumatra. Some remained at court and provided alternative foci for ambitious courtiers.

The ruling line of the Melaka sultanate was not a straightforward genealogy, especially in a system where father-to-son succession was not the only path to the throne (younger brothers and senior male relatives were also acceptable). At a court where the ruler had more than one royal wife, as well as numerous concubines, there was never a shortage of potential male heirs. Theoretically, the mother of a royal heir was one of the ruler's queens, but at least one ruler was descended from a mother who was not recognised as a queen and this injected an element of weakness into the whole line thereafter. Rival princes from the senior female line could challenge the incumbent line based on their ancestry. This did happen during the 17th century.

A further element of instability and uncertainty which existed during and after this period, centred round the power, wealth and prestige of the *bendaharas*. Their wealth was well attested and this was combined with very close blood relationship with the sultans—either grandfather, uncle, cousin, or by marriage with female relatives. They were obvious candidates for the throne and this was recognised by their official role as regents, if the ruler were a minor. Ambitious courtiers might support the *bendahara* in the belief that he would come to power and take them with him.

The ability of the elite to amass wealth for their own purposes and the flexibility of the royal line during this period contributed to a climate around the ruler that was tense and volatile. The physical separation, symbolic of the distance between the status of the elite and the non-elite, which was a feature of the political culture during this time also contributed to a sense of tension in the community. The ruler was literally isolated from the people and probably also from all but the most senior of his chiefs. This would have made it difficult to inspire the very close ties of loyalty which were an essential part of the ruler–subject relationship in Malay political culture. As well, the special links which the rulers of Srivijaya developed with the *Orang Suku Laut* were no longer the sole preserve of the sultan. The *bendahara*, for example, had the allegiance of the *Orang Suku Laut* groups in his territory of Bentan, and the *laksamana* could also command his own following. During the 15th century, the growth in access to material wealth and the greater diversity of power relations resulted in much greater potential for competition within the Melaka elite, as well as between external centres which were keen to attract the Straits trade to their harbours and away from Melaka.

When the Melaka elite withdrew from the Portuguese onslaught of 1511, they were dependent on the local maritime people (*Orang Suku Laut*) and the local *Orang Asli* the 'Original people', to help them escape. An old story in the Philippines relates how a relative of the sultan of Melaka escaped with his followers and, taken by the *Orang Suku Laut*, reached Mindanao. Establishing allies there, he settled, and the *Orang Suku Laut* returned to their domain in the islands south of the Malay Peninsula. For the Malay sultan himself, it was probably too risky to attempt to leave Melaka by sea because the Portuguese fleet was still active. The main group of retreating nobles, therefore, took the ancient overland route to Pahang (see map 2, page xvi), a six day trip using river tributaries to cross the Peninsula from west to east. They would have relied on the local *Orang Asli* for directions and assistance as porters. As already mentioned, the languages of some of the *Orang Asli* groups—those following the Malayic sociocultural pattern and living in the south of the Peninsula—show that they have long been in contact with Malay speakers, extending back to at least the 16th century.

The displaced Malays from the Melaka court seemed to have believed the retreat was not permanent for they did not attempt to resettle for some years but spent the time with relatives at royal centres in Pahang and on Sumatra's east coast. They did, however, make bases in the islands of the Riau archipelago and worked with the *Orang Suku Laut* to raid Portuguese ships, prompting reprisals from the Portuguese forces, now well established at Melaka. At some stage during this early period of retreat, Sultan Mahmud ordered the execution of his son, who was also his co-ruler, an indication that the old divisions among the ruling elite were continuing. On Sultan Mahmud's death in 1529, another son, who ruled as Sultan Alauddin Riayat Shah, succeeded him and reigned for over 30 years. This sultan established settlements along the Johor River (see map 2, page xvi) and, with him, began the next phase of the Melaka dynasty. In a new location, it was known thereafter as the kingdom of Johor.

5
JOHOR AND KEDAH: CONTRACTS AND ALLIANCES

In the year 1096, on the 28th day of the month Rabi'al-akhir [April 3, 1685] . . . I Paduka Raja [royal prince] who rules Johor and Pahang, have concluded this contract with Francois van der Beke, Syahbandar, and Lieutenant Jan Rosdom when they came as ambassadors to the Yang Dipertuan [the One who is Lord], asking to trade in cloth with the Minangkabaus up the Siak River.[1]

Rulers of kingdoms in the Malay world were skilled in relations with foreigners and the diplomatic activities of the Melaka elite during the 15th century indicate how assiduously they worked to keep open a wide range of options in their local and foreign relations. Complex ceremonies were developed to honour visitors to royal courts and Europeans participated in these ceremonies and conducted business on local terms.

The permanent settlement of the Portuguese in Melaka, followed by the Dutch in eastern Indonesia and Java, brought some changes to the way business was conducted. Europeans considered precisely worded contracts important and tried to gain exclusive trading rights to certain products. Misunderstandings were later to occur because of basic differences in attitudes to the status of contracts. Dutch merchants, for example, believed in 'the letter of the law and the fine print of their eternal treaties'.[2] Malay officials did not view the contracts in the same way. For them, solemnly sworn oaths were the most binding form of agreement. The earliest evidence of the sanctity of oaths comes from the inscriptions of the Srivijayan period when the *datus* and others swore eternal allegiance to the ruler, believing that supernatural retribution would befall them if they broke their word. The penalties for departing from the terms of contracts with strangers were not held in similar awe. After Islam became the official religion of the Melaka court 'oaths were sworn in the sight of Allah, who was evoked as the ultimate guarantor of sincerity and justice' and contracts made with non-Muslims may not have had the same 'profound significance'.[3]

The continuing presence of Europeans in Southeast Asia demanded some adaptation on both sides and the Portuguese victory of 1511 offers an appropriate moment to pause and briefly survey the historical context of the Malaysian territories and the neighbouring regions during the 16th, 17th and 18th centuries and to note the realignments and responses which were occurring during that time.

Although the Portuguese aimed to keep Melaka operating as the entrepôt it had been under the Malay elite, many of the Muslim merchants from India and from the Middle East, as well as local traders, moved their business to alternative ports. This strengthened the position of several centres on Sumatra's north and east coasts which had long been Melaka's rivals. The *Malay Annals*, for example, acknowledge that the only kingdoms which were Melaka's equals (during the 15th century) were Aru (Haru) and Pasai, both on Sumatra's northeast coast and centres which could collect and exchange the resins, aromatic woods, pepper and gold which were staple entrepôt items.

Pasai was absorbed into its more aggressive neighbour, Aceh (see map 2, page xvi) and, from 1520, the rulers of Aceh energetically promoted their ports at the expense of others in the Straits area. They competed with the Portuguese by trading directly with centres in the Red Sea, thus bypassing Melaka and Portuguese ports on the west coast of India. This also threatened the trading networks of the ex-Melaka elite now in the Johor region, and in 1540 they formed an alliance with their former rivals in Aru against Aceh. During the 1560s, Aceh retaliated by attacking and overwhelming the small settlements and royal sites along the Johor River. Aceh was now the major power in the Straits region.

From the 1580s until the 1630s there was a resurgence in international trade involving China, Japan, India and Europe. Contributing to this intensified activity, merchants in both England and the Netherlands began to engage directly in voyages to the East. English and Dutch interest in Southeast Asia begins from this period. In 1607, the most successful of Aceh's rulers, Sultan Iskandar Muda, assumed power. He responded to the international demand for increasing amounts of pepper and tin by attacking Kedah and Perak, the tin-rich areas of the Malay Peninsula, as well as Pahang, whose upland gold deposits must have been very attractive.

Sultan Iskandar Muda ruled Aceh until his death in 1636. He is Aceh's most famous sultan and his reign is celebrated in several Malay prose works, which he commissioned from scholars at his court. He also brought scholars from India and the Middle East to strengthen Islam in his kingdom and to write religious treatises in Malay, the earliest examples we have of Muslim texts written for Malays. He established Aceh as a glorious centre for trade and religion but this was achieved at the expense of his neighbours. Large numbers of people were taken from the Malay Peninsula—11 000, it is said from Pahang alone—to serve as labourers and cultivators in Aceh. In 1613, his forces again destroyed the Johor royal centre on the Johor River and the royal family was taken to Aceh where a Johor prince was forced to marry an Acehnese princess and returned to Johor to rule under Aceh. This prince was no obedient son-in-law and, in 1615, joined an alliance against Aceh which consisted of Melaka's old allies, Pahang, Palembang, Jambi, Inderagiri, Kampar and Siak. The alliance continued to form a close-knit group of Malay kingdoms in the south of the Peninsula and on the east coast of Sumatra, sometimes at odds with each other and jostling for status within the group, but sharing the same traditions of kingship based on versions of the *Malay Annals*. Each of them claimed sacred the links with Palembang-Srivijaya and regarded its dynasty as as their common point of origin.

During the early part of the 17th century, the royal family of Johor made marriage alliances also with Patani, the rising Malay centre in the north of the Peninsula which provided entrepôt facilities for regional and international trade passing through the South China Sea and the Gulf of Siam (see map 2, page xvi). A court chronicle in Malay records the establishment of this port and the conversion of its ruler to Islam, at about the same time as the ruler of Melaka converted. The Thai kingdom of Ayutthaya, which had already threatened Melaka, also actively tried to govern Patani but was appeased with pledges of co-operation. From the mid-16th century, however, Ayutthaya had to defend itself against attacks from Burma and was concerned with its own defence until the end of the century. During the 17th century, the Thais were again active in requiring the Malay kingdoms in the southern reaches of their sphere of influence to send symbols of submission, and Patani and Kedah were particularly targeted.

In the southern part of the Peninsula, the Acehnese continued to menace rivals, including the Portuguese at Melaka. After several attempts, the Portuguese succeeded, in 1629, in defeating a large Acehnese fleet, thus curbing their ambitions and activities in the Straits. The former Melaka elite (or their descendants) in Johor sought any opportunity to reactivate their own trading links and networks and seized the moment to attract merchants and make Johor a major trading centre. With Aceh no longer patrolling the Straits, this left the

Portuguese at Melaka as the only other hostile presence to these plans and, before long, it became clear that the increasing Dutch presence in the region could be used against the Portuguese.

During the 16th century in Europe, the United Provinces of the Netherlands had prospered and its experienced merchants had capital to invest in a United Netherlands Chartered East India Company (Vereenigde Oostindische Compagnie or VOC) which was established in 1602. The VOC was governed by a Board of Seventeen which was represented in the East by a governor-general. Despite his instructions not to engage in local politics, he nevertheless used his men and funds to dislodge a local ruler in west Java and establish his headquarters at Jayakarta, which he renamed Batavia. For the Dutch governor-general, as for the Malays and other local powers, the Portuguese control of Melaka was a factor inhibiting their own trading plans. In 1640, the Johor ruler agreed to assist the Dutch to blockade Melaka in return for Dutch support to build several armed and fortified centres on the Johor River.

It took six months for the Portuguese to surrender but in January 1641 they withdrew and the Dutch occupied the site established two centuries earlier by Paramesvara. They used the port as a centre to collect tin from the neighbouring regions to supply the demand which had begun earlier in the century. The operations of the VOC in Southeast Asia were more centralised and better organised than previous commercial networks, except perhaps, for those of Srivijaya. It was Dutch policy, however, to develop Batavia as the central focus for all their trade and treat other ports as feeders for the centre. This was to have negative repercussions for Melaka and would be the determining influence on VOC policies in the Malay Peninsula.

The late 16th century saw a major increase in the number of Chinese junks trading with Southeast Asia and this level of activity lasted for almost a century. In 1571, the Spanish, in accordance with the Papal Bull which defined their sphere of influence as the Philippines and western South America, developed their interests and founded Manila. The implications for north Borneo, especially Brunei, were considerable. A new and very profitable network developed and became known as the (Spanish) 'galleon trade'—Chinese silks, porcelains and other luxury items were transported from Macao to Manila where they were traded for silver from Mexico and Spanish America. The Brunei sultanate (for it was now an Islamic court) and the Tausug of the Sulu archipelago (see map 2, page xvi) collected local products such as pepper, birds' nests, mother of pearl, tortoiseshell, sea cucumbers (trepang), camphor and wax as items to be traded for goods brought by the Chinese junks. Brunei flourished on this trade and the elite strengthened their links with their chiefs and representatives to ensure their networks of supply for local products were secure.

The Tausug also specialised in human captives and conducted raids themselves or purchased slaves from neighbouring maritime peoples such as the Bajaus. From the late 18th century, slave raiders worked the coasts of Borneo, Sulawesi, the islands of eastern Indonesia and Papua, northern Java, southern Sumatra and the east coast of the Malay Peninsula up into the Gulf of Siam and through the southern Philippines, seizing men, women and children who were sold to wealthy Southeast Asians and to Europeans. It was a profitable trade which terrorised local populations throughout the region and earned the people of Sulu a fearsome reputation as warriors. They were hired as mercenaries in Johor and Kedah in the late 18th century.

Movement of peoples is a recurring theme in the history of Southeast Asia. When Paramesvara migrated from Singapore he must have been accompanied by a number of followers and, after he settled at Melaka, it grew from an unknown settlement to a major centre within half a century. Immigration was essential for its development. The Malay Peninsula had a long-standing *Orang Asli* population but their need for mobility militated against large population increases. Sizable increases in population, therefore, had to come from immigration and it is not clear where the 11 000 carried out of Pahang by the Acehnese early in the 17th century came from. We do know that at about this time groups from east Sumatra and from Minangkabau areas on Sumatra's west coast were crossing the Straits and beginning to settle in the valleys of what is now called Negeri Sembilan. They maintained close contact both with their original villages and with the Minangkabau royal family as well as preserving the matrilineal descent system which is regarded as characteristic of the Minangakabau.

The Bugis of southwest Sulawesi were another major ethnic group which also began dispersing through the region during the 17th century. The exodus of considerable numbers out of Sulawesi (the Celebes) was precipitated by the aggressive policies of the VOC which, having expelled the Portuguese from Melaka, turned its attention to the eastern archipelago and tried to enforce a monopoly on spice trading. The VOC was determined to control Makassar, which was the centre of this eastern trade, but had to fight a bloody war over three years before negotiating a treaty with the sultan in 1669. This coincided with a period of intense rivalry between several leading figures in the Bugis homeland and the less successful leaders found it expedient to migrate with their followers and establish new ventures outside Sulawesi. During the 17th century the Bugis became known for their exceptional skills as navigators and pilots as they sailed, like their Austronesian ancestors, across the Indonesian archipelago, even reaching northern Australia. They were skilled with firearms and fearless fighters so many found employment as mercenaries, with the VOC as well as with local rulers. Their qualities earned them respect and, in many of the places where they settled, they married into the families of the elite and became permanent members of those societies. They were particularly successful in the region of the Straits of Melaka, including Johor.

The kingdom of Johor

The Portuguese defeat of the Acehnese fleets in 1629 opened the way for more diverse trading opportunities. The ports along Sumatra's east coast served as outlets for gold, tin and pepper from the interior and local leaders gained prestige if they associated themselves with the charismatic royal centre of the Minangkabaus, called Pagar Ruyung. As the rulers of Melaka had done, the Minangkabau royal house claimed descent from the ancient and legendary rulers of Srivijaya at Palembang. Thus, when leaders from the east coast of Sumatra claimed they had the blessing and authority of the rulers of Pagar Ruyung, they were accorded respect and several joined the diaspora of Minangkabau who migrated to the Negeri Sembilan areas of the Malay Peninsula. They were accepted as leaders by the Minangkabau migrants there and founded lineages which can still be traced. In the early years of the 18th century, the opportunity arose for another east Sumatran leader to attempt to gain a following among Malays in the kingdom of Johor.

The decision of the Johor elite to support the Dutch attacks on Portuguese Melaka had long-term benefits. The Dutch not only fulfilled their agreement to help fortify Johor settlements, they also negotiated trading agreements with the Johor elite which granted the Dutch special privileges and gave the Johor nobles rights to trade in goods which elsewhere were restricted to Dutch monopolies. One of the treaties granted the Dutch rights to trade with Siak, on Sumatra's east coast, suggesting that Johor claimed authority over this important export region. The authority of the Johor nobles at this time seems to have been very strong and there was intense rivalry among them.

In 1699, one of the nobles murdered the reigning sultan of Johor, Sultan Mahmud. Contemporary reports indicate that the ruler was a cruel and brutal man, and apparently without heirs. He was succeeded by the *bendahara*, the chief noble, who was closely related to the Melaka ruling line. Nevertheless, this provided the opportunity for the authority of the Johor sultanate to be questioned and rumours circulated that the royal line of Melaka, with its reputed links back to Srivijaya, had been broken. The accession of the *bendahara*, who traditionally had the right to replace the sultan if he was without heirs and who acted as regent if the sultan were underage, was 'legal' in the context of Malay political culture. However, the dissension which the 1699 accession aroused reflects the prize which the Johor throne represented, as well as the inter-elite rivalry which had long been evident. These internal divisions were, in part, made possible by the access to profits from trade which the nobles enjoyed, as they had in Melaka times, and the support they could call on from their individual domains which the sultan had granted them.

A decade after the *bendahara*'s accession, Raja Kecil, a chief from the east Sumatran region of Siak, claimed he was the legitimate ruler of Johor because he was the posthumous son of the murdered sultan. He announced that he was recognised as such by the Minangkabau royal family and had their support. Many believed him and he attracted a following of Minangkabaus along Sumatra's east coast. Raja Kecil's claim to be descended from the royal line of the Johor also drew the allegiance of many of the *Orang Suku Laut* who had maintained their respect for the Srivijaya-Melaka rulers. With their assistance and with a force of Minangkabaus, Raja Kecil succeeded in displacing the sultan of Johor who retreated to Terengganu, which had very close links with the Johor elite. In about 1720, Raja Kecil married one of the sultan's daughters, proclaimed himself ruler of Johor and invited the former ruler to return. When the former sultan reached Pahang he was murdered, allegedly on Raja Kecil's orders. The Johor elite who had stayed with the sultan announced that Raja Sulaiman, the young son of the murdered *bendahara*-sultan, would succeed him and they negotiated with a group of Bugis mercenaries to remove Raja Kecil from Riau where he was ruling and replace him with Raja Sulaiman.

The Bugis warriors had links with their fellows in the various Bugis settlements which had been established as a result of their diaspora from Sulawesi, in the tin areas around Melaka, particularly Klang and Linggi (see map 2, page xvi). They had made money trading in Borneo and Java and along the coasts of the Peninsula but had no power-base in the Straits region. They agreed to assist the Johor nobles in return for a permanent and senior position in the Johor government. It was agreed that one of them would be appointed as under king (*Yang Dipertuan Muda*), second only to the sultan in rank. The Bugis began their attacks on Raja Kecil and fought a series of battles on land and sea which succeeded in dislodging him from his Riau centre from where he retreated to Siak. Raja Sulaiman was installed as sultan of Johor and one of the Bugis warriors was married to his sister and installed as under king. Other Bugis warriors married Malay princesses and assumed senior positions in the kingdom. Their children, with royal Malay and Bugis blood, provided Johor with its rulers and senior officials into the 20th century.

The events of the kingdom of Johor from 1699 until the 1860s are recorded in an epic chronicle entitled *Tuhfat al-Nafis* (*The Precious Gift*), compiled in the 1860s by Raja Ali Haji, a talented and intelligent descendant of the original Bugis under king. His account, unsympathetic to the claims of Raja Kecil of Siak, the enemy of his ancestors, is the first Malay history to name the primary sources on which it draws and to present varying versions of an event. Raja Ali Haji's scholarship, his consistent use of dates and careful attention to veracity established a standard for Malay historiography and rekindled interest in the history of Johor and its status as heir to Melaka. In *The Precious Gift*, it is clear that the 18th century was a period of strong competition for the trade of Sumatra's east coast, control of the tin resources of the west coast of the Peninsula and access to the networks linking the east coast of the Peninsula with the Gulf of Siam.

Raja Kecil and his sons continued to attack Johor and its dependencies until the 1740s but thereafter the Bugis were in full control of the security of kingdom. Once free of the Minangkabau harrassment, the Bugis turned their attention to Dutch monopoly practices at Melaka and launched several attacks on the city in 1756. In 1766, one of the Johor Bugis was installed as the first Sultan of Selangor, thus ensuring Bugis dominance of the tin-rich rivers in that region and making the Dutch even more nervous about Bugis designs on Melaka.

Bugis contacts and the strategic position of the Johor capital on the island of Bentan (see map 5, page xix), with all the advantages of modern Singapore, attracted Asian and European traders who could buy spices, tin and pepper there more cheaply than from the Dutch at Melaka. The commercial success of the Bugis created dissension between them and the Malay elite, many of whom had been displaced when the Bugis were granted senior court positions. Some of these disgruntled nobles withdrew to Terengganu, always a haven for the elite Malays of Johor, and persuaded its sultan to try and oust the Bugis. His failure only strengthened the position of the Bugis who were openly masters of the kingdom. In 1784, the fourth Bugis under king, Raja Haji, renowned for his valour and with alliances with Pontianak (on Borneo's west coast) and southeast Sumatra, and supported by his brother, the sultan of Selangor, laid siege to Dutch Melaka. The city was very hard-pressed for nine months and was saved only by the arrival of a fleet sent from Europe. Raja Haji was killed in the fighting and was buried on the island of Penyengat, offshore from Bentan, where his grave is still revered.

The Dutch followed up the defeat of the Bugis by making a contract with the Malay sultan, whose residence was at Riau, on the island of Bentan, to establish a Dutch office and trading centre. *The Precious Gift* records that the sultan employed a fleet of Sulu warriors (Illanun) to destroy the Dutch post in 1787. Knowing Dutch retaliation was inevitable, the Malay sultan left Riau and re-established his court on the island of Lingga, considerably to the south, while other leading Malay nobles moved to Terengganu and Pahang. Lingga remained the site of the sultan's court until the late 19th century and the remains of his palace are still visible. After the Sulu warriors left Riau, the Dutch returned and, in 1788, declared Riau a toll-free port in an effort to restore its trade. There was already a considerable Chinese population of 5000 from Canton and Amoy and these people became the backbone of Riau's commercial life. Events in Europe, however, were to affect Dutch activities in the Straits and reshape the political map of the archipelago.

The kingdom of Kedah

The kingdom of Kedah provides an interesting comparison with Riau-Johor. Geographically, it is a land-based kingdom whereas Johor, until the mid-19th century, was predominantly a maritime entity. The soil and latitude of Kedah were favourable for agriculture and by the late 16th century, European visitors were commenting on its rice and pepper production, and by the late 18th century the flat areas of Kedah were described as having plenty of rice, bullocks, buffalo and poultry. During the 15th century, while Melaka was growing, Kedah seems to have kept a low profile. Towards the end of the century, however, the *Malay Annals* record that the ruling prince of Kedah made a personal visit to Melaka, which the sultan of Melaka recognised by granting him honours. This Kedah ruler, according to Kedah's own chronicle, *The Story of Merong Mahawangsa*, was the first to embrace Islam which replaced Buddhism as the official religion of the kingdom. Melaka may also have provided the model for Kedah's own system of ministers and nobles. The Kedah court had four senior ministers, with similar titles to those of Melaka, and eight less senior ministers. Each had their own domain, living from its revenues and sending some to the ruler.

Like Melaka, Kedah's main port had a cosmopolitan population of Chinese, Javanese, Acehnese and Indians. The Portuguese at Melaka regarded it as being under the sway of Siam (with whom they wanted good relations) but attacked it once in 1611, possibly on behalf of Siam and to punish Kedah for showing sympathy to Burmese interests. This was the period of Aceh's aggressive and expansionist policies. It attacked Kedah in 1619, probably to control its pepper and tin trade (competition for Aceh's own), and took an estimated 7000 Kedah people back to work in Aceh as labourers. By linking the trade of Aceh with that of Kedah and surrounding ports, the sultan of Aceh was creating a triangle of trading networks, or in modern terminology, a 'growth triangle', in precisely the region that the governments of

Thailand, Malaysia and Indonesia planned to create a special trade zone in the 1990s.

The Dutch capture of Melaka in 1641 controlled the agression of Aceh and removed the Portuguese, but initiated a new trading regime. The Dutch negotiated for trade monopolies under which the major ports in the Straits had to sell as much as half their tin to the VOC for fixed prices and agree to trade only with merchants carrying Dutch passes. While Kedah agreed to these conditions, it nevertheless continued to pursue its traditional trade with ports in south India and also to use the ancient land route across the Peninsula, activities which the Dutch could not control.

From the 1620s, the Kedah royal court suffered a series of succession disputes. A century later they were still a problem. In 1720, learning that the Johor nobles were using Bugis warriors to assist in their dispute with the Minangkabaus, a Kedah prince invited them to Kedah with the promise of a handsome payment if they would dislodge his younger brother from the throne. The Bugis came, installed the older brother and departed, unlike their behaviour in Johor, where they stayed. However, the use of outside aid established a precedent for the resolution of succession disputes in Kedah.

The 18th century was a time of relative peace and consolidation for Kedah because its northern neighbours were occupied fighting each other. The Burmese ruler attacked key Siamese centres and, in 1767, destroyed the capital of Ayutthaya taking thousands of Siamese back to Burma and devastating the land. This was a traumatic event for the kingdom of Siam which did not begin to recover until the 1780s when a new line of kings came to power and moved the capital to the vicinity of modern Bangkok.

In the meantime, centres like Nakhon Si Thammarat (Ligor), Patani and Kedah developed their own interests, particularly in trade and commerce. Kedah benefited from the presence of British traders around the Bay of Bengal, where privately financed British trade was being carried out by 'country traders', whose enterprise often far outstripped that of their fellow countrymen working for the 'official' English East India Company (EIC). The British traders traded opium and Indian textiles for tin, rice and pepper which they needed for the markets in China, and Kedah could provide good supplies of these commodities.

During the 1770s, there was another serious dispute over the royal succession, with various factions seeking external support for their candidate. One faction called on the Bugis from Riau and Selangor, who responded and raided the capital, Alor Star, burning the settlement. It was also in the interests of the Bugis to do anything they could to inhibit Kedah's trade, which at this time was attracting not only English country traders but also Danish, Swedish and French. The Bugis forces later returned to Selangor but, as a result of their presence, another faction in Kedah entered into an agreement with the EIC. Sultan Muhammad of Kedah was personally involved in the negotiations and although ostensibly he seemed to want British support against the Bugis of Selangor, he was aware that he was risking retribution from Siam by negotiating with a foreign power without its knowledge. Anticipating Siamese or Burmese aggression against Kedah, he may have been trying to protect himself with a British alliance. In 1772, a contract was signed which gave the EIC full jurisdiction over the port of Kuala Kedah and a monopoly of Kedah's exports of tin, black pepper and elephant ivory. In return, the ruler of Kedah had the right to purchase unlimited amounts of opium from the EIC at a fixed price, and it was agreed that the company's warships would guard the coast of Kedah. Thus, Kedah entered into a defensive agreement with a non-Malay power while retaining control over its own affairs, unlike the Malay nobles of Riau-Johor who agreed to install a Bugis as under king in perpetuity and had to learn to co-exist with the Bugis.

By the 1780s, it was clear that Siam was recovering from the wars with Burma prompting the new ruler of Kedah, Sultan Abdullah, to send the ornamental gold and silver trees as a symbol of his respect.

He also made overtures to the EIC and, like his predecessor, offered them the lease of Penang in return for East India Company assistance should Kedah be attacked. As in the earlier negotiations with the EIC, the British merchant Francis Light served as intermediary. There was some tension in Kedah about these overtures when it was realised that if the English leased Penang and developed it as a port, this would divert trade from Kedah and result in loss of revenue. For several reasons, therefore, a formal lease was not signed, but the sultan gave Light permission to occupy Penang on a temporary basis until a proper agreement was reached. Nevertheless, Light took formal possession of the island of Penang on 11 August 1786 in the name of King George III, an action which was legally in breach of international law.

Penang developed rapidly as a trading port. Contemporary accounts describe how the island's virgin jungle was cleared by the marines and lascars of three East India Company ships in July 1786, almost immediately attracting settlers from the peninsular mainland. Among the first were Chinese and Indians from Kedah who set up a small bazaar near the English settlement. Thereafter, a regular series of small boats came from Kedah with goods and food for sale. Just one year later, there were 60 Chinese families running shops in the bazaar, Malabari merchants also permanently settled there and Malay small traders who came from Kedah with goods to sell. Under the very capable Francis Light (whose relative, William, was later to design the city of Adelaide in the colony of South Australia), Penang developed rapidly as an attractive transit port on the India–China trade route and, as the merchants of Kedah had predicted, some of their trade was diverted to the new port. Opium, cloth, steel, gunpowder and iron from Britain and from India were sold for rice, tin, spices, pepper, gold-dust, ivory, ebony and rattans, which were still the specialities of the Malaysian territories.

In 1791, the sultan of Kedah attempted to reoccupy Penang but failed and was then forced to sign a treaty guaranteeing the East India Company a lease for as long as it wished. In 1800, a strip of the Peninsula opposite Penang, known as Seberang Perai (renamed Province Wellesley by the British), was also leased to the company for 10 000 Spanish dollars per annum, an amount which was also to cover the lease of Penang. Only a few years earlier, the Dutch had signed an agreement with the sultan of Riau-Johor for a Dutch post in Riau, and one with the sultan of Selangor for a post in his territory. Adding these to their settlement at Melaka, the VOC felt it had established a real presence in the Straits. They had been concerned about the increasing amount of British activity in the area, including the occupation of Penang by the EIC. However, it would be events in Europe, not Southeast Asia, which were to have a more immediate impact on the course of European action in the Straits.

The enduring nature of the Malay sultanate

Many descriptions of Malay world in late 18th century claim that the traditional forms of government were in disarray and decline. On the basis of the evidence presented in this chapter, it can be argued that even though the 'fall' of Melaka was followed by a proliferation of Malay centres, the preferred form of government was one which maintained the sultan as the central authority, with power delegated to chiefs and local headmen. In fact, the Srivijayan *datu*/mandala system of circles of allegiance still underpinned the concept of governance in the 18th century. The Malay centres remained linked by marriage and diplomatic ties and when called on, could create small alliances against a variety of threats. The acceptance of Bugis leaders into the Johor-Riau royal family did not succeed fully in integrating this non-Malay group into the elite and they remained available as mercenaries for any Malay leader who could pay them.

Succession disputes in the royal line, a characteristic of the Melaka sultanate, continued in Johor-Riau and were evident also in Kedah. As at the Melaka court, contests for leadership seem to have reflected divisions within the nobility who had much to gain if their favoured candidate occupied the throne. In 1760, the Bugis faction at the Johor-Riau court installed a very young Malay prince as sultan, and he ruled for the next 52 years, eventually bringing stability to the kingdom by dividing it into two spheres, one ruled by the Bugis under king and the other (centred on the island of Lingga) ruled by himself as Malay sultan. This division of spheres of influence resolved the problem of succession until the late 19th century.

6
PRESSURES FOR CHANGE

. . . I felt that the period of my lifetime had witnessed so many wonderful changes and new things which our grand-parents had never seen. Such events provided me with much food for meditation.

Abdullah bin Abdul Kadir,
Abdullah's Story (Hikayat Abdullah), 1849[1]

From the early 19th century it is as if there was a change in pace in the region, as if the tempo of events was quickening. In part, this was the result of the sense of urgency which Europeans expressed in their reports about the East—the competition for access to items for the trade with China had increased and more traders were arriving to bid for them. This commercial competition was linked with European politics and the rise of Napoleonic France, which had repercussions for how Europeans viewed the strategic importance of the Malaysian territories.

The change in pace was due also to the increased amount of documentation in English about the region. A series of major reports about the Peninsula and Borneo was published in English and received wide circulation in Britain. Among the best known are the writings of Sir Thomas Stamford Raffles, the British colonial administrator, but there were many others, and the intellectual climate in Britain, formed in the Age of Enlightenment, was receptive to and very interested in descriptions of foreign peoples and their social and economic organisation. Although there were preconceived theories about how civilisations 'developed' from primitive to advanced, there was also an emphasis on the 'scientific' recording of nature and peoples for the sake of knowledge. This was the age of Royal Societies, whose members published their findings in learned journals which were widely read and keenly followed. The collection of information about the Malaysian territories served a dual purpose: to increase scientific knowledge and to attract British commercial investment to the region.

Sir Stamford Raffles

The decision of Raffles to publish an English translation of the *Malay Annals* illustrates this dual purpose. The first translation into English of the Malay epic was accomplished in about 1810 by John Leyden, who died in the following year. He was one of Raffles' closest friends and, although Raffles had the manuscript of the translation in his possession, he did not publish it until 1821. He claimed at the time that he published it to make better known the history of the Malays, and it was indeed influential among readers of English. The timing of its publication, however, reflects Raffles' need to convince his critics in Britain that his choice of Singapore, as the site for an international British entrepôt, was based on evidence that it had been a major port in earlier times. Political and commercial motives were probably uppermost in his mind.

Raffles tried to learn about the Malays from their own writings. From his reading of works like the *Malay Annals*, he believed that the Malay kingdoms he saw in the early 19th century were poor representatives of earlier kingdoms, especially Melaka, whose greatness and influence had been described in such glowing terms in the earlier texts. His view of the Malay world as being 'in decline' and 'decaying' coloured the views of many Europeans and even had some influence on the Malays themselves. Raffles (and other British administrators who followed after him) assumed that the only pattern for a Malay kingdom was that of centralised rule under a sultan. So, somewhat ironically, the British 'discovery' of indigenous Malay accounts of the past was taken by them as a model for what the Malay present should be. On the other hand, indigenous scholars who came in contact with Europeans and with travellers and scholars from the Middle East, India, China and Japan, as well as with Javanese and Sumatrans, realised that the range of options for methods of administration and education was increasing rapidly.

The previous chapters described how the strategic position of the Malaysian territories brought them into contact with foreigners in transit to further destinations. Local people were in constant touch with prevailing fashions in ideology and religion, as well as responsive to the latest demands of international traders. Just as in much earlier times, the survival of centres within the region depended on their flexibility, powers of adaptation and responses to external change.

Abdullah bin Abdul Kadir

From the early 19th century, we are fortunate to have accounts written by local people themselves, recording their impressions of the world around them. In several cases, it seems that these individuals were motivated or encouraged to put their impressions in writing by the Europeans with whom they came in contact. Often it was European interest in the writings which brought them to prominence and, either in the form of printed and circulated versions or manuscripts donated to European libraries, they have survived and are available for us to read.

One of the best known texts from the early 19th century, lithographed in 1849 and written in Malay for the benefit of ordinary Malays as well as with an eye to European readers, is *Abdullah's Story* (*Hikayat Abdullah*). When it first appeared, *Abdullah's Story* was considered sufficiently important for the English governor of Singapore to purchase 12 copies immediately, sending half of them to Bengal and giving the rest as gifts to Malay 'chieftains'. It was read as a textbook in schools in the Malay world from the mid-19th century onwards and is still studied in Malaysia and elsewhere for the views of its author and the picture it gives of life in his time. Abdullah's life (1797–1854) spans the change from Dutch to British influence in the Straits of Melaka and the founding of the British settlement of Singapore. He visited also the east coast kingdoms of Pahang, Terengganu and Kelantan. *Abdullah's Story*, with its very personal evaluation of conditions in the Malaysian territories and efforts to understand European strengths and weaknesses, makes it a unique account of its times.

Abdullah bin Abdul Kadir was born in Melaka in 1797 into a family of mixed Arab and south Indian origins. His grandfather came to Melaka from south India and there married an Indian Muslim woman who ran a very well-attended school. Their son, Abdullah's father, was talented in business, religious teaching and languages. Because he was proficient in Arabic, Tamil and Malay he was in demand as a professional letter-writer and also taught Malay to foreigners, at a time when British administrators and merchants, realising the opportunities the Malay world offered them, began to seriously study the language and customs of Malays. Abdullah's mother was of Malay and Indian descent (her father was an Indian from Kedah who had moved to Melaka) and thus Abdullah grew up being able to speak several languages and mix confidently with foreigners, learning from them anything which would enhance his livelihood. The cosmopolitan and multiethnic milieu of 15th century Melaka was still evident in the late 18th century, when Abdullah was born, although the population numbers had greatly diminished.

Penang, Kedah and Siam: 1790–1842

The activities of the Illanuns, mercenaries, slave raiders and exceptionally skilled seamen, were feared throughout island Southeast Asia. They operated under the patronage of the sultans of Sulu who had their base in the southern Philippines. The Sulu rulers worked with the Illanuns (also known as Iranuns), originally from central Mindanao, paying them to bring in slaves who were used to assemble products for the international trade. The Illanuns sailed double-decked ships, over 130 feet (40 metres) long, and used slaves as oarsmen when extra speed was necessary. There were probably more than 200 such vessels which set out annually to raid ships and villages. As the numbers of commercial ships sailing through Southeast Asian waters to trade with China increased, so too did the number of Illanun raids. The growth of new centres like Penang and Singapore increased their opportunities for piracy. It has been pointed out that they were quick to modernise their fleets and tactics and adopted the technologies and equipment of their victims including compasses, charts, telescopes and the latest firearms. The number of people they took in raids on villages across the region has been estimated at tens of thousands. To effect their raids, they established land bases within striking distance of the major ports and thus had centres in the Melaka Straits area and along the east coast of the Peninsula, as well as on the Borneo coasts, particularly in the northeast and west.

Some British traders based in India had contact with groups of Illanuns. They provided them with opium and firearms in return for information about the activities of the Dutch, or any other competitors in the archipelago. The Illanuns were thus trading in information as well as cargoes and slaves and were obliged to no central authority for the success of their operations. They were feared by everyone because of their ruthless and violent methods and the efficiency of their raids. Commercial losses attributed to piracy, mostly (but not all) by Illanuns, have been estimated at several million pounds sterling a year. Many of their victims were absorbed into the Muslim sultanate of Sulu where they were given new roles and eventually assumed new identities.

The sultan of Kedah had used a force of Illanuns in an attempt to dislodge the English East India Company from Penang in 1791. It was when this failed that the sultan finally agreed to sign a Treaty of Peace and Friendship with Francis Light on behalf of the EIC. Several points in the treaty are relevant in the light of later events. First, the sultan of Kedah did not cede—but only leased—Penang to the company. Second, although the company made no direct promise of protection, the clause 'Kedah and Penang shall be as one country' allowed the sultan to think there might be aid in the event of a Siamese attack.

The nature of the relationship between Siam and the peninsular Malay states was, and is, complex. The population in the northern districts of the Peninsula and in what is now the southern provinces of Thailand is very mixed—*Orang Asli*, Thais, Mons, Burmese, Chinese, Indians and Malays—among whom intermarriage has occurred for centuries. Religion (Islam and Buddhism in particular) is one major focus for allegiance and group identity and, since the late 18th century, this has largely determined political allegiance: Buddhists looking to Bangkok and Muslims to the Malay states. However, during the 17th and 18th centuries the Siamese considered parts of the Malay Peninsula to be in their sphere of influence and expected that this would be acknowledged. Malay rulers usually responded by sending regular tokens of the relationship in the form of the gold and silver trees knowing that if they did not, there could be active enforcement by the Siamese.

Sultan Abdullah, who had negotiated with the EIC over protection for Penang, died in 1798 and his death was followed by a prolonged dispute over the succession. In 1802, Sultan Ahmad Tajuddin Halim Shah travelled to Bangkok and was confirmed by Rama I as ruler of Kedah. The internal disputes among the Kedah nobility continued into the reign of Rama II, with various factions seeking support from any likely outsiders. The sultan was in contact with the Burmese at their court in Ava, and this was reported by one of his half-brothers to the Siamese. The Siamese could not afford to risk losing their access to the Bay of Bengal via the Isthmus of Kra, if Kedah succumbed to Burmese influence. In 1821, therefore, Bangkok gave orders to the Thai governor of Nakhon Si Thammarat, who was responsible for the supervision of Kedah and Kelantan, to attack Kedah. The sultan was forced to flee and went into exile in Penang. One of the sons of the governor of Nakhon was placed in charge of Kedah, which was ruled as a Siamese province under Nakhon. Sultan Ahmad Tajuddin took refuge with his tenants, the British at Penang, and spent his time planning how to regain his kingdom.

Meanwhile, the British declared war on the kingdom of Ava in 1824 and in 1825 succeeded in annexing Burmese territory on the border with Siam. The Siamese were persuaded that it was prudent to come to an agreement with the British and, in 1826, signed the Burney Agreement granting the British trading concessions in Bangkok. In return, the British agreed to recognise Siam's special relationship with the northern Malay states and Siamese suzerainty over Kedah, but no further south. In essence, the British decided to advance their commercial interests in Bangkok and to recognise Siamese occupation of Kedah, particularly since the Siamese agreed that the British could continue to purchase food and supplies (for Penang) from Kedah free of duty.

In Penang, Sultan Ahmad Tajuddin organised many unsuccessful attempts to expel the Siamese from Kedah. In 1838, a large-scale uprising succeeded briefly in expelling the Siamese but they returned with a vengeance and tens of thousands of Kedah people fled, moving to the British territories of Province Wellesley and Penang. Contemporary estimates of the departure of 70 000, leaving only 20 000 people in Kedah may be exaggerated, but the effect of the mass migrations was to leave Kedah severely impoverished.

After an exile of over 20 years, the Siamese were persuaded by the British and by delegations from the sultan's eldest son to allow

Sultan Ahmad Tajuddin to return to Kedah in 1842. His kingdom was diminished by the loss of its northernmost districts of Setul, Langu and Perlis and by the loss of so many of its people. Sultan Ahmad Tajuddin died soon after his return. He was succeeded by his son who, in recognition of Siam's power, travelled to Bangkok for his installation. The Siamese and the new sultan recognised that continuing hostilities would weaken both sides and they cooperated to try and rebuild Kedah.

Melaka, Singapore and Riau-Johor

Francis Light had established a British base for the East India Company in Penang through direct negotiation with the sultan of Kedah. The resulting arrangement, an agreement between a reigning sultan and a foreigner, for the 'rental' of Penang (followed by Province Wellesley), was the first of its kind in the Malaysian territories. The Portuguese and the Dutch had taken Melaka by force and since 1642 it had been regarded by Europeans, at least, as Dutch. However, this changed in 1794, shortly before Abdullah bin Abdul Kadir was born.

Britain and France were at war in Europe and when France attacked the Netherlands in 1794, its ruler, Prince William of Orange, fled to England. He gave instructions that the Dutch overseas should allow the British to take over their posts on the understanding that they would be restored after the war. In 1795 therefore, British forces from India officially occupied Melaka and lifted many of the excise taxes enforced by the Dutch. According to *Abdullah's Story*, Melaka became quite prosperous during this period and there was lively trade with the east coast of Sumatra (as in much earlier times). After 1802, when Napoleon installed his brother as king of the Netherlands and had plans for capturing British and Dutch settlements in India and Southeast Asia, the governor-general of the EIC in Calcutta was persuaded by Raffles to pre-empt French moves by taking Java, then under

Napoleon's marshal, Daendels. The governor-general entrusted the planning of the Java campaign to Raffles, and late in 1810 he moved to Melaka using it as a base to collect intelligence about French and Dutch activities in Southeast Asia.

When Raffles established his headquarters in Melaka, Abdullah was 13 or 14 years old, and his recollections of Raffles' activities at that time are recorded in his *Story*. Abdullah joined the group of copyists and scribes employed by Raffles to transcribe information as it came to him and to make copies of local manuscripts. During the early months of 1811, the British expedition for Java assembled at Melaka and Abdullah watched them training and then the departure of the fleet in August. By September 1811, the Dutch forces had surrendered and the governor-general appointed Raffles as lieutenant-governor. One of Abdullah's uncles who had accompanied Raffles as a scribe died at Batavia, probably a victim of malaria.

The young Abdullah stayed in Melaka and as part of his professional work as a letter-writer and teacher, agreed to work as assistant to a group of Christian missionaries who believed education was one way to conversion. Abdullah taught the missionaries Malay and helped them prepare Malay translations of a wide range of material which they were able to duplicate on a printing press. This was one of many Western inventions which fascinated Abdullah. He could see its advantages and recommended it to Malays as a more reliable way to produce texts than handwritten manuscripts which were prone to scribal error.

While Abdullah was working with the missionaries, extending his knowledge of English and considering the information about Western civilisation they were bringing to his attention, peace had been made in Europe. Under the terms of the Congress of Vienna (1816) Dutch possessions were returned and Raffles, now with the reputation of a reformer and administrator, departed from Java. The Congress of Vienna left Penang as the only British base in the Straits of Melaka. When the Dutch returned, they came in the name of the Dutch government which had taken over the bankrupt Dutch trading company, the VOC. Both Raffles and the merchants in Penang believed the Dutch would again enforce their policy of trade monopolies, shut the British out of many ports and forbid local traders to do business with the British. Raffles and William Farquhar, British resident of Melaka, were eventually given permission by the directors of the EIC to negotiate discreetly with local rulers for a site for a second British base. Strategically it had be in the southern part of the Straits—the critical region which Srivijaya had once controlled.

Farquhar, whom Abdullah notes was popular among the local residents of Melaka, sailed from Melaka before the official handing over to the Dutch, and local rumours had it that he was looking for a new site for a British settlement. He did, in fact, negotiate with the Riau nobles to be allowed to establish a post on one of the islands at the southern end of the Straits, all of which were considered to be under their jurisdiction. Melaka was handed back to the Dutch in September 1818, with Abdullah watching (and later recording) the sorrow he witnessed on the faces of the English officers.

What followed is regarded now as a great cloak and dagger event and a triumph for the tenacity of Raffles and Farquhar. The story has its British versions but it is also recorded in Raja Ali Haji's epic history, *The Precious Gift*. Raja Ali himself would have been only nine or ten years old at the time of the events, but his father, who was also involved in compiling the epic, actively participated in the drama. *The Precious Gift* describes Farquhar's mission to Riau, his discussions with the Bugis under king about the return of the Dutch, and his negotiations for a settlement on one of the islands under Riau's control. The Dutch return to Riau in 1818 is described as well as the reactions of the Riau nobles, some wanting to side with the British and others not daring to oppose the Dutch. One of the nobles, the *temenggung*, withdrew from Riau to his own domain and visited one of its islands, Singapore. On learning that he was there, Raffles and Farquhar who were still sailing in the area to identify a suitable site came ashore. Recognising its potential as a toll-free port, they negotiated with him for a lease on the island. Although Riau's newly signed treaty with the Dutch specifically precluded any agreements with foreign nations, the *temenggung* signed a preliminary agreement in late January 1819. Realising that only a treaty with a ruling prince had real effect, Raffles and Farquhar exploited a succession dispute in the royal line of the sultanate. The *temenggung* agreed to bring the elder and uncrowned royal prince to Singapore secretly and make every effort to evade the Dutch. Saying that he was leaving on a fishing expedition, the prince sailed to Singapore and was taken on board Raffles' ship. The following day, according to *The Precious Gift*, with all the appropriate ceremonies and in the name of the governor-general of Bengal, Raffles and the *temenggung* installed the Malay prince as Sultan Husain Shah, ruler of Singapore and its surrounding territories, a reference to the southern parts of the Peninsula which traditionally had been considered part of the Kingdom of Johor. Raffles was then able to sign a formal treaty with the sultan and the *temenggung*. Under its terms, the EIC would pay $5000 annually to Sultan Husain and $3000 to the *temenggung* in return for the cession of Singapore, which would be administered jointly by Sultan Husain, the *temenggung* and the English resident.

When the Dutch learned that one of the Riau princes had been proclaimed sultan of Singapore by the British, they made known their displeasure. But they had also to look to their own position because the heir-apparent in Riau, Abdul Rahman, had not been formally installed as sultan. The Dutch urged the Riau nobles to install Abdul Rahman and, after his marriage to a Terengganu princess, this was accomplished.

The details of the founding of Singapore are important for the later relationship between Malaysia, Singapore and Indonesia. The British decision to declare Singapore a free port bore results and some estimates place the value of trade at the end of its fourth year at over two million pounds sterling. Much of this was at the expense of Riau's own trade and therefore a loss to the Dutch. They did not recognise

Sultan Husain as the legitimate ruler of Singapore and therefore, in their eyes, the cession to the British was not legal.

One of the most vivid accounts of the first months of Farquhar and his men on Singapore comes from Abdullah, who visited the island during its first year of British settlement and thereafter travelled regularly between Singapore and Melaka. In his *Story* he records that the only inhabitants of the island were *Orang Suku Laut*, who were so frightened of the British that they jumped in their boats and fled (possibly thinking they were slave raiders). Only when the *temenggung* ordered them to sell fish to the British did they make contact. The island itself was not well suited to agriculture because it was covered in dense scrub with soil of mud and clay. According to Abdullah, the people of Melaka realised the profits to be made from taking food and supplies to Singapore, despite the Dutch forbidding them to go. A steady stream of traders, labourers and craftsmen began leaving Melaka, braving the pirates who were attracted by the increased traffic and between 1821 and the time of the first census in 1824, Singapore's population doubled to 10 000. Abdullah describes the trials and hardships endured by the pioneering settlement—rats, fires, robberies and violence. But the traders were undeterred as Abdullah writes: 'The port of Singapore was crammed full of shipping, ketches, sloops, frigates, two-and-a-half masters, schooners, junks from China, Annam and Siam and boats from Borneo.'[2]

The burgeoning growth of Singapore caused considerable tension with the Dutch who were now faced with a British base almost midway between Melaka and their port on Riau. Singapore's status as a free port attracted more trade than their own ports. Negotiations began in Europe to try and find a solution to European jurisdiction in the region. In 1824 the Anglo-Dutch Treaty of London was signed dividing the land on each side of the Straits of Melaka between Britain and the Netherlands. Dutch Melaka became British territory while the British enclave, Bencoolen (in Sumatra) was transferred to the Dutch. The local rulers were not consulted. Under the 1824 treaty, the previously homogeneous cultural and economic region of the Peninsula, Straits of Melaka and Sumatra was divided artificially and administered by Europeans.

The nobles of Riau and Lingga realised that they would lose authority over their traditional territories on the Peninsula. The *temenggung*, now on Singapore, lost some of his traditional islands which fell in the Dutch sphere. He compensated for this by resurrecting his 'rights' to the southern parts of the Peninsula. Likewise, the *bendahara* who had traditional domains in the region of Pahang, began strengthening his position there. Despite Dutch warnings not to enter British territory, many of the nobles from Riau and Lingga continued to move freely (as they still do) between Riau-Lingga, Singapore and the east coast of the Peninsula. Some established businesses in Singapore and purchased property there.

The 1824 Treaty of London was later criticised by some Europeans. James Low, a colonial administrator of note, published a stinging rebuke in the late 1840s claiming that the it was 'an act of political and mercantile suicide' to give Sumatra to the Dutch. He also questioned the morality of the treaty: 'What right in an era of international justice can any nation possibly have to thus barter away extensive countries, with their independent populations?'[3] But the treaty endured and became the international boundary which determined the territory of the modern nation states of Singapore, Malaysia and Indonesia.

On Singapore, Farquhar was succeeded by a second administrator, John Crawfurd, who further strengthened British control of the island by making a new agreement with the *temenggung* and the sultan in 1824. In return for a cash settlement, they ceded their rights to Singapore and the adjacent islands to the EIC but retained their land on Singapore—the *temenggung* and his extensive following lived at Teluk Belanga, while the sultan maintained his residence and mosque at Kampong Gelam, where a few of his descendants can still be found in the 21st century. The EIC was now faced with having to administer Penang (and Province Wellesley), Melaka and

Singapore. In an attempt to rationalise this, in 1826, they combined the territories into a new unit called the Straits Settlements, to be administered from Penang.

The *temenggung*

Before the British occupation of Singapore, the *temenggung* had been one of the inner circle of officials in the Riau-Johor elite but he had chosen to remain on Singapore (rather than return to Riau) when the 1824 treaty came into effect. Formerly, the domain of the *temenggung* was a maritime one and his incomes had been derived from marine produce and from taxes on shipping. When the *temenggung* signed the treaty with Crawfurd he forfeited his rights to Singapore and his income from commercial shipping was eroded by the British. Unlike Sultan Husain, however, he did not take this passively but reacted and devised alternative means for making money. He was receiving some income from revenues derived from the Chinese growers of gambier (a resin used as an astringent and in the tanning process) and pepper who established themselves in Singapore but soon needed more land. He allowed them to move across the narrow strait to the southern parts of the Peninsula, also his domain, but almost totally uncleared. It was here that they discovered they could tap sap from wild-rubber trees and harvest gutta-percha (a multipurpose gum). In the 1840s this fetched good prices and the *temenggung* made his fortune.

The next *temenggung*, Ibrahim, who assumed the title in 1841 after his father's death, turned his attention increasingly to the Peninsula territories, known as Johor, and employed a bureacracy to administer his 'tenants', the Chinese cultivators. This more formal kind of administration had not been necessary for the *Orang Suku Laut* who had previously provided the main source of his family's income. The change in environment necessitated a new system of administration and new ways of ensuring that the *temenggung* maintained the loyalty of the Chinese. Thus the *kangchu* system was developed in Johor. The *temenggung* negotiated with Chinese leaders and granted monopolies to *kangchu*, or 'river lords', who were contracted to develop and control certain stretches of territory along the rivers of Johor. The *kangchu* were responsible for looking after their workers and for ensuring that the taxes on revenue-earning activities such as plantations, gambling, opium sales, alcohol and pork were paid. A similar system of revenue farming was used in Kedah, after the restoration of the sultan in 1842 so that the British came to regard Johor and Kedah as models of good practice in income-earning activities.

James Brooke and the Sea Dayaks (Ibans) of Sarawak

The story of James Brooke and his successors in Sarawak is also a study in transformation and adaptation, but without the model of Raffles and Singapore, it may never have happened. In 1839, a young, wealthy and patriotic Englishman travelled to Singapore. He was inspired by the achievements of Raffles and determined to find a territory he could develop (as Raffles had Singapore) for the greater glory of Britain. He had some experience of the East, being born in India and having served in the Indian Army during the Anglo-Burmese war when he was wounded. After extended convalescence in England, he resigned from the Army and returned to the East intending to pursue his mission. On hearing that there were considerable stretches of territory in Borneo as yet unexplored by Europeans, he set sail in July 1839, in his own vessel, heading eastwards.

When he reached the Borneo coast near the Sarawak River, intending to take a message from the governor of Singapore to the Brunei governor at Kuching, he found the latter embattled in a drawn out conflict with the local chiefs. James Brooke agreed to intervene on behalf of the Brunei governor in return for the title 'Rajah' and permission to govern the area himself. Brooke succeeded in negotiating a settlement with the chiefs, was granted the governorship and in 1842 paid an official visit to the sultan of Brunei to have his title confirmed. Under the terms of the 1842 agreement, Brooke was to make annual payments of $1000 to the sultan of Brunei and the former governor with lesser amounts to three chiefs. For the British government, Brooke's position was troublesome. They feared his territorial ambitions would create tension with the Dutch and although he persistently requested it, official British recognition of Brookes's authority in Sarawak was not forthcoming.

James Brooke assumed his new position with little awareness of how greatly local conditions in Borneo differed from those in Penang and Singapore. The territory around the Sarawak River was known to have deposits of gold and from the mid-18th century Chinese gold miners had moved into the upper reaches of the Sarawak River, particularly into the region known as Bau (see map 5, page xix). In 1824, antimony-ore was discovered and in response to interest from merchants in Singapore, the Brunei nobles had organised the working of antimony for export, using local people as labourers. This much Brooke knew. However, the ethnic situation was more diverse than on the Malay Peninsula. By the early 19th century, the Ibans or, as Brooke called them, the 'Sea Dayaks', were the most aggressive and active of the local peoples in the southern parts of Sarawak. They seem to have been centred in the Kapuas Valley (see map 5, page xix), but over several centuries, perhaps beginning in the mid-16th, they began to spread into what is now Sarawak, where they encountered pre-existing populations. Some of those populations inter-married with the Ibans, others moved towards the coast where, coming into contact with Muslim peoples, they converted to Islam and were considered to be Malays.

The Iban lifestyle centred round shifting agriculture and temporary outward migration by young men. Iban groups moved regularly to preserve the fertility of the soil and they were widely feared for their courage in combat and their practice of taking human heads, necessary for rituals central to Iban culture. Young men were encouraged to travel and seek their fortunes as a way of bringing home material wealth and gaining status. Those who had reached coastal areas of western Borneo and come in contact with Muslim peoples there, sometimes raided with them and at other times raided against them. The Ibans of the Saribas and Skrang Rivers (see map 5, page xix) were particularly effective sea raiders and caused terror along the Sarawak coasts.

Before James Brooke's arrival, the Ibans working land around the middle reaches of rivers had points of exchange with coastal Muslims along the rivers. Some of the rivers were controlled by Muslim chiefs on the coast, who claimed the river and its peoples were theirs to adminis-ter and control. Some of these Muslim chiefs in their turn were subject to the sultan of Brunei and delivered part of their revenues to him as was done in other Malay kingdoms. Other ethnic groups occupying ter-ritory in early 19th century Sarawak included the 'Land Dayaks', more correctly known as Bidayuhs. The Bidayuhs kept themselves separate from the Ibans by maintaining very distinct cultural practices and a more settled form of agriculture.

The Rejang, north of Kuching, is Sarawak's longest river and was sparsely populated at the time of Brooke's arrival (see map 5, page xix). The upper headwaters were inhabited by Kayans and Kenyahs, who constructed massive longhouses and, like the Ibans, practised shifting agriculture and headhunting. The middle reaches of the Rejang to the coast, as well as along the Mukah and Oya Rivers slightly northwards, were the territories of the sago-producing Melanaus. The demand for sago in Singapore stimulated Brunei contact with these peoples and some converted to Islam. The Melanaus in this region were particu-larly vulnerable to attacks by the Skrang and Saribas Iban sea raiders.

When Brooke took up residence at Kuching in 1842, he consid-ered his most urgent task was to stop the violence and raiding of the Saribas and Skrang Ibans. Assisted by Henry Keppel, then a captain in the Royal Navy, he led expeditions against these warriors. The most serious confrontation was in 1849 near the mouth of the Saribas River where 500 Ibans were killed and most of their 98 vessels destroyed.

Earlier, in 1846, forces hostile to Brooke at the Brunei court had threatened his position in Sarawak, but again with the assistance of the Royal Navy, he survived. As a result, the sultan of Brunei ceded the territory around Kuching to Brooke and his heirs in perpetuity and ceded the island of Labuan to Britain. After the major battle of 1849, Brunei agreed to cede also the Saribas and Skrang districts to Brooke. By the middle of the 19th century, therefore, the Brunei sultans had transferred their power over much of the southern reaches of their territory to James Brooke and his successors. One legal aspect of the Brunei agreements with Brooke distinguished his position from other colonial authorities in the Malaysian territories. In the Brunei transfer of 1846, Brooke was specifically granted not only rights to territory, but also personal sovereignty over it. This he accepted as the basis of his rule and that of his successors. Brooke's heirs remained rulers of Sarawak until the Japanese occupation of Borneo during World War II.

Pahang, Terengganu and Kelantan

Singapore's status as a free port greatly enlivened its links with the trading networks of the east coast of the Malay Peninsula. The Singapore merchants relied on the east coast particularly for supplies of gold dust, tin and pepper, items still in demand for the China trade. In 1838, however, a civil war in Kelantan interrupted the smooth flow of trade and some vessels sent by Chinese and Jewish merchants in Singapore were detained during the fighting. The hostilities in Kelantan were just one in a long series of similar incidents in a number of the Malay states which 'interfered with' the smooth operation of businesses centred on Penang and Singapore. The merchants in both places regularly lobbied the British government to intervene in local affairs and use force to settle disputes which threatened their trading operations. In general, however, the British adamantly refused to step in or become in any way officially embroiled with local politics in the

Importers of General Merchandise · Shippers of Rubber, Tin & Tropical Produce.
Steamship, Airline and Chartering Agents · Sunker Coal Contractors.

BOUSTEAD & CO LTD
INCORPORATED IN THE FEDERATION OF MALAYA
Insurance Agents · Secretaries and Agents for Rubber and Coconut
Estates and Tin Mining Companies · Agents in Singapore for Lloyd's of London
SINGAPORE · PENANG · KUALA LUMPUR · MALACCA · PORT SWETTENHAM
IPOH · TELUK ANSON · TUMPAT · KOTA BAHRU · KUALA TRENGGANU · KUANTAN · KUCHING

*An advertisement for one of the oldest and most successful of the British merchant firms
to have established branches in Malaya during the 19th century. Originally operating as
agents, it gradually expanded its interests into the wide range of activities listed here and
played a major role in developing plantations, mining and communications networks.*
(*Source:* Straits Times Annual, 1956)

peninsular states. The Chinese and Jewish merchants took matters
into their own hands and sent a mission to negotiate the return of their
vessels in 1838.

Abdullah bin Abdul Kadir was employed by the Singapore merchants to serve as an interpreter for their mission. He kept a journal
while travelling and later wrote an account of his observations of the
Malay states on the east coast of the Peninsula which was published as
Abdullah's Voyage (*Kesah Pelayaran Abdullah*). He formed his impressions of Pahang from his brief visit to the first main port on the Pahang
River, Kampong Cina ('Settlement of the Chinese'), also known as

Pekan Bharu. It was one of the places of residence of the *bendahara* of Pahang, who was recognised by the Riau-Lingga sultanate as having authority in Pahang. At the time Abdullah's mission visited, the *bendahara* was touring the interior regions of the Pahang River and was reported to be at Jelai (see map 5, page xix). Abdullah was informed that Jelai was a major centre with tens of thousands of Malays and Chinese who traded in forest products and gold (from the Jelai and surrounding mines). Abdullah may not have known that the chief of the Jelai region was regarded by the *bendahara* as his equal and it would have been important for the two leaders to be on good terms so that vessels could go freely up and down the river. Abdullah's notes, perhaps unwittingly, reflect the dual nature of Pahang: a very active and potentially prosperous interior under its own chiefs, populated by *Orang Asli*, Chinese and Malays, and a coastal region developing in tandem with Singapore which looked outwards to passing trade as well as up the river for its supply of trade items.

Abdullah diligently notes the goods traded: gold, tin, silk weaving, rare timbers, resin and rattan were exported while opium, silk, salt, rice and some cloth from Europe were imported. The currency was in the form of tin coins in only one denomination, making transactions rather difficult. The Chinese, he noticed, had intermarried with Malays and Balinese (perhaps brought to Pahang as slaves by the Illanuns) and there were many Arabs who had their own mosque.

As an avid reader of the *Malay Annals*, Abdullah would have known that the first sultan of Pahang was a Melaka prince who had committed a crime and was exiled to Pahang by his father, a 15th century sultan of Melaka. Pahang's history remained intertwined with that of Melaka and its relocated kingdom, Johor, so that by the late 17th century the sultans of Johor were known also as sultans of Pahang. Some time during the 18th century, the Malay rulers of Riau-Johor, perhaps to secure the support of their senior chiefs at a time when they feared domination by the Bugis under kings, confirmed the domains of the *temenggung* as the islands and territory around Johor, and for the *bendahara*, the coastal areas of Pahang. The division of the Johor-Riau kingdom under the Anglo-Dutch Treaty of 1824 meant that the *bendahara*'s domain (as well as that of the *temenggung*) fell in the British sphere and was in effect separated from the sultan's authority. As a direct consequence of that treaty, the independence of both senior ministers of the old Riau-Johor kingdom was facilitated so that, by the end of the 19th century, their descendants dropped the title of *temenggung* and *bendahara* respectively and assumed the title of sultan. When Abdullah visited Pahang in 1838, the *bendahara*, named Ali, was maintaining his links with the Riau-Lingga court as well as with the *temenggung* of Singapore. Both men had benefited from the British development of Singapore through increased trade and the desire of the British to maintain stability in the region.

Abdullah's mission left Pahang and sailed north for the next major centre, the port of the kingdom of Terengganu. The town of Kuala Terengganu, he thought, was not neatly laid out (as he was used to in Melaka and Singapore) but had winding paths, piles of rubbish, puddles and uncleared undergrowth. Always an advocate for the orderliness of the British, he made a point of noting what he considered were signs of disorder. He was pleased, however, that there were 'occasional places' where children could study the Qur'an and copyists who could write Arabic script extremely well and produce beautiful copies of the Qur'an, for which Terengganu had an excellent reputation. These comments suggest that during the 19th century, perhaps linked with the active Muslim scholars of Patani, Terengganu had an established system of *pondok* (local religious schools) where Muslim students studied and copied the Qur'an and other Muslim texts.

As in Pahang, Abdullah notes the imports and exports: opium, linen, undyed cloth and dyed European cloth were imported while gold, tin, coffee, sugar, rattan resins, pepper, dried betel, silk and cotton cloth, trousers, jackets, sashes and headcloths, as well as kris, swords and spears, were exported. The richest merchant was a Chinese who had converted to Islam, which implies he had married a local Malay woman.

Abdullah was surprised by the size of the fishing boats of Tereng-ganu, each carrying a crew of 30 or 40. His brief visit did not allow him to learn more, but he had, in fact, identified a particular characteristic of Terengganu. The coast of Terengganu was (and remains) famous for its fishing industry, and for the skill of its men at making and sailing vessels. Terengganu craft traded north to Cambodia and Siam, east to Sulu, Brunei and Labuan, south to parts of the (now) Indonesian archipelago, and to all ports of the Peninsula including Penang. The fishing and trading enterprises became interdependent because the Terengganu fishing catch had to be preserved for use during the stormy months when boats could not put to sea. Salt from ports along the Gulf of Siam was necessary for the preservation of the fish and for making the special shrimp paste, *belacan*, which is an essential item in much of the cuisine of Southeast Asia. Rice was imported in large quantities, brought to Terengganu in the large local vessels and then redistributed to other regions of Southeast Asia. Kuala Terengganu was thus the centre of a varied and profitable local trade as well as an entrepôt for foreign vessels engaged in the China trade. The skills of the fishermen as sailors were also undoubtedly used by the Illanun pirates, who must have made use of their knowledge of local conditions. In Abdullah's time, there was at least one settlement of Ibans on the Terengganu coast (interaction with the west coast of Borneo had been ongoing since at least the mid-18th century). Later, in Kelantan Abdullah noted that one of the religious teachers there was from Pontianak (south of Kuching) who had settled in Terengganu before being invited to teach in Kelantan. The silk cloth and specialised weapons described by Abdullah were distinctive products of Terengganu which is still famous for its decorative arts.

Abdullah records that shortly before his visit, in 1838, the ruler had died and had been succeeded by a 15-year-old prince known as Sultan Muhammad. He reigned only three years before being deposed by a relative who, under the title Baginda Omar, ruled Terengganu until 1876. Like Pahang, Terengganu is mentioned in the *Malay*

Annals, but its relationship with Melaka is unclear. Both Patani (southern Thailand) and Riau-Lingga claim they were responsible for installing the first sultan of Terengganu in the early 18th century and these claims reflect their respective influences on the Terengganu elite. Marriage alliances were made with both Patani and Riau-Johor and numerous times during the 18th century, when the Malay sultan of Riau-Johor was under pressure, he withdrew to the haven which Terengganu provided. The links were renewed in the 19th century as a result of Raffles' interference in the succession of Riau-Johor, when he installed Husain as sultan of Singapore. The prince, who regarded himself as the rightful heir to the throne, had not been officially installed by his court and in 1821 he withdrew to Terengganu where both he, and his son, married Terengganu princesses. The result of his son's union was the prince Mahmud. In 1839, the year after Abdullah's voyage, Mahmud's uncle, Baginda Omar, became sultan of Terengganu. Two years later, when Mahmud was only 18 years old, he became sultan of Riau-Lingga, in the Dutch sphere of influence.

Leaving Terengganu, Abdullah's group continued up the east coast, to his final destination, Kelantan. The mission planned to deliver letters from the governor of Singapore to the Kelantan leaders, requesting the release of the trading vessels. Abdullah records the continuous exchange of fire between the stockades of the opposing sides and the damage which had been done to the settlements as a result. He describes the port of Kelantan as if it were a frontier town—full of cockfighters, gamblers, opium smokers and prostitutes. To readers in the 21st century, aware of Kelantan's current reputation as the most Islamic of the Malaysian states, this description of un-Islamic behaviour may be surprising. Abdullah's visit, however, came before the reforming zeal of several later rulers of Kelantan. In his notes, Abdullah makes special mention of the livestock—cattle, buffaloes, goats and sheep—which abounded, and the export of gold, coffee, rice and silk garments which attracted ships from Europe, Madras and China. During the first half of the 19th century, Kelantan was, in fact, the richest and most populous of the Malay states.

Like Pahang, Kelantan has a vast interior of heavily forested, upland areas which are the domain of groups of *Orang Asli*. In that terrain and environment, boundaries have no significance and the inland borders between Pahang, Terengganu, Kedah, Kelantan and southern Siam (now Thailand) are creations of the 20th century. Unlike Pahang, however, Kelantan has an extensive coastal plain with various points of access to the sea and is not dominated (like Kedah, for example) by one major river, up which most traffic had to pass. As a result, Kelantan is characterised by a number of fairly autonomous groups with a sultanate centred on the Kelantan river entrance, members of the royal elite having their own territories in surrounding areas of the rich coastal plain. Until the early years of the 19th century, large sections of the interior were in the hands of very powerful chiefs and only after that time was the ruling sultan able to extend his authority into the surrounding districts. He moved the capital to its present site of Kota Bharu (see map 5, page xix) and gained the recognition of large sections of the coastal plain. It was the death of this sultan which gave rise to the civil war and the detention of the Singapore vessels in 1838.

The new sultan was resisted by two nephews of the former sultan, one the *bendahara* and the other the *temenggung*. Together they forced the new sultan out and, when Abdullah arrived, they were awaiting instructions from the king of Siam about who should take over the kingdom. This underlines another distinctive feature of Kelantan: its relations with Siam were much closer than all other Malay states (excepting Kedah) and it had to maintain a working relationship with its immediate neighbours, the southern Siamese provinces. After Abdullah's mission had departed, news came from Siam advising the *bendahara* and *temenggung* to rule together. They each assumed the title of sultan but it was not long before the former *temenggung* ousted the former *bendahara* who fled to Siam. Thereafter, under the title Sultan Muhammad II, he began a rule which was to last until 1886. This sultan is credited with 'creating the machinery of a central government'.[4] He established a central Land Office for the registration of land titles, a central religious court and, most importantly, a Siamese-based system of tax collection using village heads, 'circle' heads and district chiefs. Although each of these systems was implemented, they were not entirely successful in centralising power in the sultanate and, in effect, the taxation system enhanced the power of the district chiefs. When Sultan Muhammad died in 1886, there was again major civil disruption with a renewed struggle for control of the sultanate. The framework for improved civil and religious administration which he initiated become the basis for Kelantan's government in the early 20th century and was a model of its day.

Abdullah's mission stayed only briefly in Kelantan, unsettled by the hostilities, and was only partially successful. The trading vessels were released, but without their cargoes or any compensation for their Singapore owners. However, the activities of the young Riau-Lingga sultan, Mahmud, were to have a more lasting impact on the east coast states and became the subject of questions in the British House of Commons. Mahmud's life is a 19th century example of the close interconnections between sultanates which were typical of the 15th century, when the Melaka royals established marriage alliances throughout the Malay world.

The activities of Sultan Mahmud of Riau-Lingga

When Mahmud was installed as sultan of Riau-Lingga in 1841, he was already married to his cousin, the granddaughter of Husain, whom Raffles had installed as sultan of Singapore. Mahmud's connections with Terengganu were strong through his mother, and his uncle Baginda Omar who, before becoming sultan of Terengganu in 1839, had spent ten years at the royal court of Riau-Lingga. The close artistic connections between the Lingga court and that of Terengganu are attributed to the musicians and artists Baginda Omar took back with him. After his installation as sultan of Riau-Lingga, Mahmud asserted his powers as ruler and set his own course. He was encouraged to do so by private individuals in Singapore who saw advantages in having a royal client. Mahmud's success in Singapore made both the British and Dutch uneasy about the stability of local politics and, in 1856, the Dutch governor-general in Batavia sent him an official warning to discontinue his visits to Singapore. When Mahmud ignored this, the Dutch deposed him in 1857 and installed his uncle as sultan of Riau-Lingga.

Both the Dutch and the British underestimated the reaction this would set in train. Mahmud had all the status of a descendant of the revered Melaka royal family and was related to the ruling lines of Singapore, Johor, Pahang and Terengganu. Mahmud left the Dutch sphere and travelled to Pahang in the late 1850s, precisely the time of a succession dispute over the position of the *bendahara*. Although Mutahir, one of the late *bendahara*'s sons, had been nominated to succeed his father, another son, Ahmad, opposed him. Mahmud of Riau-Lingga had his own interests at heart and may have been planning to assume control of Pahang himself, possibly supported by the great chief of Jelai. After some initial manoeuvring, Mahmud agreed to support Ahmad in his bid for the leadership of Pahang and tried to persuade his uncle Baginda Omar of Terengganu to assist. The British in Singapore were alarmed at the prospect of an escalation of the Pahang conflict and urged Terengganu not to participate. Dependent on Singapore for much of his trade, Baginda Omar overtly complied.

Mahmud next made overtures to Bangkok, apparently seeking aid for Ahmad and for himself. He pledged that in return for Siamese aid to put himself on the throne of Pahang, he would acknowledge Siamese overlordship. The official Thai archives have records of these contacts—as they do for most of their dealings with the Malay states. King Mongkut, it is recorded, replied that he did not wish to interfere in the affairs of Pahang, which he regarded as a British Protectorate, because he was on friendly terms with the British. However, he invited Mahmud to visit Bangkok, an invitation he accepted in 1861. When Siamese ships appeared off Terengganu, the British feared an extension of Siamese influence over the entire east coast and despatched a warship. The Siamese vessels left, but shortly afterwards, the British signed treaties with both Pahang and Johor to bring their foreign relations under British control. Mahmud's activities had resulted in the British being forced to become more formally involved with Pahang and Johor than they had anticipated.

In Bangkok, Mahmud presented one of his sisters to King Mongkut, and her presence among the royal ladies was noted by Anna Leonowens (whose story became famous in *The King and I*) when she was a governess at the court. In 1862, Mahmud returned to Terengganu in the role of Siamese governor of both that state and Kelantan. He was now able to offer substantial support to Ahmad in Pahang and the British demanded that Baginda Omar expel his nephew. Omar refused and, in November 1862, two British gunboats shelled the fort and palace of Terengganu for four hours, an attack which was later censured in the House of Commons. The Siamese sent a vessel to collect Mahmud but he stayed only briefly in Siam before returning secretly to Pahang to share Ahmad's triumph as victor in the war. Not long afterwards, Mahmud died in 1864, aged only 41. The British were extremely relieved because they considered him the main cause of the disturbances which had been occurring in Pahang, Terengganu and beyond. Clearly, as a sultan whose lineage commanded respect throughout the Malay world and as a strongly motivated individual who was not intimidated by threats from the British or the Dutch, Mahmud was a force to be reckoned with. He was perhaps the most tenacious of any of the Malay sultans in pursuing what he considered were his rights in the face of European opposition.

Naning, Negeri Sembilan, Selangor and Perak

While the states on the east coast of the Peninsula were reaching accommodation with Bangkok and Singapore, centres on the west coast were experiencing their own local conflicts. In May 1831, Abdullah sailed from Singapore to Melaka because he had heard that there might be a war between the British forces there and the *penghulu* (chief) of a nearby region called Naning, and he wanted to protect his home and family. Abdullah found the inhabitants of Melaka in great commotion, expecting an attack from Naning (see map 5, page xix). In response, the British magistrate, W.T. Lewis, left with an armed force of Indian soldiers but returned after only three days after a humiliating ambush and defeat. This was the prelude to a drawn-out engagement between the British and the *penghulu*, which resulted from a total misunderstanding of the local situation by Mr Lewis and led to a costly and embarrassing campaign. It is one example of the effect a conscientious, but under-informed, foreigner can have on local (Malaysian) affairs.

The *penghulu* of Naning, also known as Dol Sayid, is celebrated as an early freedom fighter in the current interpretation of Malaysian history and Abdullah provides some background to the war in his *Story*. The district of Naning lies inland from Melaka and was known to the Dutch during their period of administration there from 1641. A productive rice area which had attracted Minangkabau settlers (among others), the Dutch and the chief of Naning had come to an agreement that the latter would deliver a portion of the annual crop to Melaka in recognition of the Dutch presence. There was no question of Dutch control of Naning and only sporadic contact, but honour on both sides was satisfied by a token amount of rice being sent annually to Melaka. When the British occupied Melaka, between 1795 and 1818, little was changed but, following the transfer of power to Britain in 1824, Mr Lewis mistakenly believed Naning was subject to Melaka and should deliver its tithes and acknowledge British authority. The *penghulu* of Naning and his people could not accept these terms and the uncertainty by the British about how to handle the situation only added to the general confusion. Various sections of British officialdom were divided about whether direct intervention and a show of force should be made, or whether the policy should be revised and greater accommodation reached with the *penghulu*. Because Melaka was losing money, it was decided the payments from Naning were essential and Lewis's force was sent to deal with the *penghulu*. The ignominious retreat, described above, was the result.

In his *Story*, Abdullah lists the 'Genealogy of the Rulers of Naning' which acknowledges that Naning was settled by groups of Minangkabau migrants from Sumatra who intermarried with local *Orang Asli*. The uncleared areas of Naning were ideal ground for guerilla tactics and the punitive forces sent by the British were ill-prepared for the overgrown conditions and for the sporadic fighting they encountered. The *penghulu* eventually surrendered when his supplies ran low and some of his allies deserted to the British. He was allowed to live in Melaka on a small pension. When he died in 1839 he was known as a successful merchant and doctor and was venerated by many Malays. The British appointed a series of new district chiefs in Naning and regarded the incident as closed. It had indicated, however, that good relations between local groups and the British had to be negotiated and that both sides needed to know more about the other.

In his *Story*, Abdullah alludes to the Minangkabau settlers of Naning but does not go on to explain how they came to dominate the neighbouring region now known as Negeri Sembilan or the 'Nine States' (see map 5, page xix). The activities of Raja Kecil, the Minangkabau-supported leader who attacked the kingdom of Johor in the early 18th century, have been described in the previous chapter. Although Raja Kecil did not succeed in gaining a permanent foothold, other Minangkabau leaders did establish themselves in the rich river valleys inland from Melaka and founded settlements. Detailed information about the early history of those settlements is difficult to obtain but we do know something about Inas, one of the districts, whose history may reflect a wider pattern.

The *Orang Asli* of the Inas area were organised under leaders called *batin*. When new settlers moved into the area, some of them were granted the title of *penghulu* by the local *batin*. Some *Orang Asli* converted to Islam (probably when they married Malay settlers) and left their *batin* groups to live under *penghulus*. In the late 18th century, the Minangkabau settlers were strengthened by the arrival of a member of the Minangkabau royal line, Raja Melewar (1773–95), who is recognised as the first *yamtuan*, or lord, of the region. He bestowed Sumatran titles and offices on loyal supporters, thus adding to the array of positions and offices available to local people.

There are now between 12 to 13 different customary law (*adat*) districts in Negeri Sembilan, covering various clan groupings (*suku*). Traditional leadership is still held by district chiefs whose succession is based on a rotation system, with elaborate rules to ensure the correct order of rotation between a select group of lineages. While this situation provides rich material for anthropological research, in practical terms the grounds for dispute over territorial and leadership rights are legion. Until the late 19th century, the various clans and districts retained a largely autonomous existence, making alliances and linkages only when it was necessary to achieve a particular end. The land in the Negeri Sembilan hills is suitable for wet-rice cultivation (and rice can be grown there without irrigation) while the headwaters of the rivers have gold and tin deposits. A particular characteristic of the Minangkabau dominated areas of Negeri Sembilan is the system of land ownership and inheritance. Following Minangkabau custom, family lands are in the hands of women and ancestral lands pass down the female line.

North and west of the river valleys of Negeri Sembilan lie the territories of Selangor. Within the boundaries of the modern state, Selangor can be divided into three major river valleys of settlement which, working from north to south are: the Selangor River, the Klang and the Langat (see map 5, page xix). Before the 18th century, Selangor was only sparsely populated until the arrival of migrants, during the 1700s, attracted by the tin for which Selangor is still famous. The Bugis groups who moved there from Riau were instrumental in developing

A rare photograph (late 19th century) of women washing for tin in a river using shallow trays. More intensive methods of mining (in pits by dredging and sluicing) required organised teams of male workers, usually Chinese coolies.
(Source: National Archives of Malaysia)

Selangor's tin trade. Despite Dutch attempts to prevent them, they traded with British country traders, receiving opium in return for the tin which the British needed for the China trade.

The establishment of Penang provided even greater opportunities for trade with the British and the leading Bugis chief in Selangor, a member of the family of Bugis under kings in Riau, asked the sultan of Perak to install him as sultan of Selangor in 1766. Thus, Sultan Sallehuddin, who began the royal house of Selangor with the assistance of the sultan of Perak, consolidated his position from his lucrative trade in tin and opium. When he died in 1782, he was succeeded by his son Ibrahim (1782–1826), during whose reign a gigantic tin mine 40 feet (12 metres) deep and with two sluices each a mile long (1.5 kilometres) was excavated in the upper reaches of the Selangor River (nowadays Ulu Selangor). It was said to have been worked not by Chinese but by Malays who were probably immigrants from Sumatra.

One of the results of the relatively late settlement of Selangor was the absence of a developed system of administration. The first sultan instituted the practice of granting rights over districts to members of his own family. Thus, in addition to the disputes over royal succession which were, as we have seen, a characteristic of Malay royal families, there were also disputes over succession rights to territories especially when the available territory ran out in the mid-19th century.

One dispute over territory was not long lived (1867–73) but it did have disastrous consequences and opened the way for a permanent and official British presence in Selangor. At the heart of the dispute were rights to the tin-rich territory of Klang, which the sultan had not passed to his grandson as expected, but to another relative. Raja Mahdi, the grandson, was the popular claimant and was able to raise forces to pursue his claims. His chief opponent was a Kedah prince (Tengku Kudin) who had married into the Selangor royal family and had the backing of leading British figures in Singapore and Penang. The fighting resulted in the destruction of major tin mines and the depopulation of agricultural districts. It was complicated by the involvement of backers in Singapore and Penang, forces from Kedah and from Pahang, incidents of piracy, and outbreaks of major violence among Chinese miners around Kuala Lumpur. The supply of tin to the merchants of Singapore and Penang was disrupted and they lobbied the British government to intervene and 'restore order'. Before outlining the results of this pressure, it is important to give a brief survey of Perak, Selangor's northern neighbour.

According to a local legend, the kingdom of Perak originated with the marriage of a Malay trader who settled in the upper reaches of the Perak River and married the daughter of an *Orang Asli* chief. Although they had no children of their own, their adopted daughter married a prince from Johor (note the links with the Melaka dynasty), who became the first ruler of Perak. Like Selangor, Perak is an area with rich deposits of alluvial tin which can be extracted by washing in trays. These deposits may have been exploited in prehistoric times and they were definitely being worked in the early 17th century when they attracted the attention of the very active rulers of Aceh. Perak, like Johor and Pahang, was raided by the Acehnese and, it is said, 5000 of the population, including the royal family, were transported to Aceh. The royal family of Perak intermarried with that of Aceh and a Perak prince was returned to Aceh as its ruler.

In the mid-17th century, after the Dutch had replaced the Portuguese in Melaka, Perak's tin was exported through a system of monopoly agreements with the Dutch. The Dutch failed to exert a total monopoly, however, and some tin was traded with freelance merchants via overland routes to Kedah. During the 18th century Perak, like Kelantan, had a number of territorial chiefs who were loosely linked with the sultan, but who had considerable autonomy in their own districts. This was also the period of Bugis activity in the archipelago and, as already noted, groups of Bugis succeeded in establishing themselves in the tin-rich areas of Selangor. They tried also to extend their influence to Perak, and for short periods had some success. However, fearful of losing his influence in his own kingdom, the Perak sultan of the day negotiated a treaty with the British in 1825, under which he would be guaranteed protection. Essentially, Perak was trying to ensure its position both against the Siamese in Kedah and the Bugis in Selangor.

Internal security was a different matter—the sultan was supposed to have his own domains under control. Like all Malay kingdoms, Perak was vulnerable to quarrels over succession and disputes over control of revenue-rich districts. The Chinese, who arrived in increasing numbers during the 19th century to work as miners had their own disputes and Kinta, the richest tin-producing district at that time, was one of the worst areas for violence. Any disruption to the extraction of tin for the British merchants caused them acute concern and for some time they had been lobbying strongly in London for official British

A Short History of Malaysia

action on the Peninsula whenever their commercial interests were threatened. The Colonial Office steadfastly refused to intervene.

The situation changed when senior members of the royal families in Selangor and Perak, in return for assistance to press their claims for territory or power, granted prospecting concessions to foreigners (a British businessman and a Chinese developer respectively). The foreigners, who stood to lose much if their concessions were not honoured, persuaded their Malay patrons that more active British intervention would further their own interests. They continued to lobby British officials in London and in 1873, in response to the repeated reports of 'violence' and 'disruption' as well as the losses caused by piracy, the Colonial Office authorised Sir Andrew Clarke, the incoming governor of Singapore and Penang, to look into the situation.

After listening to the local British lobbyists, Clarke was persuaded that the time was right to present a treaty to the chiefs of Perak. The treaty would endorse a new sultan—who had several competitors—and put an end to the Chinese disputes by stationing a British official permanently in Perak's main mining districts. In return, the sultan had to agree to accept, and pay for, a British administrator, known as a resident, whose advice he was bound to follow. The new agreement, known as the Pangkor Treaty because it was signed on a British vessel anchored off the island of Pangkor, was concluded on 20 January 1874 by the eight senior ministers and several of the chiefs of Perak and Clarke, governor of the Straits Settlements.

The Pangkor Treaty has assumed a special importance in Malaysian history because it is regarded as marking the beginning of official British intervention in Malay affairs. Similar understandings were reached with Selangor and Sungai Ujong (Negeri Sembilan) where British residents were also accepted. In Perak, the first resident, J.W.W. Birch, moved swiftly to introduce a new system of taxation and revenue collection. His policies and direct manner aroused the hostility of the new sultan and senior chiefs, whose traditional rights were threatened by Birch's new regime.

British officials seem to have learned little from earlier clashes with local chiefs—for example, the Naning incident between Lewis and the *penghulu* of Naning in 1831 provided lessons about the importance of local interests and of extended negotiation rather than aggressive action. Despite evidence that both the sultan and senior chiefs were extremely hostile to him, Birch continued with the implementation of the new tax regulations in Perak. On 2 November 1875, he was assassinated early one morning while bathing in the river. Official British retribution was swift and violent. The chiefs implicated in the assassination and the sultan were exiled and the alleged perpetrators of the murder were hanged. These actions were designed to serve as an example of British response to lack of cooperation from local authorities and thereafter, in Perak at least, there was greater support for British policies. The intro-duction of new revenue-collecting measures, which struck at the basis of power and authority for both chiefs and sultans, continued to arouse hostility elsewhere in the Malaysian territories and lasted well into the 20th century.

Islamic connections

Although Islam had been adopted by some Malays during the period of the Melaka sultanate, there are few details about its administration and propagation. From the late 18th century onwards, there is more evidence about how Islam was being practised. In the 1780s and 1790s, we know that some Malays were travelling to Mecca to participate in the rituals of the pilgrimage. The sultan of Selangor, for example, was writing letters to the East India Company requesting assistance and safe passage on EIC vessels for several of his subjects who were trying to reach Mecca. The pilgrimage to Mecca (the *hajj*) is one of the five basic principles enjoined on all Muslims and its successful completion brings individual Muslims spiritual benefits, as well as status in their home community.

It is not surprising then, that Abdullah bin Abdul Kadir, the diligent clerk, language teacher, translator and educator, should himself embark on the pilgrimage. Singapore had become the centre for a great deal of Muslim activity for the whole of the Indonesian archipelago as well as the Malaysian territories. Its role as a shipping centre meant that it was the major port of embarkation for the *hajj* and it had also attracted an active group of Hadrami Arabs and Indian Muslims. Some of them were highly regarded as religious teachers and they contributed to the publishing industry, which was well established in Singapore, by printing religious texts and journals and circulating them to their fellow Muslims.

In February 1854, Abdullah left Singapore in an Arab vessel. He kept a journal of his voyage in which he recorded his arrival in Mecca and his deep emotion at being present in the Holy Land. However, he died suddenly in October 1854 and left the journal incomplete, to be returned to Malaya by a friend and later published. Always an apologist for the achievements of the British and their orderly system of government, as he had experienced it in Melaka and Singapore, he would probably have approved of the British system of residents ushered in by the signing of the Pangkor Treaty in 1874, just 20 years after his death. However, he may not have approved of the clause which limited the resident's advice to secular matters and clearly delineated 'Malay Religion and Custom' as remaining strictly under the sultan's authority. Abdullah had been critical of the Malay rulers for what he believed were old fashioned and autocratic attitudes and he had urged them in his writings to educate their people in the ways of the contemporary world. Reform of the sultanates, he believed, was necessary and the 'protection' provided by the Treaty of Pangkor for the maintenance of royal privileges was not in the best interests of the future development of the Malays.

By the early 20th century, an articulate and well-educated group of modern-minded Muslims was also urging Malays to adapt to the needs of a changing world. This could be achieved, it was argued, if the Qur'anic injunction, 'God helps those who help themselves' was actively applied by individual Muslims.

7
RESPONSES TO COLONIALISM

Then came to our eastern countries the Europeans from the north replete with the weapons to win the battle of life and equipped with knowledge of the ways and means to make profit . . .

Syed Shaykh al-Hady, 1907[1]

By the early 20th century, it was clear to the majority of the inhabitants of the Malaysian territories that the presence of the British was not a temporary phenomenon. The Brooke family was entrenched in Sarawak and the British North Borneo Company was trying to administer Sabah, while on the Peninsula, British businesses, plantations and a colonial civil service were in embryonic form but growing rapidly. The responses of several regions in the Malaysian territories to British colonial rule enable us to gauge the effects a permanent and institutionalised Western presence was having on the local populations. In recent times, the impact of the colonial period has been reassessed and it is being recognised that the contact between colonisers and colonised was very much a two-way interaction: the colonisers were affected and influenced by the process as much as the local peoples.

The term 'colonialism' generally conjures up images of repression, authoritarianism and paternalism. The quotation above reflects the views of an influential and articulate group of local people within the Malaysian territories in the early 20th century. During the 19th century, foreign-dominated rule was a widely spread phenomenon throughout Asia although the degree of colonial influence, even within one major region, could vary greatly. Malaysia's neighbouring states, the Netherlands Indies, Burma and the Philippines were all subject to a European power. Thailand remained independent but, in the early years of the 20th century, traded some of its territory to the British in return for recognition of its sovereignty over other areas. It is this concern for control of territory which has led one prominent writer of Southeast Asian history to identify the creation of national borders as one of the most important features of the European advance into the region. As Milton Osborne notes, the colonial powers created borders 'that, with minor exceptions, have become those of the modern states of Southeast Asia'.[2] British policies did indeed have a permanent effect on the Malaysian territories through the fixing of their international and many of their internal borders, as well as on the way they were governed.

Making borders: dividing and governing peoples

The Anglo-Dutch Treaty of 1824 divided the Malay Peninsula and island Southeast Asia into British and Dutch spheres and established the major international boundary between what were to become Malaysia and Indonesia. When Sultan Mahmud of Riau-Lingga (Dutch territory) ignored the European-derived boundaries and, during the 1850s, travelled freely through the Peninsula and to Bangkok he was deposed by the Dutch and was subjected to gunfire from British warships off Terengganu. He could be described as one early victim of the new international boundaries. At the time of his death in 1864, the geographical components of modern Malaysia were beginning to be drawn together.

Siam, the Straits Settlements and Borneo

The boundaries between the Anglo-Malay and Siamese spheres of influence were laid down in the 1826 Agreement of Bangkok (the Burney Agreement). Siamese rule was acknowledged in Kedah, but in Kelantan and Terengganu, it was agreed that the British would not interfere in the internal affairs of either kingdom and the Siamese would not obstruct British trade there. In the same year, 1826, the EIC decided to combine the administration of Penang, Melaka and Singapore into one unit, to be known as the Straits Settlements. The commercial success of Singapore and Penang soon became evident, as a leading historian of the 19th century noted: 'By the mid-19th century the Straits Settlements offered striking justification of the theories of free trade, light taxation and *laissez-faire* government.'[3] Abdullah Munshi was convinced that the Straits Settlements were an example of what could be achieved by planning and control. For him, and for many of the successful merchants operating there, the Straits Settlements represented the antithesis of the 'chaos' and 'disorder' of the Malay states ruled by Malay sultans. In 1858, after years of lobbying in London, Singapore's leading businesses directly petitioned the British Parliament for the Straits Settlements to be separated from India and the India Office. This was achieved finally in 1867 when the Straits Settlements became a Crown Colony under the Colonial Office, with an executive council of senior officials and a legislative council whose members were nominated by the governor.

Meanwhile, some of Brunei's territories were being transferred to James Brooke, starting in 1841 with the grant of Kuching and the mineral-rich territory around it. Brooke's troubles with the local peoples (particularly the aggressive Skrang Iban groups) had made him a vocal supporter of Crown Colony status for the Straits Settlements. He saw this as opening the way for British protection of Sarawak, possibly even linking Sarawak with Singapore. But this did not eventuate and Sarawak's borders remained limited to Borneo, where Brooke's influence expanded steadily into Brunei's territories. By 1906, Sarawak had assumed its present borders and encircled what was left of Brunei. The latter kingdom was saved only by a British treaty with the sultan in 1906, under which the sultan accepted a British Resident as adviser and Brunei became a Protectorate.

By the 1870s, other European groups were interested in Brunei's territories in the region now known as Sabah. The Dent brothers had a successful private British Trading Company in the Far East and sent their partner, Baron von Overbeck, an Austrian businessman from Hong Kong, to negotiate with the sultan of Brunei for the lease of some of his territory. As in Sarawak, the sultan of Brunei did not have personal rights to all territories under his influence and many important areas were controlled by individual ministers or other members of the Bruneian elite. However, he could bring his influence to bear and so, in late December 1877, the sultan of Brunei and one of his ministers agreed to lease large areas of the west coast of Sabah to the Dents' syndicate, in return for an annual rent.

The Dent brothers turned next to Sabah's east coast and negotiated with its nominal overlord, the sultan of Sulu, for further leases for which they also paid annual sums. In 1881, the British government granted the Dents' 'Provisional Association' a Royal charter to establish the North Borneo Chartered company. Under the charter, the company had wide powers to govern 'North Borneo' providing the conditions of the charter were respected. These included protecting the rights, customs and interests of native peoples; developing the territory; promoting public works and irrigation; granting land to investors, free access to British shipping and allowing free trade. In addition, all issues concerning external relations would be conducted by Britain. The company's administration was supervised by a Court of Directors in London represented in Sabah by a governor and his officers. The extent of company-controlled territory grew through the 1880s as more Brunei nobles leased portions of their territories in Sabah directly to the company. A degree of administrative 'neatness' was created in 1888, when Sarawak, Brunei and Sabah officially became British Protectorates. By the early 1900s, the borders of modern Sabah had been defined but the inland areas, particularly along the southern border—a region inhabited mostly by Murut peoples—was almost entirely unknown to outsiders.

Internal borders

The Protected Malay States (1874–95)

On the Peninsula, the 1874 Pangkor Treaty with Perak (the model for later agreements with other Malay states) did not establish international boundaries. It did, however, become the cornerstone for a major new administrative alignment of the four regions which had agreed to accept and support a British resident to work in concert with the reigning sultan through a State Council. Perak and Selangor, then Negeri Sembilan and, in 1888, Pahang, were administered under the 'residential system' and were known collectively as the Protected Malay States.

In the late 1880s, after Pahang had also accepted a resident, several British officials believed that an amalgamation, or loose confederation of the four similarly governed and adjacent states, would benefit their development as well as rationalise their administrations. It made sense, they suggested, for common services such as roads, railways and communications networks to be organised together rather than separately. The idea was put into effect in 1896.

The Federated Malay States (FMS)

The agreement consenting to a federation was signed by the sultans of the four kingdoms in 1895 when the arrangement was presented to them. In reality, the implementation of the agreement resulted in an amalgamation of the four kingdoms by combining their administration, services and, above all, their finances. Under the latter arrangements, richer kingdoms could subsidise the poorer, and Pahang needed to be bailed out during the 1890s. The head of the federation was a British resident-general, who was theoretically under the governor of the Straits Settlements and who was appointed also as high commissioner for the Malay states. An annual meeting (or durbar) of Malay rulers and British officials was the only official opportunity for the component parts of the federation to come together.

Sir Frank Swettenham, a forthright ex-resident with over 20 years' service in Malaya, was appointed first resident-general (1896–1900) and established a style of centralised control from the new administrative centre of Kuala Lumpur. His personality ensured that the resident-general was not seen as subservient to the governor and for the four years he held the position he aggressively pursued major development policies for the federation. The four sultans concerned, especially the articulate Sultan Idris of Perak, resisted the idea of amalgamation of finances and administrations and the federation was not accomplished as completely as the British government had envisaged. When the Colonial Office recognised this in 1910, they supported amendments to the 1895 agreement with the result that the governor was unambiguously in charge of the FMS. Bifurcation of policy between the Straits Settlements and the FMS was to be strenuously avoided.

The Unfederated Malay States (UMS)

Only four peninsular kingdoms had agreed to accept British residents and were thus involved in the federation. By 1910, however, the situation began to change, largely as the result of the new Anglo-Siamese Treaty of 1909. The negotiations for the treaty seem to have been conducted directly between Siam and Britain, without reference to the Malay kingdoms involved, a situation which would later be a cause for dissension. Under the treaty, Siam agreed to transfer its authority over Kedah, Perlis, Kelantan and Terengganu—but not over Patani—to the British. The treaty thus established Malaysia's northern international border and like the Treaty of London (1824) divided culturally and ethnically related peoples into different international jurisdictions. After World War II, unsuccessful attempts were made to reunite the Malay peoples by pressing for Patani's incorporation into Malaya.

Kedah, Perlis, Kelantan and Terengganu also agreed to accept British advisers (who had less authority than British residents) into their administrations, largely because they needed assistance to pay large state debts. In 1910, Johor too agreed to allow a British officer to be stationed in the state but without any official position. British influence in Borneo was being formalised at this time with Brunei accepting a resident in 1906 and Labuan, North Borneo and Sarawak each coming under the authority of the governor of the Straits Settlements. None of these areas, whether in Borneo or on the Peninsula, would agree to join the FMS. In effect, however, they were ultimately under the same authority (the governor) and they were very much influenced by the style of administration in the FMS. In some senses, the Unfederated States enjoyed the best of both worlds: their sultans retained more control over domestic affairs than their counterparts in the FMS and they were able to change some aspects of their internal administration to incorporate innovations from a number of sources which included Britain, Siam and Ottoman Turkey.

Cooperation or resistance

Treaties made between Britain and the Netherlands, or Britain and Siam, or even treaties between local (usually Malay) rulers and foreigners, were agreements unlikely to have been widely known beyond the circles of officials who negotiated and administered them. In 1910, European knowledge of inland areas of the Peninsula, let alone Sabah, was minimal. In Sarawak, the Brooke administrators had made more forays into the interior than most of their counterparts elsewhere in the Malaysian territories, yet a map from the period shows how much land was still unknown to outsiders (see map 4, page xviii).

These regions, although blanks on the map, were populated, their peoples interacting with others in the Malaysian territories. However, tracing this interaction through either Malay or European documents is very difficult. The interactions were not always positive and in some regions Malays, Minangkabaus, Bataks, Rawas and others captured non-Malay peoples for slaves. Many of those groups developed elaborate avoidance procedures which allowed them to trade without direct contact. The effect of increased colonial influence produced very different responses among the indigenous peoples in different areas.

The Semais

The Semais represent a fairly large population of *Orang Asli*, who from at least the late 19th century, have lived (and continue to live) in the foothills and mountains of southern Perak and in the adjacent areas of northwestern Pahang. Today, the Semais number about 30 000 and form the largest group of the *Orang Asli*.

As shifting cultivators, the Semais were vulnerable to the effects of colonial 'development' policies which demanded increasing areas of land. Foreign investment in mining increased the numbers of Chinese and Indonesian workers being brought into the peninsula and efforts to locate new mineral deposits took them into areas which were traditional domains of the Semais. As well, the British policy of encouraging intensification of rice production and the spread of plantation crops brought Malays and others into competition with the Semais for agricultural land. The colonial officials wanted to see development accomplished with the utmost speed so that revenue would flow and infrastructure (roads, railways) could be established. Negotiation with the Semais over access to their lands was not part of colonial policy.

The arrival of new peoples into the Malaysian territories has always been a characteristic feature of its history and degrees of accommodation and adaptation have developed over time. One important example concerns rights to land use. In the region now known as Negeri Sembilan, and possibly also in parts of Kedah, Kelantan and Pahang, some Malays and other peoples recognised the traditional rights of the *Orang Asli* to particular territories and intermarried with them so that their descendants participated in local land usage practices. Customary law in Negeri Sembilan included specific recognition of *Orang Asli* 'ownership' of jungle and interior land and allowed for compensation if the *Orang Asli* were displaced. It is more difficult to learn what *Orang Asli* themselves thought of these arrangements.

There is some information from the early 20th century which indicates how relationships between *Orang Asli* and Perak Malays were negotiated. The sultan of Perak at that time contacted a group of Semais through his local Malay chiefs and conveyed to them letters of appointment as headmen with Malay titles. The Semais thus appointed responded by implementing some features of Malay political culture: they organised a headman for each local group of Semais and arranged for annual meetings of the headmen. At these meetings, produce they had collected was delivered to the Malay chiefs as a token of mutual accommodation. These Semais also implemented a dispute resolution procedure where public meetings were held to hear 'trials' of alleged *Orang Asli* offenders. This procedure extended an existing Semai tradition of consensus through discussion at public meetings but refined it for the more specific purpose of dealing with wrongdoers. This degree of interaction between Semais and Malays provided sufficient latitude for the Semais to maintain their own integrity and identity, unless they chose to settle permanently with non-*Orang Asli* groups (Malay or Chinese, for example) and adopt their religion and lifestyle.

Unfortunately, relations between the Semais and outsiders were not always peaceful. There are many European reports about raids on *Orang Asli* to capture women and children, who would then be sold to become labourers or household servants. In these raids, it was not unusual for male *Orang Asli* to be murdered. Information on the per-petrators of the raids is less clear—Malays were certainly involved in the procurement and sale of the *Orang Asli* but some *Orang Asli* groups themselves may have been coerced by Malays to raid others. In the northern parts of the Peninsula, Thais sometimes captured *Orang Asli* for their curiosity value as well as for their labour.

Some groups of *Orang Asli* negotiated ways of protecting them-selves from the raiders by appointing selected Malays as their agents. The Malays acted as intermediaries between the Semais and outsiders. The intermediaries inherited their positions and good working rela-tionships of trade and exchange operated in some Semai territories in Perak and Kelantan up until the late 1940s, when more bureaucratic links were established. It has been suggested that the present divisions of the Semais into 'highland' and 'lowland' Semais is the result of slave raiding and increasing intensification of settlement by outsiders. Those groups who retreated in the face of advancing threats to their lifestyle remained in the more remote and upland areas. One of the long-term effects of slave raiding has been *Orang Asli* distrust of dealings with Malays. In many of their oral traditions, outsiders are depicted as dangerous, untrustworthy and to be avoided. In Malay stereotypes of *Orang Asli*, the image of a less developed, uncivilised, culturally inferi-or group may well be linked to Malay folk memory of the time when many of the slaves and dependents in Malay society were *Orang Asli*.

The rights of *Orang Asli* to their traditional lands were threatened not only by colonial development policies but also because the British negotiated for territory only with the Malays. Although some Malay chiefs had made agreements with the *Orang Asli*, the British regarded the Malay sultans as the sole source of authority over land, and therefore dealt only with them. The implications of this policy are still being played out in contemporary Malay politics. The *Orang Asli*, like most of the world's other tribal peoples, had the choice of withdrawal into remote areas or assimilation.

The Bajaus

The largest group of *Orang Suku Laut* in Sabah waters are the Bajaus who are widely dispersed around the Sulu archipelago (southern Philippines), the northeast coast of Sabah, and eastern Indonesia. From at least the late 18th century (if not much earlier), the Bajaus served the sultan of Sulu as seamen, pilots, traders and raiders and in return were awarded titles and positions at court. One of the points in their network of collection and exchange was an island in the Darvel Bay region of Sabah's east coast (see map 5, page xix). This was a collection point for sea products and birds' nests. During the 1880s, the settlement attracted neighbouring peoples who did not wish to come under the influence of the British North Borneo Company, at that time extending its operations in Sabah.

The expanding community in Darvel Bay which had links with the Bajaus, whom the British officials regarded as pirates, alarmed the North Borneo Company. In their view, there was no reason why the Bajaus should not replace their 'piracy' with a 'settled' life. Company officials, therefore, rewarded those Bajaus who started growing coconuts for the copra trade. The company also devised a system of boat registration which would enable the British to track boats from the registration labels attached to their bows. At the same time, the governor of the British North Borneo Company began replacing chiefs who had been installed by the sultan of Sulu with men who undertook to be loyal to the company.

But administration is expensive and revenue was not flowing to the company so in 1887 the governor also introduced a tax on the lucrative Bajau trade in birds' nests. Faced with having to pay to register their boats *and* with a tax on their main trade item, many Bajaus resisted. On the grounds that he was dealing with a piratical people, the governor summoned several Royal Navy ships to shell and destroy Bajau settlements. The local chiefs responded by sailing to Sulu to seek the sultan's assistance. In their absence, the governor decided to establish a new trading centre to attract more passing trade to the Darvel Bay region. He selected a mainland site not far from the Bajau island and named it Semporna, appointing a Chinese trader to represent the company and promote the settlement. Unfortunately for the Bajau chiefs, the Spanish authorities in the Philippines had been attacking Sulu and their navy chased away the Bajaus who then decided that settlement in Semporna was not such a bad option.

Between the late 1880s and 1910, Semporna attracted a large influx of Bajaus who used it as an alternative to their former Sulu market. The North Borneo Company also introduced cash (rather than barter) for transactions in Semporna which enabled local trade to be linked more effectively into the wider regional markets. The adoption of a cash economy as a major economic innovation 'greatly expanded the value and volume of local trade, in some cases intensified economic specialization, and effectively linked local trade to global markets well beyond the district'.[4] The facilities and opportunities for making money which Semporna represented transformed the lifestyles of those Bajaus who chose to trade and settle there. Others maintained their existing lifestyle but the company's policy of boat registration and their use of police to enforce it resulted in fewer Bajaus making extended trips to eastern Indonesia and more choosing to operate closer to Borneo and the southern Philippines. The combination of changed circumstances in the Sulu sultanate (coincidentally caused by another colonial presence) so that it no longer served as an alternative to the authority of the company, the initiative of the governor in identifying and appointing key individuals as company agents and the success of the cash economy in Semporna provided conditions which the Bajaus found favourable for their own purposes. Unlike many other minority communities under colonial influence they did not disintegrate. On the contrary, they adapted to the new conditions and exploited them to their own advantage.

The Chinese miners of Bau

The British North Borneo Company, through the policies of an astute governor, had some success in its interaction with the Bajaus in the late 19th century. But the company was also criticised for looking too much to developing maritime relations at the expense of administering the inland and interior people of Sabah. It was proving difficult to introduce new administrative practices to the region. In Sarawak, 30 years earlier, James Brooke (referred to in Sarawak as the rajah) had experienced a surprise attack on Kuching which strengthened his ideas about methods of local administration.

In the late 1840s, James Brooke was occupied with the pacification of the Saribas and Skrang Dayaks and with developing a policy for administering his territories. In 1852, he appointed his nephew, Charles Johnson, as his deputy (*tuan muda*) and Charles began a long career dedicated to implementing his vision of what Sarawak could and should be. Charles (who later took his uncle's name of Brooke) personally led 50 expeditions against 'hostile' Iban groups, using friendly Ibans as his warriors. One of the objects of the campaigns was to stop the Iban practice of headhunting but it has been suggested that the campaigns themselves, during which heads were taken, 'perhaps served instead to perpetuate the practice'.[5]

James Brooke developed a system of administration in which the few Europeans in Sarawak worked through local chiefs to interfere as little as possible with traditional practice. He described himself as the 'governor' (*tuan besar*) and personally promulgated the first written laws in 1842, basing them on existing local laws which he obtained through discussions with headmen. His aim was to separate abuse from custom and through free trade and respect for the Dayak, Malay and Chinese communities to promote local prosperity.

The Chinese were administered through their own leaders. It is important to differentiate between various Chinese ethnic groups because each had their own specific customs, occupations and language. In Sarawak, seven distinct dialect groups were recognised. The first Chinese mining settlements in Sarawak were established by Chinese who had already been mining in the Sambas–Pontianak districts of Dutch West Borneo since at least the 1760s (see map 5, page xix). These early mining communities were mainly Hakka Chinese from southern China. In the early 1820s, when the demands of Dutch administration became burdensome and when the gold began to show signs of being worked out, many moved north into Sarawak after learning that antinomy and gold had been discovered.

By the 1840s, considerable numbers of Hakkas from the Sambas fields had settled at Bau, a rich gold area in the upper reaches of the Sarawak River. In the same period, Hokkien traders and Cantonese market gardeners settled in Kuching. By 1857, migrants from the Dutch territories had swollen the numbers at Bau. The miners were under the influence of an aggressive secret society and were smuggling opium, for which some miners were convicted by Brooke's representatives. The situation was tense but became critical when new taxes were announced on gambling, opium and the export of gold. Each tax directly affected the Chinese miners. All kinds of rumours circulated in this heated context and the angry miners expressed their frustration by mounting a surprise attack on Kuching in February 1857. Europeans were captured and two children and several British settlers were murdered. The Malay quarter of Kuching was sacked and totally destroyed. James Brooke escaped by swimming across the Sarawak River and the town was saved by the arrival of a European vessel owned by a mining company. Charles Brooke returned from a tour of the interior with his Iban force and pursued the Chinese across the border into Dutch territory where many were captured by the Dutch. Some estimates put the number of miners killed at about 1000 and the disruption which the incident caused meant that the gold mining never regained the former levels of production. Chinese immigration slowed and it took a further decade before numbers reached the levels of 1857. Although Hakkas remained the dominant group, they were closely followed by Foochows (people from Fuzhou in southeastern China), with increasing numbers of migrants coming directly from China as well as from the Straits Settlements.

The Bau miners had shown that Kuching was vulnerable to attack and the Brookes took note. Charles soon embarked on a major expedition against an influential Iban leader called Rentap, around whom Iban opposition to the Brooke presence was focused. Rentap and his followers successfully resisted attempts to capture their long-house headquarters in 1857 and Charles launched another attack in the following year, again without defeating Rentap. But, from the Brookes' point of view, worse was to come.

In 1859, two British officers were murdered in a fort on the Rejang River in the Third Division (see map 5, page xix). Charles Brooke led an expedition which resulted in the execution of ten locals suspected of being implicated in the murders but others remained uncaptured. The European community in Sarawak, aware of the success of the Indian Mutiny and hearing also that Europeans had been massacred in Banjarmasin (south Borneo) in the middle of 1859, were afraid of a mass uprising by local peoples. Many Europeans were unnerved by rumours a war was being organised by disaffected Muslims who were planning to restore the rule of Brunei. Indeed, it became evident that Brunei nobles were being supported by some local Malay chiefs in a bid to oust Brooke rule. Using a display of naval force, James Brooke finally negotiated an agreement with the leaders of the disaffection and a *modus vivendi* was established.

During this period in Sarawak history, all contenders for power relied on being able to persuade Iban warriors to fight for them. Charles Brooke decided to change this by winning the loyalty of as many as possible. His third expedition against Rentap was more carefully planned and supplied with special cannon. Although he still did not succeed in capturing Rentap, who escaped and lived a further few years in remote jungle, the Ibans of the Saribas and Skrang Rivers were considered finally to be 'pacified' (that is, more tolerant of Brooke rule).

Rentap's name lives on in Sarawak and in the national history of Malaysia as one of the first freedom fighters for his people. In 1993, a special monument was unveiled to commemorate nine Heroes of Sarawak. Among the nine names were Rentap, Liew Shan Pang, leader of the Bau uprising, and the leaders of several other movements to resist Brooke rule. Formerly 'rebels', they are now heroes.

In 1863, six years after the attack by the miners of Bau, James Brooke handed his authority to Charles and retired to England where he died in 1868. Charles went on to rule Sarawak for 49 years until his death in 1917. His experience in the country was therefore exceptionally long and his policies, implemented over more than 50 years, have shaped modern Sarawak. A historian of Sarawak has summed up the Brooke legacy in this way:

> . . . the effect of Brooke rule had been to entrench a European ruling family at the expense of traditional Malay and Chinese leadership . . . While the Brookes and their officers railed against 'vested interests', their own interest was to preserve their position by resisting change. They were not so much opposed to economic development as to the resulting social and political changes which would inevitably undermine the basis of their authority and prestige. Nevertheless, for the most part, they carried out their work for little financial reward and with a sincerity of purpose seldom found in orthodox colonial systems.[6]

Populating the Malaysian territories

Even though the Hakka miners of Bau had murdered and wrought so much destruction in Kuching, Charles Brooke still believed the key to developing Sarawak was to attract large numbers of Chinese settlers. In 1867, he wrote in his diary: 'We are going to reduce the price of the cooked opium in the country and if this report be true will be the means of bringing many hundreds perhaps thousands of people into the country. We want population to turn our waste land into shape and create bustle and industry.'[7] But attracting permanent settlers was not easy even though Charles used Chinese merchants as agents and from 1871 offered land grants. However, from about 1910 groups of Christian Chinese began arriving with their families to settle near Kuching, Sibu and on the Baram River and cultivate vegetables, pepper, rubber and some rice. When the Miri oil wells went into production in 1910, more Chinese came as labourers and as skilled workmen. Further north in Sabah, Chinese merchants were operating on the coasts and from the 1880s arrived in greater numbers. At that time, when it was rare for women to accompany them, many Chinese married local Sabah people and mixed race children were quite common. By the 1920s, Chinese women were also migrating and mixed marriages became comparatively rare.

The pattern of immigration to Penang serves to illustrate how Chinese migration contributed to the rapid development of new centres. When Francis Light leased Penang from the sultan of Kedah in the late 18th century, it had few inhabitants but it quickly attracted Malays from the Peninsula and from Sumatra, and Indians from southern India, particularly Chettiars (moneylenders) from Madras as well as labourers. However, it was the Chinese who emigrated in the largest numbers and by the 1850s there were 24 000, compared with 20 000 Malays, and 12 000 Indians. Some of the earliest Chinese migrants to Penang were already extremely wealthy and later became benefactors and highly respected community figures. Those who assimilated with local (predominantly Malay) culture were known as Babas (Straits Chinese) and contrasted themselves with the Chinese who arrived later, usually direct from China, and who were referred to as *sinkeh* (newcomers). From about the 1850s, the pace of Chinese immigration increased due to a constellation of factors: unrest in China (associated with the Taiping Rebellion), poverty in the southern provinces of China and a dramatic increase in demand for tin (for plating containers—'tins'—for the food canning industry). This meant that Chinese could be induced to leave their homeland by promises of employment and a better life. The period of so-called 'coolie' migration began.

Contractors and agents in China located men (or lured them into gambling debts and then 'saved' them) who would leave their villages to travel overseas. They were shipped to the Malaysian territories where they would be 'bought' by a local employer. Totally at the mercy of this employer, the coolie had to work for fixed wages until the amount of his purchase had been covered. Such a system thrived on abuse and it was common for coolies to have paid off their original 'debt' but not be told they had done so. Furthermore, the employers owned the services which the coolies needed: foodstores, opium dens, brothels and gambling houses. Using any one of these increased the coolies' debt and kept them tied to the employer. To obtain some kind of protection, the majority of coolies turned to secret societies either as full members or as sympathisers. These societies originated in China for local political purposes which, in the Malaysian territories, had little meaning. The particular features of the societies, such as strict obedience to the leader, comprehensive codes of conduct and secrecy with elaborate rituals, together with a fierce resolve to protect members from interference by members of other secret societies, meant that violent clashes and brutal attacks between rival groups were common.

The disruptions caused by the secret society wars and the shocking conditions under which many coolies lived and worked resulted finally in British legislation, in 1877, to control immigration and to

The altar of Kwan Yin, goddess of mercy and protector of seafarers, in Melaka's 17th century Cheng Hoon Teng Temple, the oldest in Malaysia. It was founded by Li Hup, a Chinese immigrant who made his fortune through commerce.
(Source: Straits Times Annual, 1959.)

monitor the activities of the societies. William Pickering, an extraordinary Englishman who spoke various Chinese dialects fluently and had worked for many years in China, was appointed the first protector of Chinese. His newly established department became known as the Chinese Protectorate. Within two years he had won the respect of the heads of the secret societies, and he used his department as a source of advice and redress for any Chinese who brought their grievances before it. In 1890, when Pickering retired, the secret societies were officially banned and dissolved but Pickering's legacy, in the form of the Chinese Protectorate, continued to work with the Chinese until the Japanese Occupation and World War II.

Although life for an average coolie was arduous, poorly paid and unrelenting, there are some success stories. Loke Yew is one example. He was a village boy born in Kwantung Province of southern China in 1845. He left for Singapore when he was 13 to work in a shop until he had saved enough to set up on his own. He invested his profits in tin mining ventures in northern Perak. He lost his first mines in one of the many outbreaks of violence between rival secret societies during the 1860s—the disturbances which had contributed to the negotiation of the Pangkor Treaty of 1874. Having lost much of his capital, he won a contract to provision the British troops brought to Perak after Resident Birch was murdered in 1875. He personally delivered the provisions to upriver sites and used *Orang Asli* as guides. After further unsuccessful ventures in tin mining, he was one of the many to make their fortunes from the development of the rich deposits at Kinta in the 1880s.

Using some of this capital, he moved to the newly established Kuala Lumpur and, in partnership with two other Chinese, won the tender for maintaining a new railway. His contacts with British officials resulted in gaining the licence to impose taxes (known as 'tax farming') on opium, liquor, gambling and pawn shops in Selangor. As these were items and services which most coolies used, he made large profits and gained the licence for the same services in Pahang. He went on to open many tin mines in various districts with the aim of becoming the richest tin operator in the FMS. His ventures in Pahang included constructing 21 miles (34 kilometres) of road to Kuala Lipis through the Genting Highlands which allowed a new flow of migrants into Pahang.

In partnership with an Indian businessman, Thamboosamy Pillai, he introduced electricity into some of his mines. In Selangor, he was granted the lease on 20 000 acres (8100 hectares) of land for agriculture and he imported Chinese workers to clear it and plant pepper, gambier and rubber. During the first decade of the 20th century, he invested also in coffee plantations and soon had many estates. He worked with the British on numerous committees concerned with developing and running Kuala Lumpur and was elected first chairman of the Selangor Chamber of Commerce in 1904. He was a philanthropist and because of his own total lack of education (he was illiterate) he established scholarships for children and donated large sums to educational institutions. When he died in 1917, he left not only mines and plantations but large investments in major enterprises such as shipping, trading and collieries.

Another success story, the Khaw family, like Loke Yew, worked through partnerships with other business groups, were diverse in their operations and established links with the local ruling elite, in their case the Thai ruling family as well as the British in Penang. They were Hokkiens, from Changzhou in China, who emigrated to Penang in the 1820s. The first Khaw made some money as a local trader (possibly selling vegetables), bought land and raised the capital to begin trading with towns along the peninsular coast north of Penang and into southern Thailand. He married a Thai woman whose money and connections enabled his enterprises to prosper so that he was able to purchase a vessel to bring goods to and from Penang. Like Loke Yew, he used capital to develop tin mines in southern Thailand and was also a tax farmer. In the 1850, he was appointed by the Thais as the local governor. He maintained his links with Penang where he also had a wife and family. Their descendants were extremely successful, highly regarded Malaysian Chinese and their imposing clan temple may be visited in Penang.

In Thailand, other members of the family were accepted into the Thai aristocracy and remained close to the Thai royal family. All the Khaw marriages established or cemented strategic links with groups which could extend Khaw business interests. The Khaws differed from Loke Yew, however, in one important respect. They developed their extensive family network in Thailand (where they were linked into local politics and the Thai elite) and in Penang (where they were connected with the leading commercial families) to establish a corporate lineage through a carefully thought through family trust.

When individual family members died, the trust continued to manage the diverse corporate interests of the clan group. Unlike Loke Yew's businesses which have not maintained their own identities, the Khaw enterprises still continue.

Indian immigration

Thamboosamy Pillai, the Indian businessman who became a partner of Loke Yew, was one of Kuala Lumpur's leading figures from the 1880s until his death in 1902. He migrated from India in 1875 to work as Treasury clerk for the first British Resident of Selangor. After Kuala Lumpur became the state capital of Selangor in 1880, he moved there to establish his own businesses. These flourished and in 1889 he personally paid for the building of an elaborate Hindu temple, Sri Maha Mariamman, which remains a major attraction in Kuala Lumpur.

Most other Indian migrants did not have his success. Small numbers migrated to the Straits Settlements before the 1880s to work on sugar and coffee plantations, but the main flow began after then. Large numbers of Indian railway workers played a vital role in establishing and running the first lines which linked interior production sites with coastal ports. The British encouraged Indians to come to the Peninsula because they were accustomed to working with them in colonial India and because many of them understood English. Indian labourers were recruited using agents who either visited India personally to select workers, or had local subcontractors who assembled men on their behalf. As with Chinese coolies, wages were fixed for a period of years making it difficult for the workers to leave their original employers. Women were also recruited from the turn of the century to work on the rubber plantations which had just been established as commercial ventures in several places on the Peninsula. When the indentured system was abolished in 1910, more Indians came as free labourers but never in the same numbers as the Chinese. Comparative figures reveal that by 1941 there were 2 300 000 Chinese on the Peninsula and in Singapore while the number of Indians was 750 000.

The majority of 19th century immigrants from India worked as labourers but Thamboosamy Pillai was a clerk who moved into commerce and died a wealthy Kuala Lumpur entrepreneur in 1902. (Source: National Archives of Malaysia)

Besides labourers, Indian professionals migrated to the Malaysian territories. Hindu moneylenders from southern India established branches of their firms in key commercial centres and their influence on the growth of commerce in their new home is evident not only in the large numbers who still practise as accountants, lawyers and financiers, but also in the words of Indian derivation borrowed into Malay to describe a range of commercial activities. Sikhs were recruited to work in security positions (especially as night-watchmen) and, from the 1870s, in the police force. One other group of people was transported from British India to work in the Straits Settlements from the end of the 18th century. It is estimated that 15 000 Indian convicts arrived between 1790 and 1860 and towards the end of that time fewer returned to India after their release. Convicts worked for the government as snake and tiger killers, firemen, *punkahwallas*, canal, well and grave-diggers, builders' labourers, tailors, smiths, syces (drivers), gardeners, draughtsmen and printers. It has been said of the Indian convicts that their

153

history is the history of the Public Works Department and that the major public colonial buildings, bridges, roads, canals and harbour works in Penang and Singapore are the result of their hard labour.[8]

Javanese and Sumatran immigration

Although Chinese and Indians provided the largest numbers of immigrants to Malaya, sizeable numbers of migrants from Java and from various parts of Sumatra also settled permanently in the Malaysian territories. The majority of Javanese who immigrated in the late 19th century came as agricultural and plantation labourers to Johor, Perak and Selangor but in the first decades of the 20th century, they took up small landholdings of their own. The British North Borneo Company encouraged Javanese migrants to work the newly established rubber plantations but when the rubber market slumped in the 1930s, this migration slowed. The possibility of obtaining grants of land seems to have been the main attraction for the considerable numbers of Rawa, Mandailing and Korinci people who migrated from their Sumatran homeland between the 1850s and the 1880s to work as small-scale cultivators along interior river stretches of the west coast states. Some of them were also very successful as itinerant pedlars who would accept rice in lieu of cash for their goods. Numbers varied, but Selangor, in particular, attracted Sumatrans and Javanese so that by 1886 they were estimated to number 12 000 out of the total Malaysian population for that state of 18 000.[9]

To summarise: the population movements into the Malaysian territories during the second half of the 19th century were the continuation of an ongoing process of peopling Malaysia's underpopulated and underdeveloped regions. The increase in numbers during this time and the specific occupations which were taken up by the various ethnic groups are linked with the British colonial presence which encouraged the 'development' of Malaya, Singapore, Sabah and Sarawak. However, once settled in their new positions, intermarriage and cultural assimilation (to Malay culture) was comparatively rare. In part this can be explained by the geographical spread. The Chinese predominated in urban areas, in tin-mining districts and in Johor. The largest number of Indians was found in rubber areas, which were located mainly in the west coast states of the Peninsula. Malays were still most numerous in the northern peninsular states (Kedah, Kelantan, Terengganu), and more lived outside towns than in urban environments. In Sabah and Sarawak, the Chinese settled in urban and rural areas. In towns, however, where representatives of many ethnic groups lived, separation between groups became the norm. Each group tended to have its own district within the town where their places of worship and social organisations were located and became the focus for their daily lives. The religious and cultural barriers to inter-marriage as an accepted practice were upheld and became the basis for the plural society of modern Malaysia.

Capital development: rubber and tin for the modern world

The demand for labour in the Malaysian territories increased dramatically in the early 20th century when world markets demanded massive supplies of tin and rubber for the automobile and other mechanised industries. Extractive techniques for tin had improved so much that small-scale investment, even at the levels at which Loke Yew and the Khaw family operated, was insufficient to develop fully the rich deposits on the west coast of the Peninsula. The small-scale production of rubber, which had begun with the collection of sap from wild rubber trees in Johor under the *kangchu* system in the 1860s, had developed into a major plantation economy organised largely by British planters and required considerable capital to cover establishment costs.

The expansion and intensification of both the rubber and tin industries were underwritten by foreign capital, usually from British

One of the first rubber trees cultivated from Brazilian seeds germinated in Kew Gardens and sent to Singapore in the late 1870s. H.N. Ridley (shown here in about 1905) developed the herringbone pattern of excisions for efficient extraction of the latex.
(*Source:* Straits Times Annual, 1968)

investors. The largest mines and plantations were foreign owned and controlled and totally dependent on cheap labour. The tin and rubber were exported as raw materials to be processed outside the Malay territories and sold at vastly increased prices to the world's markets. The profits in large measure were paid as dividends to their foreign sources of investment, with only minimal amounts being returned to Malaya to develop the infrastructure needed to facilitate production and export.

Commercial networks, responsive to the specialised needs of global markets, have long been a feature of the economic life of the region. However, large-scale foreign investment in the Malaysian territories produced at least two kinds of long-lasting changes. First, whereas the earlier networks had circulated profits back into the region through a variety of mechanisms, the profits derived from foreign investment flowed largely back to sources outside the region which developed at the expense of the Malaysian territories. Second, the earlier networks were characterised by diversity which enabled them to respond rapidly to changes in global tastes and needs. The selective nature of large-scale investment in long-term enterprises (particularly in the plantation sector where time before productivity is measured in years) made them very vulnerable to natural disaster, economic depression and changes in demand. The world demand for rubber and tin in particular had several major slumps during the 20th century. The most severe occurred in the 1930s and 1980s and precipitated corresponding downturns in the local economy. The retrenchment of workers during the 1930s in the mining and plantation sectors caused massive unemployment, poverty and squatter settlements, providing fertile ground for nascent communist and trade union movements.

In terms of immigration, quite clearly the hundreds of thousands of Chinese and Indians who were brought in as indentured labourers or who came to escape catastrophes in their homelands made a major contribution to the modern economy of Malaysia. Without their industry and manpower Malaysia could not have become the world's largest producer of tin by 1900 and producer of half the world's rubber by 1924.

Kelantan and Terengganu

Unlike the states on the west coast of the Peninsula and Sabah and Sarawak, the east coast states did not experience the same degree of immigration. The coastal plain of Kelantan, for example, supported a Malay population which in the early 20th century was estimated to be larger than the combined Malay population of the Federated Malay

States. Lack of population was not an issue. On the contrary, at the beginning of the 20th century, there was a problem supplying the local population with sufficient rice and the traditional method of dry rice cultivation began to be replaced by the more productive irrigated rice system. The implications of the change were soon apparent: irrigation required more intensive and more organised labour input and benefited the landowners (the Kelantan elite) rather than the peasant workers.

These were not the only changes occurring in Kelantan. At the level of international politics, the governments of Britain and Siam negotiated a new Anglo-Siamese Treaty in 1909. The sultan of Kelantan lost some territory but apparently found it in his interests to sign an Anglo-Kelantan Treaty in 1910 under which he agreed to accept British protection and a British adviser (not a resident). The sultan and the Kelantan elite were wary about the encroachment of British authority and, although senior British authorities encouraged it, the Kelantan establishment resisted suggestions that they join the Federated Malay States.

The sultan's acceptance of a British adviser and his officials complicated the administration of the state. There was the immediate challenge of adapting to a new relationship with an adviser who was responsible to the governor in Singapore and replaced the Siamese officials with whom the Kelantan court was accustomed to negotiate. The local leaders and district chiefs were now subjected to the authority of British-appointed district officers (the majority of whom were not from Kelantan) and forfeited most of their power to levy taxes. The pressure on local elites spread into the ranks of their patrons and increased the rivalries which were characteristic of the Kelantan ministers and members of the royal family. Some of the elite found new opportunities to maintain or develop their influence. One of these was in the sphere of religious administration which, during the 1890s, was expanded with more Islamic religious courts, public lectures and the establishment of religious police who actively encouraged the faithful to fulfill their religious obligations. Some of the elite played an active role as muftis and preachers but others felt displaced by the new district officers who worked under the British adviser to collect revenues and maintain order.

An often quoted example of local reaction to the many changes occurring in Kelantan is the 'Tok Janggut rebellion'. 'Tok Janggut' (Mr Long Beard) was the familiar name of Haji Mat Hassan, a charismatic local personality who was believed to be invulnerable and who, after making the pilgrimage to Mecca, grew a long white beard. His family had long been associated with the local elite of a district in southern Kelantan near the Terengganu border and when a district officer was appointed to this region in 1905, the traditional chief lost his authority to collect taxes and therefore the source of his power. Tok Janggut and several others persuaded villagers to boycott the new system and to withhold their taxes. However, little seems to have happened until 1913 when a Singaporean Malay was appointed district officer and was extremely diligent in his revenue-collecting activities insisting that the taxes be paid. The situation was compounded by a further factor: in 1915 taxation was changed from a produce tax (which was flexible in the event of poor harvests) to a fixed land rent (which was paid by land owners who were, in general, the aristocracy). It was the introduction of a new tax by a foreign power, rather than the amount of the tax per se, which aroused local resentment. When the district officer learned that 2000 people were willing to follow Tok Janggut and resist paying the tax, he ordered Tok Janggut to appear before him. However, one of the police sent with the order was stabbed to death by Tok Janggut, whose followers then sacked the D.O.'s office and began burning buildings, including the houses of several European planters. It was said later that many Kelantanese were emboldened by the belief that Britain was losing the war against the Germans (World War I) and might soon be defeated.

Attempts by the sultan to negotiate were unsuccessful and it was three weeks before a force of 200 armed men from Singapore reached the district. Tok Janggut led his followers against the force but was shot

*HH Sultan Ismail of Kelantan (reigned 1920–44) on upper step of the
royal dais in his palace, flanked by dignitaries and government officials.
(Source: National Archives of Malaysia)*

and killed. Some of his followers escaped to Terengganu and Siam and
others melted away. During this period there were several other small
incidents of armed Kelantanese gathering in Kota Bharu and up river,
but none developed into major confrontations.

While the causes of the movement led by Tok Janggut can be
associated with the displacement of the traditional elite and the
implementation of new forms of taxation, there was also resentment
about 'foreigners' (non-Kelantanese, both Europeans and Malays
from elsewhere) being appointed to administrative positions over
Kelantanese. Tok Janggut was said to have announced he would
drive out all Europeans and all foreigners. Associated with this was
the suspicion that the British were trying to force Kelantan to join
the FMS and be more closely administered through the residential
system. Possibly as a result of the Tok Janggut movement and the
other incidents of armed Kelantanese confronting representatives of

British administration, the British were very cautious about appearing to coerce Kelantan (and later Terengganu) into joining the federated system and, as it eventuated, they never became members. The aversion to foreigners in Kelantan had the significant outcome of ultimately enabling Kelantanese to fill positions in their own administration, which the British ran with the minimum of outside appointments.

One further event of long-term significance for Kelantan was associated also with the Tok Janggut affair. The sultan of Kelantan had tried to negotiate with Tok Janggut but had failed to reach a settlement. However, during this period one of the palace officials impressed the sultan, who promoted him and in time he became chief minister. More immediately, this official (Haji Nik Mahmud) persuaded the sultan to allow him and his brother-in-law to establish a new body to administer Islam on behalf of the ruler. The organisation, known as the Kelantan Council of Islam and Malay Custom (*Majlis Ugama Islam dan Istiadat Melayu*) took over the existing administration of religion and centralised the collection of religious taxes, giving a proportion to the sultan, returning some to individual mosques, but also retaining a considerable amount for its own purposes. The council established a printing press and several schools in Kota Bharu, one of which was an English school where sons of the Kelantan aristocracy could be educated to work in the British administration. This had the dual purpose of increasing the status of the traditional elite by preparing them for positions in the administration organised by a colonial authority and at the same time maintaining their links with the Council of Islam. However, for the displaced former administrators of Islam (the local mosque leaders and local religious scholars) and for non-elite Kelantanese, the Council of Islam was regarded as a tool of the aristocracy and an enclave of conservatism. They, and other non-elite Malays elsewhere in the Malay territories, sought different avenues to express their views on the role of Islam in Malay life in the early 20th century.

Terengganu, like Kelantan, had a large Malay population. In 1912, the British estimated there were 154000 Malays in Terengganu. The main centre, Kuala Terengganu, described as the largest in the Unfederated Malay States, had a population of 25000. Despite its population size, in 1909 (following the signing of the Anglo-Siamese Treaty) when the British informed the sultan of Terengganu that his kingdom was now under their influence, they judged it not sufficiently advanced to receive an adviser, and sent instead an agent.

The crown prince of Terengganu maintained the close connections which had long been established between his family and the royal family of Riau-Lingga as well as with relatives in Johor and Singapore. He was fully aware of the independent stance the Johor sultan had adopted in his dealings with the British. In 1911, supported by a group of the Terengganu elite, he introduced a Constitution, closely modelled on that of Johor, which proclaimed Terengganu's sovereignty and laid the way for administrative reform. In 1912 and 1913, a cabinet and state council consisting of the ruler and his senior advisers was established and the crown prince instituted a system of government departments staffed by permanent officials to take over the details of state administration. A secular school had been set up in 1908 under a Johor-trained teacher, which educated the sons of chiefs in reading and writing and prepared them for administrative work.

The crown prince continued the restructuring of Terengganu's administration by replacing the hereditary chiefs with district officers under the direct control of his officials in Kuala Terengganu. The chiefs were promised compensation for their lost revenues but the kingdom's resources were not adequate and when the money was not forthcoming the chiefs felt not only displaced but also cheated. The crown prince needed more funds and the British agreed, but on their terms. In 1914, a loan was arranged between the crown prince and the government of the Straits Settlements on condition that the crown prince reform his fiscal administration. The British were also concerned that foreign-run (Chinese and European) mining ventures in Terengganu were being obstructed by Terengganu officials. The munitions being manufactured in Britain for World War I needed supplies of wolfram (from which tungsten, an essential item in steel alloys, is extracted) and there were rich deposits in Terengganu but the Chinese mine owner was being controlled by the Terengganu officials. These difficulties increased Britain's desire to have greater authority and this was achieved through a special commission sent to Terengganu to examine various aspects of its administration. The report recommended an extension of British influence to improve efficiency and it was decided to negotiate a new treaty under which Terengganu would have to accept an adviser.

Before this could be done, the sultan died and was succeeded by the crown prince. After initial resistance, he unwillingly agreed and in 1919 signed and agreed to the placement of a British adviser. The newly installed sultan felt humiliated by the adviser's behaviour and took the unexpected step of abdicating. He was replaced by a younger brother, Suleiman, who was sultan from 1920 until the Japanese Occupation in 1942. He ruled in a context of increasing readjustment in response to British policies. The former crown prince had installed Terengganu Malays, members of the elite, to positions in the bureaucracy but during the 1920s the adviser replaced some of the heads of key ministries with Europeans. The adviser tightened the administration of outlying districts and created a new adminsitrative unit in Ulu Terengganu, the most remote and independent region in the kingdom. The adviser failed to recognise the local authority of the influential al-Idrus family, long established Muslim leaders in the region and pressed on with opening the district through roads, police, schools and new land regulations. However, the local people who were cultivators of hill rice and not accustomed to a cash economy, could not pay the new land taxes. They were encouraged by a charismatic religious leader, Haji Drahman, who had studied with a famous scholar from the al-Idrus family. His work as an entrepreneur, travelling to all the east coast ports, as well as to Siam and Borneo, meant that he was attuned to the most recent trends of the times and he criticised the new British administration as being contrary to Islamic law (*shari'ah*). He urged people not to follow the laws of the infidels and successfully defended three people arrested by the British for breaking their laws. Although major incidents seem to have been avoided for a few years, later evidence showed that from 1925, at least 800 individuals across a widespread area of the east coast joined a secret Muslim movement (*Sharikat al-Islam*) and that Haji Drahman and other religious leaders were involved.

In 1926, a major flood destroyed the crops and livestock of many peasants and in 1927 the Ulu Terengganu rice growers again resisted paying their land tax. Although the sultan tried to pacify them, in May 1928 a large number of Malays gathered at Kuala Brang and, chanting prayers and carrying banners, began to travel down the river towards the capital. Meeting a police party sent to stop them, a clash occurred and 11 were killed. The similarities with the Tok Janggut movement in Kelantan are revealing: unwelcome change associated with a foreign presence; the introduction of a new tax system and charismatic leaders who acted in the name of Islam against non-Muslims. One of the results of the Terengganu 'rising' was the sultan's decision to establish closer contact with the people and after 1928 he undertook more ceremonial tours. He, and other members of the traditional elite, seemed anxious to ensure that they, rather than popular, non-elite Malays, remained leaders of Terengganu.

Modernising through administration and reform

As we have seen, rulers drew on a variety of sources (Johor, Singapore, the Middle East and Turkey) to find new models for their administrations. Kedah, like Kelantan and Terengganu, remained outside the system of Federated States. Its rulers had also instituted changes to the older style of Malay rule by adopting features of Siamese administration. The sultan maintained control of all revenues and avoided being dependent on his chiefs for their collection. From the late 19th century, the royal family was at pains to maintain very close relations with the Thai royal family and some of the Kedah princes were educated in Bangkok. However, the sultan began to amass considerable debts and, in 1905, was forced to negotiate a loan from the Siamese government. Under its terms, he agreed to accept an adviser appointed by the Siamese to assist with financial management and to establish a State Council. Under the Anglo-Siamese Treaty of 1909, already referred to in the context of Kelantan and Terengganu, Siamese 'rights' over Kedah were transferred to Britain. Like its fellow Unfederated States, Kedah accepted a British adviser and, like Kelantan, the sultan insisted that local Malays be trained for administrative positions. In 1923, Kedah signed a Treaty of Friendship with Britain under which the British adviser remained but it was spelled out that no major decisions concerning Kedah's sovereignty or future could be made without the sultan's agreement. By this time, British officials seem to have come to a realisation that not one of the Unfederated States would join the federated system without being coerced to do so.

The kingdom of Johor provided the British administration in Singapore with a dilemma—by keeping abreast of British 'reforms' in the nearby Straits Settlements and Federated Malay States and adopting an ordered administration, the rulers of Johor provided no excuses for British intervention. Johor was the last kingdom to accept any form of official British presence. The *temenggung* of the Riau-Lingga kingdom chose to settle in Singapore and then to work with officials and businesses in Singapore to extend his own influence. He was so successful that in 1855, having made a fortune by granting leases to Chinese groups to work land along the rivers of Johor, he paid a monthly allowance to the sultan of Singapore in return for full rights to the territory of Johor, excluding the small district of Muar. In the 1860s, he moved his establishment from Singapore to Johor and established a new capital, taking with him a strong team of advisers and assistants, both Malay and European.

The *temenggung* was succeeded by his son Abu Bakar (born 1833, ruled 1862–95). He was educated in Singapore at the school run by Benjamin Keasberry, a Protestant missionary, and dealt confidently and firmly with representatives of all races. The British could not complain about his attention to his administrative duties and he implemented an efficient system of bureaucracy, earning him the reputation of an exemplary ruler. Moreover, most of this was achieved without official British advice. One of Abu Bakar's innovations was his Johor Advisory Board which he established in London to represent the interests of Johor without reliance on the British officials (including the high commissioner) in Singapore. He found ways to bypass British official-dom in Malaya if it suited him and employed a range of agents, lawyers and advisers. It was possibly on their advice that he dealt directly with London in 1885 and signed an alliance with the Colonial Office. Under its terms, he was recognised as sultan of Johor, the kingdom's sovereignty was respected and its external security guaranteed. The sultan felt at home in England, visited Queen Victoria and her family at various times and was a seasoned traveller to Europe, the Middle East, Turkey, Greece, China and Japan. Although he was regarded by his fellow sultans in the Malay territories as an upstart, he was recognised overseas, being decorated by Queen Victoria, the royal courts of Europe and the emperor of China. In 1894, the sultan instituted a Constitution for his kingdom, which set out the powers of the ruler, the duties of a Council of Ministers and a Council of State (a legislative body).

When Abu Bakar died, it was discovered that his extravagant lifestyle had severely drained the kingdom's revenues but his heir, Ibrahim, managed to maintain the hospitals, schools and police force and law courts introduced by Abu Bakar and sent his sons to England for their education. He was unable, however, to maintain economic momentum and, in 1914, was forced to agree to accept a British adviser. Ibrahim had a long reign, and lived to see Malaya's Independence before dying two years later in 1959.

Syed Shaykh al-Hady

Sultan Abu Bakar had been exposed to an eclectic range of 'modern' thought during his period at Benjamin Keasberry's school in the 1850s. One of the textbooks he studied there was *Abdullah's Story*, whose didactic passages criticised Malay rulers who neglected their subjects and praised the advantages of learning and modern science. When he became ruler, Abu Bakar did respect learned people and on his visits to Cairo and Constantinople, the centres of Muslim intellectual life, he was impressed by the achievements of modern-minded Muslims. He did not live to see the full effect of these two centres on the Malay world.

The life and work of Syed Shaykh al-Hady, one of the most famous Arab–Malay Muslim scholars and teachers, illustrates the renewed energy flowing into Islamic thinking in the early 20th century. Born in 1867 to a Malay mother and a father descended from an Arab family which migrated to Melaka in the late 18th century, he was educated in a religious school in Terengganu and later worked and studied with the Bugis-Malay literati of Riau. The Riau elite, like their counterparts in Johor and Terengganu, were travellers and kept in regular contact with events in the Middle East and Egypt. On these visits, Syed Shaykh came in contact with the writings and teachings of the energetic and innovative grand mufti of Egypt, Shaykh Muhammad Abduh. Since 1882, Egypt, like Malaya, had been dominated by the British, and Muhammad Abduh urged his fellow Muslims to select what was of value from European thought and use it to further the glory of Islam. He also chided those Muslims who were held back by conservative views and superstitious practices, which were not part of Islam as taught by the Prophet Muhammad (Blessings and Peace be Upon Him). These views attracted idealists like Syed Shaykh and during the early 1900s a group of modern-minded Malays centred in Singapore founded a journal called *al-Imam* (*The Leader*) which included Malay translations of some of Muhammad Abduh's works and also carried strongly worded articles by local writers.

The spirit of the journal, which had 31 issues over its life of two years, was in line with Muhammad Abduh's teachings that all Islamic peoples (including Malays) were being overtaken by advances in the West. Muhammad Abduh warned that Muslims were not following God's holy laws (*shari'ah*) particularly His injunction to use the gift of reason and intelligence to implement the true teachings of Islam, a guide to life in this world and the next. *Al-Imam* carried news from the two most advanced Eastern nations of the day, Turkey and Japan, to prove to its readers what could be accomplished by non-European cultures. In the same vein as Abdullah Munshi, more than half a century earlier, the journal urged parents to attend to the education of their children and funds were raised to start a progressive school in Singapore which taught Arabic, English, Islam and a range of secular subjects such as mathematics, geography and history. *Al-Imam* was extremely influential, with a readership throughout the Malaysian territories, into southern Thailand and throughout the Indonesian archipelago but it aroused criticism from conservative Muslims who did not agree with its 'modernist' views.

Syed Shaykh al-Hady was one of the regular contributors to *al-Imam* but when it folded, due to lack of funds, he moved to Johor in about 1909 and worked as a *shari'ah* lawyer. From about 1916, he lived in Penang where he was active as an educator, writer and publisher until his death in 1934. He left lasting legacies in the form of the well-known progressive school, Madrasah al-Mashhur (which extended the ideals of the Singapore school and educated girls as well as boys) and his writings, which he published from his own publishing house. He used a range of genres to convey his message of modern Islam—detective stories, erotic love stories, didactic texts, pamphlets about the rights of women according to the Qur'an, and a booklet on Islam and rationalism. The erotic love stories, which were actually cleverly composed didactic texts, were bestsellers and went into a number of reprintings, enabling Syed Shaykh to finance further publications. One of these, *Saudara* (*Brother*), outlived him, appearing between 1928 and 1941. Its aim was 'to seek brotherhood or friendship in many Muslim communities' and, like *al-Imam*, its readership spread beyond the Malaysian territories into southern Thailand and Indonesia. It was proof of the effectiveness of publications in bringing together like-minded individuals and it provided a means of communication for those who believed Islam could raise the status of colonised peoples and lead them into better ways of life. This was the beginning of a more general interest in advancing the cause of colonised nations and led many of 'the colonised' to believe Islam was not the only way forward, but that secular nationalism might be more effective in displacing the colonial powers.

8
TRANSITION TO INDEPENDENCE

Today one hears 'Merdeka' shouted by men, women and children of all races in every nook and cranny of Malaya. Let their call be answered.

Tunku Abdul Rahman Putra, 1955[1]

A period of just less than 30 years separates the Independence of Malaya (*Merdeka*) from the 1928 Terengganu 'rebellion', a relatively small people's movement against an alien presence and a new taxation system. In that brief period, the peoples of the Malaysian territories experienced the effects of the Great Depression, the Japanese Occupation, a communist insurgency movement which led to a state of emergency being declared, and the formation of a broad range of new political, religious and nationalist organisations. The leaders of the new movements had to convince the diverse peoples of the Malaysian territories that their future interests would be served best by a new federation of all the Peninsula states—in other words, they had to create a sense of national unity which would transcend district and state loyalties. Merger with the Borneo territories was to come later.

Education

A major factor in the rapid transformation of Malaysian society at this time was the availability of education and the explosion of reading material—newspapers, journals, booklets—which accompanied the growth of schools and colleges. Education created bonds between individuals who otherwise might have little in common and newspapers and journals brought readers into contact with international events and, through letters to the editors' columns, into contact with one another.

As well as the journal *al-Imam* and the new-style Anglo-Islamic schools (*madrasah*) which modern-minded Muslims like Syed Shaykh al-Hady supported, there were two other important streams of education for Malays: Malay vernacular schools organised by the British for 'ordinary' Malays, and an elite Malay College established to provide the children of the Malay aristocracy with sufficient English education to enable them to participate in the administration of colonial Malaya. Clearly, pupils in each of the three streams would have very different educational experiences and could expect very different career paths. Only the *madrasah* and *pondok* (village religious schools run by local Muslim teachers) were outside the colonial system and drew their inspiration from the Middle East, Egypt and Turkey. Graduates from the *madrasah* became religious teachers or leaders of modernist Muslim organisations. Those from the *pondok* were usually more conservative in their thinking and maintained the institutions of Islam in Malay villages.

The Malay vernacular schools were under a colonial Department of Education whose policy was to teach basic literacy and skills, such as handicrafts and gardening which, most colonial officials argued, would not disrupt the traditional lifestyle of the Malays nor lead to changes which might result in 'social unrest'. However, despite these intentions 'unrest' was fostered by the lively atmosphere of the Sultan Idris Training College, established in Perak in 1922 to train teachers for the Malay schools. Its graduates believed Malays were not keeping up with the changes of the modern world and needed to work hard to catch up with the progress they believed was happening around them. In touch with anti-colonial and nationalist student movements in Indonesia, they went out into their communities determined to inspire change through their teaching and through their writings.

The elite Malay College at Kuala Kangsar was attractive to those members of the Malay aristocracy who saw the advantages of an English education for the future advancement of their sons under colonial rule. The aim of the college was to Anglicise and modernise the Malay upper class so as to consolidate their position as leaders. Although most of the pupils were from the traditional elite families of the Malaysian territories, some scholarships were offered to exceptional commoners. Many graduates were able to go on to tertiary education in Britain and returned to work as civil servants, lawyers, doctors, business people and later, as politicians. Many became so Anglicised that they lost contact with much of their own traditional culture and would rarely, if ever, read the Malay booklets and journals published by their fellow Malays who had attended the Sultan Idris Training College. This split between English and Malay-educated Malays reflected differences in attitude to British authority and would later be expressed in strong differences about the way Independence should be achieved.

In the major towns of the Peninsula and therefore beyond the reach of all but the most exceptional village children, there were a few English schools, some run by missionaries and others by the government. They were attended by Chinese, Eurasians and, to a lesser extent, Indians but only very rarely by Malays who, even if they could travel to the schools, feared they might be pressured to convert to

Top:
Kelantan and Terengganu preserve the traditional Malay art of making large decorative kites from bamboo and paper. Formerly believed to be a means of contacting the spirits of wind and sky, the kites are now flown for recreation and in competitions after the rice harvest. (Getty Images)

Bottom:
A Malay house (near Melaka) in traditional style. The raised floor and steeply pitched roof are for ventilation, while the front steps at the main entrance lead to the verandah where visitors are received.
(Virginia Matheson Hooker)

Top: An enterprising Malay woman makes snacks as a business enterprise run from her home. (Virginia Matheson Hooker)

Bottom: · The Petronas Twin Towers (Kuala Lumpur) at 451.9 metres was the tallest building in the world in 1996 and is the most advanced building constructed in Malaysia. The shape of the floor plate is based on Islamic geometric patterns, while the interior motifs reflect traditional weaving and carving designs. (AP Photo/Andy Wong)

Top: The decoratively lit Mogul-style Sultan Abdul Samad Building (Kuala Lumpur) was constructed in the 1890s originally as offices for the Federated Malay States and the Selangor State government. It now houses the Judicial Department and the High Court. (Courtesy Tourism Malaysia)

Bottom: Kuala Lumpur's central business district featuring the Maybank Tower (far left) in the form of a Malay dagger or *kris* and the 421-metre high Menara Kuala Lumpur (Kuala Lumpur Tower) with its tower head based on Islamic geometric patterns. While Kuala Lumpur will remain the business capital of Malaysia, the new 'smart city' of Putrajaya will become the political, administrative and diplomatic centre for the federal capital. (Courtesy Tourism Malaysia)

Top:
Malaysia's prime minister, Mahathir Mohamad, delivers the opening address to the 2002 UMNO general assembly. (AP Photo/Andy Wong)

Christianity. Tamil children of rubber estate workers were provided with some Tamil schooling on the estates, but the standards were apparently not good.

After the government-run vernacular Malay schools, the most numerous schools were Chinese vernacular schools organised and financed by Chinese communities themselves. There were no schools provided for any of the *Orang Asli* groups who remained outside all formal educational institutions and were therefore untouched by these changes.

The educational opportunities available to each ethnic group were therefore determined by the pupils' gender (there were some schools in each system for girls but the emphasis was on educating boys), ethnic background, religion and class. The sons of the Malay elite were trained for senior administrative posts, English-educated Chinese and Indians staffed the lower ranks of the colonial administration, and those with a vernacular education (in Malay, Tamil or Chinese) were limited to working within their own communities. Many of the Chinese schools used textbooks from China, celebrated Chinese national days and, because of their lack of status in Malaya, considered themselves as belonging to China and dedicated to serving it. These feelings intensified when Japan invaded Shanghai in 1932 and the progress of the war was closely followed by all pupils. These educationally-based social and economic divisions continued in broad terms until the 1970s.

Anxiety about the position of the Malays

In the mid-19th century, Abdullah bin Abdul Kadir had compared the position of the Malay peoples with that of the Europeans he encountered in Melaka and Singapore. He was so disturbed that he wrote at length urging Malays to educate themselves and their children so they could participate in the developments around them. The journal

Son and successor of Sultan Idris of Perak, HH Sultan Iskander (reigned 1918–38), one of the first Malay sultans to be educated in England, shown here in 1926 with Sir Hugh Clifford (British colonial official in Pahang 1887–99 and High Commissioner 1927–29). (Source: National Archives of Malaysia)

al-Imam, inspired by modernist Islam, also admonished those who neglected education and the application of God's laws to improve their lot on earth. The same concerns are evident in the Malay booklets, newspaper articles, editorials, letters to the editor and short stories and novels which appeared from the 1920s onwards. By that time, Malays believed British policies had contributed to the poverty and backwardness of the Malays and they blamed the large-scale immigration of Chinese and Indian workers into the country for taking jobs from the local population. They did not note a further fact which became obvious only much later—that by encouraging Malays to cultivate rice as a livelihood, the British were restricting them to the least lucrative of pursuits and one which tied them to a rural and restricted economic existence.

The demographic evidence added to the anxiety of those who were worried about the position of the Malays. The census figures for 1921 revealed that together, Chinese and Indians outnumbered Malays. The official figures were: Malays 1 627 108, Chinese 1 173 354 and Indians 472 628. The original British assumption that Chinese and Indian workers would return to their place of origin was undercut by the fact that increasing numbers were changing their occupations as labourers to become shopkeepers, clerks and small-scale financiers, with assets that were not readily portable. It became evident that they were making their homes in the towns of the Peninsula and their children were being absorbed into the lower levels of the colonial administration. Educated Malays from a non-elite background, particularly those who had been trained as teachers, were deeply worried by the condition of rural Malays whom they saw as backward and oppressed. They were concerned also that the Malay elite, the traditional aristocracy whom the British had maintained as rulers of the peninsular states and were educating at the elite Malay College to continue to rule the Malays, seemed closer to the British than to their own people. They spoke English, dressed like Europeans, enjoyed English sports (including horse racing and gambling) and sent their sons to England for higher education.

Haji Abdul Majid (1887–1943)

A few Malays from non-elite backgrounds did enjoy an English education and used its benefits to assist their fellows. Two interesting examples of their times are Abdul Majid, who worked with the British to provide support for other Malays, and Ishak Haji Muhammad, who worked against the British and believed colonialism was destroying the moral fibre of all the peoples native to the Malaysian territories.

Born in 1887, Abdul Majid was the son of a Sumatran trader who owned a shop in a suburb of the rapidly expanding centre of Kuala Lumpur. In 1895, he was one of only ten Malay boys who joined the 201 pupils at the new English language Victoria Institution. After completing his schooling, he worked for two years as a clerk. He must have been a confident and ambitious person because in 1905 he succeeded in being accepted at another English institution, the newly opened Malay Residential School (later renamed the Malay College) in Perak. After graduating at the top of his class, he stayed on for 11 years as the Malay master and in this capacity met many of the leading colonial officials and members of the Malay aristocracy of the day. He was appointed as the first Malay assistant inspector of schools but in 1924, left the education service to accept the important new position of Malay pilgrimage officer. His responsibilities included performing social welfare work for the increasing numbers of Malay pilgrims who took advantage of the improved shipping services to travel to the Holy Land as well as also reporting any anti-colonial political activity to the British. He held the office for the next 16 years working in Jeddah for half the year and returning for the remainder to Malaya. He retired due to ill health in 1939 but in 1941 started a journal in English called *The Modern Light*, to help Malayan Muslims understand their religion and aspects of modern life, such as banking. He died in 1943 during the Japanese Occupation. His role as a mediator between cultures—he wrote dictionaries for Malays explaining the meaning of key English terms for government, science and technology, and Teach Yourself Malay books for English speakers—played an important but underestimated role in improving relations during the colonial era. He could not have done this without his access to an English education and without his high standing in the Malay community.

Ishak Haji Muhammad (1909–91)

Ishak Haji Muhammad was born in Pahang in 1909 and attended the local Malay vernacular school before winning a place in the English school system and being sent to English schools at the bigger centres of Kuala Lipis and Raub (see map 5, page xix). In 1930, he was selected as one of the most promising of his generation and sent to the Malay College in Perak to be prepared for the Malay Administrative

Service. Although he moved rapidly through several promotions in the service, he resigned in 1935 to travel widely through the Malaysian territories working as a freelance journalist and mixing with Malayans of all occupations. As a result of what he saw, he became active in nationalist organisations and journalism in the late 1930s and also published two political satires. Together with two other young activists, Ibrahim Yaakob and Ahmad Boestamam (both to become leading Malay nationalists) he established the Union of Malay Youth (*Kesatuan Melayu Muda* or *KMM*). Ishak's anti-British and explicitly radical activities angered colonial officials and he was imprisoned. Under the Japanese Occupation he was released and continued his work as a journalist writing for the Japanese-sponsored Malay newsagency *Malai Shinbun Sha*. After the surrender of the Japanese, he continued his work to end colonial rule and was active in a range of radical Malay nationalist organisations. When the Communist Emergency was declared in 1948, he was imprisoned by the British for five years. After his release in 1953, he worked as a writer and journalist and led two socialist movements. He continued his critical commentary of Malayan society after Independence and, under the pen-name 'Pak Sako', became one of Malaysia's most popular columnists.

Ishak Haji Muhammad was one of a group of intelligent, idealistic young Malays who were in contact with the nationalist movements in the Netherlands East Indies and were critical not only of British colonial policies but also of those Malay aristocrats, whom they considered were cooperating with the British and were thus betraying their own people. The members of the *KMM* believed in a union of Malay peoples which would bring together all the Malay peoples of the Malaysian territories and the Netherlands East Indies in a Greater Malay nation state. Although the Japanese disbanded the *KMM* they supported another radical youth group (Defenders of the Homeland *Pembela Tanah Air* or *PTA*) which after the war fed into a new and very determined movement called 'Generation of Aware Youth' whose acronym in Malay meant 'Fire'. By the late 1940s, these radical groups had been active for over a decade with little to show for their struggle but an increasing sense of frustration.

Ishak Haji Muhammad's two satires in novelette form, published in 1938 and 1941, present his ideology through engaging fictional stories. His characters show how indigenous skills and experience, which pre-date Western influence, are not only more appropriate for modern Malaya but also more effective because they are in harmony with the culture and with the natural environment. While many Malays, his stories argue, have lost touch with their own culture, the *Orang Asli* have not and can teach Malays how to regain many of the skills they used to know. Ishak's attitudes were radical in their day—he was suggesting that indigenous knowledge was superior to that of the West and, even more daringly, he proposed that Malays turn to *Orang Asli* to revive the skills they themselves had lost. In the 1930s, as in the 1990s, the majority of Malays believed *Orang Asli* to be undeveloped and uncivilised, so that the idea that they could hold the key to the future was incredible. Ishak was far ahead of his time by promoting conservation of indigenous knowledge, the environment and the indigenous peoples of Malaya. Ishak's resignation from his colonial service position occurred during the period of severe economic downturn in the 1930s which is now referred to as the Great Depression. His decision to leave a well-paid job and to rely on freelance journalism for his livelihood reflects his deep commitment to working for better conditions for his fellows.

Concern about the position of the Chinese

While Ishak Haji Muhammad was concerned primarily with the condition of *Orang Asli* and Malays under colonial rule, the Chinese Malayan Tan Cheng Lock was concerned about the lack of recognition given to the locally born Chinese in the Malaysian territories and he dedicated much of life to redressing this. Like Ishak Haji Muhammad, he had an English education which he used to challenge many British policies. He became one of the best-known members of the Chinese community in Malaya.

Tan Cheng Lock

Tan Cheng Lock was born in Melaka in 1883, the fifth generation of a Chinese family who had settled in Melaka in the late 18th century (perhaps a decade or so earlier than Abdullah Munshi's grandfather) and built up a regional network of trading junks. By the time Cheng Lock was born, his family was integrated into the Melaka community of locally born Chinese, known as Babas. Cheng Lock grew up speaking the local Malay dialect, not Chinese. The Babas (and their wives, known as Nyonyas) saw themselves as distinct from two other groups of Chinese: first, those Chinese born in China who moved to Malaya and settled but maintained their Chinese customs, and second, those who were born in China and would probably return there. In general, it can be said that only members of the Baba community were interested in being involved in local politics, the other groups being more committed to their homeland.

Tan Cheng Lock was educated at the English school in Melaka and the Raffles Institution in Singapore, staying on as a teacher from 1902–08. He left, however, to work with Chinese rubber enterprises in Melaka and did well. During the period of World War I, he used his money strategically to win favour with the British: he raised money for the British war effort and revived the Straits Chinese British Association. His reward came in 1923 with an offer from the governor of the Straits Settlements to become an unofficial member of the Straits Settlements Legislative Assembly, representing the residents of Melaka. For the next 12 years he pressed hard for reforms in the areas of education, medical services and the civil service. While he was prepared to work initially within the framework of a colonial government, he believed steps should be taken towards elections and self-government. The final aim, in his view, should be a federation of all of British Malaya which would become a member of the British Empire and Commonwealth. He was insistent that locally born Chinese be recognised for their contribution and commitment to Malaya and treated more equally. He pressed for better education for all peoples in Malaya and for an education in English for all who desired it. He believed also that Chinese language instruction should be available for Chinese children in English schools so they could preserve their own customs and heritage.

Tan Cheng Lock was outspoken in his criticism of British discrimination towards the different groups in Malaya. He called for more local people to be included in the civil service and warned that society would be divided into a hierarchy of British, Malays and others unless there was more equal treatment of all peoples in Malaya. He moved his family to India before the Japanese occupied the Peninsula and was impressed with Gandhi's moves for independence. By the time he returned to Malaya in June 1946 he was ready to push even more energetically for self-rule.

The Great Depression

The crash in the New York stock market in 1929 had repercussions for most world economies and those which were based on raw materials were particularly hard hit. When America's automobile industry collapsed, Malaya lost a major buyer of its rubber and tin. The unemployment of Chinese, Indians and Malays which followed 'affected race relations; it led to serious labour unrest and it damaged the confidence of the Malaysian population in the British government'.[2]

The Malaysian territories were more affected by the slump in world trade than the neighbouring regions of the Netherlands East Indies and the Philippines because the latter two had developed food crops in tandem with export crops and thus did not suffer the food shortages which were to engulf Malaya. The British had encouraged an expansion of the rubber industry so that by 1929, almost half of all cultivated land was planted with rubber. The foreign exchange generated from rubber sales was used to import food, including rice. Only the northern Unfederated States of Kedah and Kelantan were able to support their populations with food.

Tin prices also plummeted and mines were closed or employed only a skeleton staff. In 1930, it was estimated that in Perak alone there were 10000 unemployed miners, the majority of whom were Chinese. By 1931, there were grounds to support a claim that almost half a million Chinese were unable to work because of the slump. Many of these migrated to the cities, especially to Singapore, seeking food and any kind of work. Others stayed in the mining districts and grew their own food on any land they could occupy and use, sometimes selling the excess in what became productive market gardens. The land, however, was not theirs and under the law they were illegal occupiers or 'squatters'. Following World War II, during the Communist Emergency period, most of the squatters would be moved into protected villages in one of the largest resettlement programs ever organised by a colonial government.

Indian labourers, particularly those on rubber plantations, were also retrenched and some returned to India. But the majority stayed and lived in extreme poverty and misery. During the 1930s, major cuts were made in government departments so that unemployment was felt also by white collar workers. Under these conditions, crime gangs flourished and robberies, extortion and kidnapping were common as desperate people tried to survive. The Kuomintang (KMT) flourished during the 1930s and established reading clubs and night schools becoming the largest Chinese organisation in Malaya. It was in this period that young Chinese, like Chin Peng, later secretary-general of the Malayan Communist Party (MCP), joined underground movements and read Chinese books smuggled into Malaya, with Mao Tse-tung's *Protected War* being very influential. The Malayan General Labour Union, with its offshoot the MCP, began to flex its muscles. Major strikes occurred in 1936 and 1937 and labour unrest combined with fears about an impending war alarmed the British.

The Japanese Occupation 1942–45

Just after midnight on 8 December 1941, in a well-planned campaign, Japanese forces landed on beaches in Kelantan and southern Thailand. The landings were synchronised with the Japanese attack on Pearl Harbor, very shortly afterwards. The Pacific War had begun.

Although the British had been making preparations from the late 1930s to counter a Japanese attack, when it came the generals were simply insufficiently prepared and the strength of their forces too weak to withstand the highly organised and effective strategies of the Imperial Japanese Army. When it was finally realised that Singapore could not be defended against the Japanese advance, British Special Branch accepted the offer of the MCP to fight behind the lines in return for official recognition of the party. Over 200 MCP men were trained and became the nucleus of eight regiments which were known collectively as the Malayan People's Anti-Japanese Army (MPAJA). Throughout the Occupation they waged an effective guerrilla war and in some areas worked with members of Force 136, an elite group of special agents landed by the British in 1943 to collect intelligence and assist the MPAJA with training and supplies. They were not the only guerrilla fighters who took to the jungles to harass the Japanese. It is now known that there were numerous small groups who engaged in anti-Japanese activities as well as smuggling, extortion and intelligence-gathering.

The three and a half year Japanese Occupation of the Malaysian territories is remembered by those who survived it as a period of hardship and anxiety during which everything changed— one Chinese writer referred to it as the 'Malaya Upside Down' time when 'even the atmosphere stank of carrion and rot'.[3] It dominated the lives of everyone in the Malaysian territories between 1942 and 1945 and 'shattered the pattern of seventy years of colonial rule'.[4] Physical devastation was widespread—Singapore had been heavily bombed and was in chaos; the population of Kuala Lumpur deserted the main parts of the city and buildings were looted and burned.

The Japanese immediately reorganised the administrative framework for the region to bring Sumatra and the Malay Peninsula together. In Borneo, which had been attacked on 16 December 1941, Brunei, North Borneo and Sarawak were administered together in a unit known as Boruneo Kita (Northern Borneo) and then, in 1943, the four northern states of the Malay Peninsula were given to Japan's ally, Siam.

The Japanese military presence affected daily life at every level. First to be singled out for attention was the Chinese community in retaliation for the anti-Japanese activities which had been organised by the Malayan Chinese when Japan invaded China in 1937. In a special operation, Chinese were identified and executed, with conservative estimates of the number killed being 40 000. Others were ordered to pay a special tax to repay their support for the British or for the Kuomintang. Any activities perceived as anti-Japanese, carried out by any member of the population whatever their ethnicity, were immediately dealt with, mostly with extreme violence.

A Japanese general was to say after the war that the Japanese had missed an opportunity 'to show Asians that as an Asian power, she was a kind liberator who would treat them better than the European powers'.[5] Instead, the brutality and hardship experienced by the majority of the population made them fearful of the Japanese and those who did not join the guerrilla and resistance movements collaborated, not necessarily because they supported the Japanese but because they had to survive. The most dreaded Japanese organisation was the *Kempeitai* (secret military police) whose horrific methods of torture and decapitation were applied especially to the Chinese and to suspected British sympathisers. An efficient neighbourhood vigilante system was set up to identify anti-Japanese activists and informers took the opportunity to settle personal grudges, creating a climate of suspicion and mistrust which would remain after the Japanese had surrendered.

For those parts of the Peninsula like Kelantan which were physically isolated and for Sarawak and Sabah, ruled by self-contained systems, the Japanese Occupation (somewhat ironically) afforded them more direct contact with the outside world. The Japanese organised schools where Japanese was taught combined with vigorous physical exercise routines. Leadership training was given to those whom the Japanese identified as likely material for administrators (some were sent to Japan for advanced courses) and special women's and youth groups were established. The Japanese propaganda machine absorbed writers and journalists and printed material which could contribute to their war aims.

Thousands of Malayans were taken to other parts of Southeast Asia to provide labour for Japanese projects. When insufficient Malayans volunteered for labour service (to work on the Siam–Burma railway, airfields and defences), people were forcibly rounded up or kidnapped, and even children were sent to the railway project. The mortality rate was probably higher than the official figure of over 51 per cent. In Sarawak, as in many other places, local militias and volunteer armies were formed, with each elite family in Sarawak being required to supply one son.

The Allied successes in the Pacific, especially the capture of Morotai (in Halmahera Islands) in September 1944, enabled Australian and American forces to reach Borneo and, despite strong Japanese resistance, to make landings at Tarakan, Labuan and Balikpapan between May and July 1945 (see map 5, page xix). Allied bombing of Tawau, Balikpapan, Sandakan, Jesselton (later named Kota Kinabalu), Brunei town and Labuan caused massive destruction. The Japanese had plans to remove the inmates from their prisoner of war camps and force them to march, or kill those too weak to travel, and some were executed. Further loss of life in the

Malaysian territories was avoided when the Japanese emperor surrendered after atomic bombs were dropped on Hiroshima and Nagasaki in August 1945. Australian forces liberated Labuan, Brunei, Sarawak and North Borneo and made arrangements for the future government of the Borneo territories.

Early in 1945, Allied planes were bombing Penang, Kuala Lumpur and Singapore and, unknown to the civilians on the Peninsula and in Singapore, the Allies were planning landings for early September. The emperor's announcement forestalled them and on 20 August Japan's surrender was reported in Malaya. British forces landed in Selangor in September and organised a military administration until April 1946, when civilian government was restored.

Post-war reconstruction

The British forces which landed in September 1944 had been prepared for anti-Japanese warfare rather than the conditions of surrender which they in fact encountered. They were faced with massive civil disorder as wartime vendettas were played out, collaborators identified and often killed, and mounting tension between members of the MCP and Malays. In late August, when it became known that the Japanese had lost the war, members of the MPAJA came out of the jungle to take control of local government in many towns and villages and the British had to admit that they were dependent on them to instil order and organise civilian life.

Members of the MPAJA particularly sought out Malays who had participated in the militia and other organisations set up by the Japanese and took violent action against them. In response, many Malays, especially those in rural areas, formed armed vigilante groups and attacked Chinese farmers and MPAJA members, causing bloodshed and hundreds of fatalities. The expression of hostility along ethnic lines fed the suspicion and mistrust which had thrived during the hardship of the Occupation and caused ill-feeling which many believe lasted well into the 1960s and 70s.

Besides the vendettas and violence, severe social dislocation had occurred as a result of Japanese labour drives which had separated family members and population movements from the countryside to the major cities, especially Singapore, in search of work. For several years after the war, many people were still trying to locate lost family members, including those who had been executed by the Japanese. As one British administrator described the immediate post-war situation:

> There was a food shortage, a worthless currency, a thriving black market, and the threat of a smallpox epidemic. On the plus side was the generally excellent quality of what remained of the pre-war public service. In Seremban, for example, the Indian street cleaning gangs began to clean up the mess, reckoning that something better would now be required.[6]

This was the context in which the people of the Peninsula tried to return to 'normal' life.

From Malayan Union to federal Constitution

The British Military Administration (September 1945 to the end of March 1946) saw itself as responsible for restoring essential services to the population of Malaya but longer term policy was the responsibility of the Colonial Office. During the war, the Colonial Office had been developing new and very different policies for Malaya. The administration would be rationalised to create a unitary state in which all races would be entitled to citizenship. To achieve this, the British had to make new treaties with the Malay sultans under which they would surrender some of their authority and jurisdiction but they would be compensated by being able to participate in a wider grouping (the Malayan Union) which extended beyond their own states.

In the context of regional politics the mood was anti-colonial. In 1945 Indonesian nationalists under Sukarno and Hatta declared Independence while in Vietnam, Ho Chi Minh seized power for the Indochina Communist Party, initiating the Vietnamese Revolution. In India, the Independence movement was both violent and unstoppable. It was therefore seen as pressing that plans for the Malayan Union be implemented without delay. There were essentially three changes which the Union would achieve: the sovereignty of the rulers would be transferred to the British Crown, the autonomy of individual Malay states would be absorbed into the Union and the privileges which had previously been reserved for Malays would be available to members of other communities. In this way, it was argued in the Colonial Office, a strong central government could be created and Malaya's peoples could be persuaded to give their loyalty to it.

In October 1945, only one month after British forces returned to Malaya, Sir Harold MacMichael was sent to persuade the Malay rulers to sign the pre-prepared new treaties. It has been said that the speed with which the MacMichael mission acted caught the rulers off-guard and all signed. Later they were to say they had not realised the full implications of the treaties and that they did not believe the British would have asked them to sign anything which was not in the interests of the Malays. In January 1946, the White Paper outlining the proposals for the Malayan Union was released and public reaction was almost immediate. The Colonial Office had completely misjudged the strength of opposition to the concept of the Union and the reaction to the loss of status for both rulers and Malays which it represented. In one stroke, the proposals captured the attention of the numerous and varied Malay organisations which had been formed all over the Peninsula and in the Straits Settlements since the 1930s and aroused an outburst of anti-colonial feeling.

The Malay press reported and amplified the concern which was growing among these groups and suggested that Dato Onn Jaafar, a district officer in Johor who had gained a reputation for leadership, should organise a general conference of all associations to respond to the proposal of a Malayan Union. On 1 March 1946, representatives of 41 associations attended the first Pan-Malayan Malay Congress. One of its first resolutions was the establishment of a new organisation of national unity, the United Malays National Organisation (UMNO) with Dato Onn as president. As a result of the congress, Dato Onn was able to lead a vigorous campaign against the implementation of the Union and to persuade the sultans to boycott the inauguration ceremony scheduled for 1 April 1946. In the face of such determined opposition in Malaya and from influential retired British administrators who had served in Malaya, the Colonial Office was forced to abandon the scheme. In July 1946, Malay leaders agreed to work with the British on the drafting of a constitution for a federation of all the Malay States and the Straits Settlements, excluding Singapore, which would remain a British colony.

After six months of heated debate and negotiation, a new federation known as the *Persatuan Tanah Melayu* (Federation of Malaya) was inaugurated on 1 February 1948. The British had succeeded in their aim to establish a unitary state which included the previously Unfederated Malay States (which many regarded as tantamount to annexation), but they had failed to gain equal rights for all the federation's citizens. The British also declined to be drawn into a strong attempt by Malay groups in Kelantan and southern Thailand to have Patani included in the Malay states which were returned to British jurisdiction after the war. The dissatisfaction of the Malays in southern Thailand with their position under Thai Buddhist rule was expressed in continuing attempts to gain independence from Bangkok and lies at the heart of a Muslim separatist movement which has never entirely disappeared.

Political organisations

The campaign which Dato Onn was able to mount against the Malayan Union scheme indicated just how far Malay political organisation and confidence had developed since the 1930s. In the intervening period, Malays had seen the British defeated by an Asian force, they had been encouraged in their nationalist aspirations by the Japanese, particularly in the closing stages of the war, and they had direct experience of leadership in military and semi-military organisations where effort and achievement were rewarded with promotion. This concept of promotion based on effort was particularly attractive for people who had been excluded from colonial networks of advancement and for whom status was based on birth and connections with the traditional Malay aristocracy. The Japanese model offered an alternative model to that of the colonial and the traditional Malay system.

There were also some harsh verdicts about the reactions of the rulers to the Union scheme. The sultans were perceived by many educated Malays as having failed to protect the interests of their people. The champions of the Malay cause were seen as the individuals who had spoken out at the Pan-Malayan Malay Congress, and in particular, Dato Onn. However, once the Malayan Union crisis had been resolved, the longer-term issues remained: the place of non-Malays (referred to as Malayans) in Malaya, poverty and underdevelopment, the relationship with the nationalist movement in Indonesia and competing ideologies.

In the turbulence of the post-war period, a number of political coalitions came into being but because of the complexities of rapidly changing contexts and conditions (including British security laws), the shifting of alliances and jockeying for supporters and patronage, only a small number of political parties actually survived into the mid-1950s. After the Malayan Union scheme failed, political allegiances generally fell into one of five groups.

United Malays National Organisation (UMNO)

The UMNO's supporters included conservative-minded Malay nationalists who supported moves towards self-government but wanted also to conserve the main features of the existing Malay power structure (including the position of the sultans). Those attracted to the UMNO ranged from Malays who held administrative positions under the British, to holders of traditional office, such as district chiefs and local headmen. Malay school teachers were particularly effective advocates, urging village parents to back the UMNO. If Abdul Majid had still lived at the time of the UMNO's founding, this would probably have been the party which he supported.

Malay Nationalist Party (MNP)

The UMNO was not the party for more aggressively nationalist Malays, people like Ishak Haji Muhammad. Malays like Ishak were highly critical of the policies of elitism which characterised much of British colonial practice in Malaya, particularly in areas such as education and the civil service. They regarded British economic policies, especially in the mining and plantation sectors, as exploitation of the local populations. For the radical nationalists, socialist ideals were very attractive. Many of them, especially Ishak's colleague Ibrahim Yaakob, were in contact with Indonesian nationalists who were working for a coalition of Malay peoples which would encompass both the Malaysian territories and Indonesia.

For these Malays, the Malay Nationalist Party (MNP), formed in October 1945, had adopted ideals they could support. The leaders of the MNP included Ishak Haji Muhammad, Ahmad Boestamam and Dr Burhanuddin each of whom had been detained by the British in the pre-war period for his anti-colonial attitudes and each of whom had used the period of the Japanese Occupation to further his nationalist aims. They argued that the concept of 'Malay' should be linked with culture rather than descent (race) and that all who adopted

Malay culture could be viewed as 'Malay'. Because many of the Malay journalists working for leading Malay newspapers sympathised with the attitudes of the MNP leaders, they wrote in support of the party and were able to boost membership. In terms of numbers of members, the MNP and the UMNO were probably very similar. The MNP worked with the UMNO to overturn the Malayan Union scheme, but then withdrew from the association, accusing the UMNO of being too close to the British and not sufficiently concerned to further the interests of ordinary Malays. Thereafter, the UMNO negotiated with the British concerning moves towards self-government and the MNP was sidelined and accused by its detractors of being too pro-Indonesian and too close to various socialist and communist groups.

Independence of Malaya Party (IMP)

Both the UMNO and the MNP were predominantly Malay organisations primarily concerned with the future of Malaya as a Malay nation. Non-Malay residents of Malaya, of whom Tan Cheng Lock is one example, also had strong views about Malaya's future. Tan's friend, Dato Onn, tried to persuade the UMNO to allow non-Malays to join and to change its name from United Malays to United Malayan (a term which embraced all who lived in Malaya) but he was unsuccessful and left the UMNO. With Tan and the leaders of other ethnic communities, Dato Onn founded the Independence of Malaya Party (IMP) in 1951. The very different aspirations and views of the various ethnic communities proved unable to be accommodated within this type of 'Malayan' coalition and it was not successful as a political force.

Islamic movements

For some Muslims, each of the above three options was too secular and not sufficiently focused on the values and beliefs of Islam. Within this group were many degrees of commitment to Islam, ranging from those who believed in total devotion to the injunctions of Islamic law, to those who considered that Malay identity could best be expressed through some form of Islamic organisation. There was considerable debate about the forms Islamic political activity could take and a number of different parties were founded. The only one which survived to the time of Independence (and beyond) was PAS (*Persatuan Islam SaTanah Melayu*, the Pan-Malayan Islamic Party).

Malayan Communist Party (MCP)

The Malayan Communist Party had been active since the 1930s and had strengthened during the Japanese Occupation by operating effectively against the Japanese in the jungle. When peace was declared, arms and supplies were stored in the well-developed jungle hideouts established during the Occupation and training was maintained. The post-war social dislocation, inflation and poor labour conditions were fertile ground for the party to recruit new members and MCP cadres appealed to Chinese and Indian workers to resist colonial exploitation. The cadres also infiltrated other organisations, including the MNP, to recruit sympathisers.

When the British organised the first elections to the Federal Legislative Council in 1955, the parties represented four of the broad strands listed here: radical nationalists (including socialists), conservative Malay nationalists, communal interest groups (Chinese and Indian) and specifically Muslim groups. One group was no longer represented officially. The MCP had been banned since July 1948 because of its terrorist activities and armed resistance to colonial authority in the civil war which became known as 'the Emergency'.

The war for hearts and minds

The decline in the social and economic conditions of many inhabitants of Malaya, evident during the years of the Great Depression and exacerbated by the war and Japanese Occupation, had reached a critical stage by 1946 and 1947. By that time, the MCP had gained effective control of 200 of Malaya's 277 registered trade unions and was effectively pursuing a campaign of strikes. Although the radical Malay nationalists were also mobilising and attracting the scrutiny of the British Security Service, it was the Malayan Communist Party which was the best prepared and best organised group to exploit the socio-economic conditions for political purposes. The MCP operated parallel lines of civilian and military branches, both controlled by a Central Executive Committee and having a descending chain of command through state, district, branch and sub-branch levels. By the late 1940s, it had a membership of about 12 500. The labour strikes attracted considerable publicity and in some cases the British responded with force and fatalities ensued. There were also stronger attempts by the Department of Labour to negotiate between workers and managers to achieve peaceful settlements, thus frustrating some of the militant party members. The MCP reviewed their tactics and, while maintaining some public activity, decided they would go underground and prepare for armed resistance.

Malaya's strategic position in the region, commanding the vital sea lanes of the South China Sea and the Straits of Melaka, and having a land link through Thailand into Indo-China, meant that the Peninsula was perceived by the British and Americans as a vital bastion against the spread of communism into Southeast Asia. It was believed that links between China and the overseas Chinese made Malaya vulnerable to communist infiltration. When outbreaks of terrorism and violence began in mid-1948, including the murder of three European estate managers in Perak, there was strong public reaction. Economic interests were also at stake because British enterprises in the mining, plantation and timber sectors were deliberately targeted by the terrorists. Of all Britain's colonies at that time, British investments in Malaya earned the most in terms of American dollars, which were vitally important for Britain's post-war balance of payments. To safeguard its economic and strategic interests, a State of Emergency was declared in June 1948, giving the government the power to detain without trial and to ban political parties. The MCP was declared illegal and there was an immediate crackdown by British Security on all known Leftist activists and sympathisers, including radical Malay nationalists. The leaders of the MNP, Ishak Haji Muhammad and Ahmad Boestamam, were arrested in 1948 and detained for five and seven years respectively, while Burhanuddin was detained in 1950. The MNP denied any official connection with the MCP but under the Emergency conditions it did not survive and voluntarily dissolved in 1949.

The Chinese

In the fear and violence of the early years of the Emergency, when ambushes, assassinations, kidnappings and extortion were happening on a daily basis, many non-Chinese in Malaya found it hard to distinguish between those Chinese who were members or sympathisers with the MCP and those who were not. In the minds of some, *all* Chinese were communists. The main victims of this confusion were the rural Chinese squatters, who were not terrorists, but many of them were being used by the guerrillas as sources of food and support.

The small group of Chinese-speaking British administrators in the Malayan Civil Service, which included John Davis, Richard Broome and Oliver Wolters, worked with British military units teaching them how to distinguish between terrorists and squatters. These administrators believed that the chronic lack of contact (and thus severe under-government) between colonial officials and the communities of rural Chinese, together with their isolation which was increased during the Emergency, lay at the heart of the insurgency problem. The rural Chinese had lived in self-contained communities with minimal or no contact with non-Chinese since the late 1930s. Many of the young men in those communities had been attracted to the clandestine life of anti-Japanese warfare during the Occupation and when the Emergency came into force, they maintained contact with their families in the rural communities receiving voluntary support or, when necessary, coercing it. The solution, the British administrators argued, was to deny those in the jungle contact with the isolated communities and to move the Chinese squatters from near the jungle and resettle them in protected villages. A report to this effect was prepared in 1948 but it was not adopted until 1950 when the policy of massive resettlement was implemented and named the 'Briggs Plan' after the British director of operations at the time.

Perhaps the most difficult years of the Emergency for the civilian population were 1950 and 1951. These were the years when the highest numbers of civilians were killed (646 and 533 respectively). When the new high commissioner, Sir Henry Gurney, was ambushed and assassinated in October 1951, morale plummeted. Gurney's successor, General Sir Gerald Templer, formerly director of military intelligence in London, arrived early in 1952 with the dual appointment of high commissioner and director of operations. He was armed with exceptional powers of authority and announced that Malaya was being prepared for self-government. He stressed, however, that it would not occur until the Emergency was over and until there was harmony between the ethnic groups in Malaya. Templer brought new vigour and organisation to the anti-terrorist campaign and although he was a highly controversial figure, his strength of personality and single-mindedness lifted morale.

The resettlement program for rural Chinese communities was a bold and risky strategy. The uprooting and relocation of over half a million people in 480 settlements in just a few years was a triumph of logistics even though the new villages were crude in design and construction and fortified against infiltration with barbed wire and spotlights. Individual families experienced enormous anxiety and resentment. Follow-up programs were implemented to educate and train the younger settlers for employment and there were specially designed courses in Civics, to introduce Chinese leaders to the workings of government and administration. Although the older generation may not have been impressed, the programs were aimed at the younger Chinese whose loyalties were crucial to the future of Malaya.

The British developed a number of psychological warfare techniques using anti-communist propaganda (distributed in leaflets, via the radio and through films) and a special interrogation centre. The mastermind behind the strategies was a brilliant Malayan Chinese, C.C. Too, who advised the British and the UMNO leader, Tunku Abdul Rahman, during the Emergency and remained in charge of the government's Psychological Warfare Section until 1983.

The British had brought in military support from the beginning of the Emergency and by 1953 there were 23 infantry battalions stationed in Singapore and Malaya, including forces sent by Commonwealth countries. The Royal Malay Regiment, consisting of seven battalions, saw heavy fighting but it was the Malayan police force which had the highest casualties because it bore the brunt of dangerous duties, including jungle patrols and manning the permanent forts which were established as outposts deep in the jungle. In 1953, there were almost 37 000 in the regular police and 44 000 in the Malay Special Constabulary, a force which protected key installations and implemented the food-control regulations which operated in the New Villages. More and more of the civilian population was drawn into village patrols, civil defence and special operations and intelligence work.

It is now known that from late 1951, the MCP Central Executive Committee decided to change its tactics. Although it had succeeded in causing death and disruption throughout Malaya and in Singapore, it had not always been able to capitalise on its successes and many of the young Chinese recruits lost morale under jungle conditions. The general population had been hard-hit by the violence and destruction and the MCP realised they had antagonised many of the 'exploitable medium bourgeoisie'.[7] The Central Executive Committee decided to move gradually from their main concentration in Pahang to the Malay–Thai border region and increase their propaganda strategies through educational movements in schools and youth organisations.

By 1957, the official casualties as the result of MCP actions were 2 890 police, 3 253 civilians and 518 military, emphasising the 'success' of British policy to manage the conflict as a police, rather than military action. An autobiographical novel, *Scattered Bones* (*Tulang-Tulang Berserakan*), by Usman Awang, one of Malaya's leading writers, written in 1962 but only published in 1966, is a graphic and convincing account of the lives of a group of Malay policemen during the Emergency. Drawing on his own experiences as a young policeman, Usman describes the jungle patrols of the Malay police, their poor conditions and their low pay. He convincingly describes their dawning realisation that many of the terrorists they kill are ordinary human beings like themselves and that the conflict is a colonial problem rather than a struggle of liberation from colonial rule. A major theme of the novel is the terrible social dislocation caused by the Emergency and the tragic losses suffered by ordinary Malayans.

The MCP had an estimated 8000 members involved in subversion activities in 1951. By 1958, only 868 remained actively involved and just over half of those had moved with Chin Peng over the border into southern Thailand. The strategies of resettlement, psychological warfare and the judicious use of amnesties had weakened the MCP to the point of powerlessness.

The *Orang Asli*

Before the Japanese Occupation, the heavily forested interior areas of the Peninsula (the jungle) were the domains of the *Orang Asli* almost exclusively. Non-*Orang Asli* peoples lacked the experience and knowledge to survive in the uplands of the interior and Malays, in particular, were terrified of the spirits they believed inhabited the jungle. During the period of the Occupation, however, members of the MCP and others serving in the Malayan People's Anti-Japanese Army, were forced to live in the jungle. They established camps and were, in many cases, assisted by local *Orang Asli* groups. A number of the individuals

In 1952, when the communist terrorists focused their strategy on jungle warfare, the British formed the 'Malayan Scouts' (later the 22nd Special Air Service Regiment) as a counter-terrorist group to parachute into remote jungle areas. They worked with and were supported by Orang Asli who served as guides and porters. (Source: Straits Times Annual, 1959)

who survived the war later used their jungle skills to continue guerrilla warfare on behalf of the MCP.

During 1952, when the MCP implemented their revised policy of retreating to the deep jungle, their relationship with the *Orang Asli* groups with whom they came in contact intensified. In some cases, *Orang Asli* served as guides, porters, intelligence gatherers and food providers in return for help to grow crops and medical assistance. The *Orang Asli* groups in the interior of Kelantan attracted the attention of zealous administrators in that state who believed the best way to control them was by removing them from the jungle and resettling them closer to 'civilisation'. The effect of the policy was deadly. Totally adapted to life in the jungle, the *Orang Asli* felt imprisoned in the new settlements, could not adapt to the hotter climate of the lower altitudes, were unused to the diet supplied to them and had no gainful means of employment. As a result, 'Hundreds died because of the mental and physiological shock to their systems; hundreds more just ceased to have the will to live, and died also.'[8] As well, when British reconnaissance flights located food plots in the jungle they destroyed them by aerial bombing to scatter MCP guerrillas and to deprive them of food resources. The bombing and resettlement policies were both so counterproductive that they were stopped by 1954.

British policy-makers then decided that rather than trying to thwart the MCP by bringing the *Orang Asli* out of the jungle, it would be more effective to send help in to them. This was to be done through a series of fortified jungle posts which would be supplied by air with medicines and food. By late 1953, seven jungle forts (as they were known) were operating and were deemed more successful as a strategy to win the trust of the *Orang Asli*. The competition between the MCP and the government for the loyalty of the *Orang Asli* led to even greater intrusions into their traditional lifestyles and proved to be the beginning of their bureaucratisation.

By late 1953, the government decided to centralise the administration of *Orang Asli* by removing them from the control of individual states to the sphere of the federal government. Two 'protectors' were appointed to oversee their welfare and the jungle forts became the distribution points for various kinds of aid, as well as propaganda, designed to persuade the *Orang Asli* that they should no longer support the guerrillas and that the government would protect them. By 1958, very few *Orang Asli* were actively supporting the MCP. The government was so confident of their loyalty that in the late 1950s they initiated a new anti-guerrilla force called the *Senoi Praak* ('Fighting Aborigines'). The force was specially trained in modern warfare in a jungle context and was so successful that it has remained a permanent part of the Police Field Force.

When the Emergency ended, government contact with the original peoples continued and had long-lasting implications. The pressure on the *Orang Asli* to leave their traditional habitats and move to settlements closer to towns intensified. Even the *Orang Suku Laut* groups who fished around the coastlines of the southern Peninsula and the islands near Singapore, were affected by the regulations imposed during the Emergency. The curfew restrictions imposed during the Emergency made it difficult for them to fish at night and they began sleeping on shore in small houses rather than living permanently in their boats. Some groups were assisted by the government to build new settlements on land and, like the original peoples of the interior, began to be permanently monitored by government.

The Intellectual Left and Singapore politics

Tan Cheng Lock, it will be remembered, had sought greater recognition for the contribution of the Chinese to the development of Malaya and the elimination of 'racial or communal feeling' so that a United Malaya could be achieved. In 1943, he had warned that unless the interests and concerns of non-Malay communities were addressed, communism and subversion would find willing followers. He worked for a Malaya in which all citizens would have equal rights with laws which would protect those rights and ensure that no community gained dominance over the others. When the Emergency was declared, he worked to unite the non-communist Chinese and in August 1949 was seriously injured in an assassination attempt organised by the MCP. Dato Onn lost his support in the UMNO for promoting the ideal of citizenship rights for all in Malaya, but when he joined with Tan in establishing a new political party, their 'Malayan' (multiracial) platform still did not attract the votes of Malays and they were badly defeated.

Another group, led by people younger than Dato Onn and Tan

Cheng Lock, was beginning to organise its members to work for a similar multiracial ideal but their criticism of the existing conditions in Malaya was more trenchant and their willingness to cooperate with the British much less. They became known as 'the Intellectual Left' and their aim was 'not only to oust the colonial power, but to win the hearts and minds of a generation to build a new nation that would rise above colonial politics'.[9] One individual who exemplified the ideals and experiences of this group was James Puthucheary.

James Puthucheary (1923–2000)

Puthucheary was born in Johor Bahru in 1923 into a well-educated Indian family and, in 1943 when Subash Chandra Bose called for volunteers to fight for Indian Independence, he enlisted in the Indian National Army. Posted to a guerrilla regiment, he fought in the Burmese jungle and survived the disastrous Battle of Imphal. He later went to Calcutta where he witnessed the excitement of Indian Independence and returned to Malaya determined to continue the struggle there. In 1948, he enrolled for tertiary training at Raffles College (later to become the University of Malaya) in Singapore. With other nationalist students, he formed the Malayan Students' Party and called for 'the development of a Malayan consciousness, a Malayan culture, and a Malayan nation'.[10] The party argued that for the sake of national unity Malayans should abandon their narrow racial identities and embrace a larger Malayan identity, in the interests of the future of the nation.

In January 1951, Puthucheary and a number of other students, the journalist A. Samad Ismail, young lawyers, doctors and teachers were arrested by members of Singapore Special Branch. The arrests were front page news in Singapore (and caused questions to be asked in the House of Commons). They were the first large group of English-speaking intellectuals to be arrested under the Emergency regulations of the Internal Security Act and several of those arrested were very well-known. James was detained without trial for one and a half years.

A Special Branch report referred to the group as the ESI (English Speaking Intellectuals), 'who undoubtedly have provided a most effective team of open-front leaders, able to argue with the best and to present their case to the world press'.[11]

Released in 1952, Puthucheary returned to university and a year later established the Socialist Club. Members included students like Wang Gungwu and Abdullah Majid who were later to become prominent public figures in Malaysia. The group became known for their dedication to improving the position of the Malay peasantry and the underprivileged in society, and some of them argued that only Malay should be spoken (rather than English or Chinese). When he graduated in 1954 with an honours degree in Economics, Puthucheary worked with other members of the Left to help establish the People's Action Party (PAP). From 1955, he became an official in one of Singapore's largest workers' unions, and became a close friend of Ahmad Boestamam who, after his release from detention in 1955, had founded the socialist People's Party (*Partai Rakyat*).

In the 1956 party elections of the PAP, the Left faction within PAP received more votes than the faction led by Lee Kuan Yew. Aware of the growing influence of the Left within the PAP, Singapore's chief minister, Lim Yew Hock, organised the arrest and detention of the leading Leftists in the PAP. James was detained for three years and the PAP was allowed to develop under the leadership of Lee Kuan Yew without the influence of the Left.

While in detention, Puthucheary wrote an analysis of the country's political economy which he called *Ownership and Control of the Malayan Economy*. He had long been interested in the link between the economy and the various races in Malaya and the constraints this posed for political cohesion. Just as he believed a unified nation could not be achieved if children were separated from each other in schools organised on communal lines, so he believed that the way labour had been organised under colonial rule also inhibited racial cooperation. He also argued against the notion that the Chinese controlled most of

Malaya's wealth and, with prophetic insight, warned that creating a group of capitalists does not automatically alleviate the poverty of the majority of the population. He sought answers to the question of why the majority of ordinary Malayans remained poor despite living in a resource-rich country. Although published in 1960, the book is still read by students of the Malaysian economy.

In 1959, Puthucheary was released and held various senior positions on government committees and boards but found himself increasingly at odds with the policies of the PAP. He resigned from his positions and from active political life to study Law. He was arrested in February 1963 by Singapore Special Branch in the notorious raids against suspected subversives in press, labour and youth organisations known as 'Operation Cold Store'. After six months in solitary confinement he was released but banned from Singapore. By this time, Singapore had left the Federation of Malaysia and was an independent nation. Puthucheary moved to Kuala Lumpur and was only allowed to return to Singapore in 1990.

Independence achieved (1955–57)

General Templer had been explicit about British conditions for independence for the federation: racial harmony and control of communist terrorism. Most colonial officials did not expect these conditions to be met for at least a decade, allowing time to negotiate the future of British commercial interests in Malaya. The British began planning for a handover by selecting some Malayans for senior administrative training. In 1951, for example, the high commissioner appointed five Malayans to head key ministries.

Malayan nationalists were keen to prove that Templer's conditions could be met in a short term, rather than a longer-term timeframe. By the mid-1950s, the majority of the radical Malay nationalists who had been in detention were released, on the grounds, it has been said, that the violent methods of the MCP made even the radical Malay nationalists appear a preferable alternative. However, when British negotiations increasingly favoured the English-educated Malay elite who had secured the top positions in the UMNO, it became clear that British influence on the shape of Malayan politics was considerable and that their preferred successors were the conservative Malay nationalists.

In August 1951, the UMNO replaced its founding leader, Dato Onn, with an English-educated member of the Kedah royal family, Tunku Abdul Rahman. The new deputy leader was Abdul Razak bin Hussein from Pahang, who, like the Tunku, had studied Law in England. They were to make a formidable team for the next 20 years. During his first years in office, Tunku Abdul Rahman made a number of public statements, possibly to distinguish himself from the multiracial position of Dato Onn, in which he claimed that 'Malaya is for the Malays and should not be governed by a mixture of races'.[12] In 1952, however, the Tunku made the surprising announcement that the UMNO and the MCA would form an alliance and contest the forthcoming municipal elections in Kuala Lumpur as a united front. Although the alliance was a hastily arranged and almost impulsive tactic by the leaders of the UMNO and the MCA to unite against the threat posed by a new party (the IMP) led by Dato Onn, it was to become the cornerstone of Malaya/Malaysia's party political system. The success of the tactic in the elections ensured the permanence of the alliance. In 1954, the Malayan Indian Congress (MIC) joined the UMNO and the MCA, the new grouping becoming known officially as the Alliance. Each of the three parties looked after the interests of their own communities and cooperated at elections, pooling the seats they won to overwhelm their opponents.

In its early years, the UMNO underwent a number of changes in ideological emphasis. The most often noted was the decision to become a Malay communal party, representing the interests of Malays exclusively. Another, not so often noted, was the breakaway of the UMNO's

Department of Religious Affairs in 1951 and the formation of PAS, a separate Islamic party. The leaders of the new group seem to have been inspired by the ideals of modern-minded Muslims such as Syed Shaykh al-Hady and his followers, and to have wanted a party which was based on the traditional sources of Islam. It took several years to settle organisation and structure but by the mid-1950s its aims were formulated as the attainment of Independence, followed by the implementation of Islamic principles in society and government. It attracted both modern-minded and more traditionally oriented Muslims, the latter having been uncomfortable with the UMNO's links with non-Muslims. The new party was not welcomed by the Malay sultans, who saw it as encroaching on their (British-given) domain of responsibility for Islam and they openly favoured the UMNO which had been diligent in upholding their interests.

One day before the important Legislative Council elections of 1955, the elections for which the main issue was independence, PAS was registered as a political party and went to the polls as an opponent of the Alliance. It was the only party to win a seat from the Alliance, which took 51 of the 52 seats and 79.6 per cent of the vote and the only non-Alliance party to survive from this pre-Independence period. In 1956, to widen its appeal and attract Malays who had earlier been drawn to the MNP, PAS elected Dr Burhanuddin as its president, a move which did succeed in lifting the party's profile. But the fact remained that the Alliance had won an overwhelming victory at the polls.

The Alliance leaders were adamant that their election win proved they had established a basis for racial harmony in Malaya, the first of Templer's pre-conditions for Independence. They then set about meeting the second condition. By 1956, it was clear that the anti-subversion tactics were lessening the effectiveness of the MCP's strategies and restrictions were lifted on increasing numbers of the New Villages. The MCP moved to negotiate for peace but the British would discuss only terms of surrender. A December meeting between Tunku Abdul Rahman and a small team (including Sir Tan Cheng

Leaders of the Alliance, Tunku Abdul Rahman, President of the UMNO, and Dato Sir Tan Cheng Lock, Founder and President of the MCA. (Source: Straits Times Annual, 1955)

Lock) with Chin Peng (secretary-general of the MCP) at Baling, northern Perak, was arranged. The British regarded this as a test for the Tunku and his team: could they resist making deals with the MCP and maintain a position of non-cooperation? In the event, the team held firm, Chin Peng could make no deal and the talks were aborted. Chin Peng returned to the jungle and remained in the region bordering southern Thailand until 2 December 1989. The majority of MCP fighters, however, melted away long before that time, and the Emergency was declared officially to have ended on 31 July, 1960.

Early in 1956, the Alliance leaders held talks in London to determine a date for Independence. The discussions included the establishment of a constitutional commission to draft a constitution and arrangements for Malaya's defence. The British finally agreed to 31 August 1957 as the official handover date. Because of its special position, strategically and ethnically, Singapore was not included in the arrangements and was to remain a British colony for a further year.

The independent constitutional commission, known after its chair as the Reid Commission, drafted recommendations for the new nation. These included citizenship rights for all who lived in Malaya (if certain conditions were met), a ceremonial and symbolic (rather than functional) role for the rulers, a limit of 15 years for special privileges for Malays and that, although Malay was the national language, for the following decade, Chinese, Tamil and English could continue to be used as working languages with the position to be reviewed thereafter. The Reid Commission also delineated the jurisdictions of federal and state governments, allocating to the central, federal government responsibility for such matters as defence and foreign relations, civil and criminal law education, health, labour and social security and the welfare of aborigines. The last represents one of the rare specific references to *Orang Asli* in the Constitution.

A Constitutional Working Committee was established to respond to the recommendations which had been received critically by many who believed their community's interests were being undermined. As a result, the 15 year limit to Malay special privileges was dropped, and the sultans were named as the special guardians of Malay interests. In the light of events in Malaysia's later history, it is noteworthy that the Reid Commission recommended direct access to the courts for appeals concerning civil liberties but the Constitutional Working Committee insisted that Parliament should be the arbiter. Critics of this decision opposed it on the grounds that 'the fundamental rights of the individual would be better safeguarded by the judiciary than by a political party in power'.[13] The responses of the committee were included in revisions to the draft Constitution and after final negotiations in London between representatives of the Alliance, the sultans and the Colonial Office, the Constitution as adopted by the new nation in 1957 was completed.

Independence was thus attained on 31 August 1957, now celebrated as Malaysia's national day. In a relatively brief period, the administratively untidy grouping of Straits Settlements, Federated and Unfederated Malay States and the diverse communities therein, had come together in a moment of nationhood. The new nation's leaders had close links with the old Malay aristocratic elites, or had been nurtured by the British for leadership roles. The arrangements they made between themselves were designed to fulfill the British demand for racial harmony and took the form of enterprise agreements for power-sharing in the new Parliament. Later commentators have emphasised that true multiracialism, as represented by popular acceptance of the term 'Malayan' (to cover all non-Malay races living in Malaya), was not achieved and the term was not embraced. There was a further failure. None of the Alliance partners consistently represented the interests of their weaker constituents. The peasants, coolies, tappers and labourers still did not have adequate representation in Alliance policy-making. There was also the question of Malaya's relationship with its sister territories, Singapore, Sarawak and Sabah.

9
MALAYSIA
IS BORN

By ties of sentiment as well as of business, we in Singapore have always been closest to the Federation of Malaya. If merger and independence could come sooner and easier through the Borneo sister territories coming in together with us into political integration with the Federation of Malaya, then we support it for it would also mean that we would have a larger and more powerful economic base for our new nation.

Lee Kuan Yew, June 1961[1]

The merger of the Borneo territories with Singapore to form the Federation of Malaysia provoked conflict inside and outside the nation and provided the excuse for armed attacks from Indonesia during the period known as Confrontation. Turbulent events followed, including Singapore's expulsion from Malaysia and inter-ethnic violence on the Peninsula. During the 1970s, under their second and third prime ministers, Malaysians experienced new economic development policies and rapid social change. Among the main issues of the 1970s and early 1980s were special policies for indigenous people (with considerable debate surrounding who was included in that category), the relationship between Islam and politics, the development of natural resources and the sharing of revenues, and strengthening support for political parties in Sabah, Sarawak and on the east coast of the Peninsula which were not members of the National Front. Sarawak and British North Borneo were taken over by the Colonial Office, making them among the last colonies in the history of the British Empire.

Sarawak: the end of Brooke rule

The second Brooke ruler of Sarawak, Charles, died in 1917 leaving a well-organised system of internal administration to his elder son and heir, Vyner Brooke, who presided over European residents assisted by both European and local subordinates. Because Vyner had three daughters and no sons, he was to be succeeded by his younger brother, Bertram and then Bertram's son, Anthony. In the late 1930s, Vyner began to have doubts about Anthony's suitability to rule Sarawak as he wished it to be ruled. When it became clear that Bertram's health would not allow him to succeed as ruler, Vyner considered various options, including the cession of his kingdom to Britain so that he could seek retirement from active administrative responsibility.

Early in 1941, before moving on the cession option, Vyner made it known that he was preparing a written Constitution for Sarawak which would 'replace Our Absolute Rule by a Form of Government on a Broader Basis and Facilitate the Gradual Development of Representative Government on Democratic Principles'.[2] The rajah (Vyner) made it clear that he was pursuing James Brooke's plan for Sarawak: that its white rajahs were ruling only as custodians of the native peoples until such time as they could govern themselves, principles which were repeated in the Constitution's preamble. Under the new Constitution, adopted in late 1941, the rajah ruled in consultation with a Supreme Council and a Council Negeri (State Council). A special agreement between Sarawak and the British government was signed by Vyner in November 1941, in which he agreed to receive a British representative, thus placing Sarawak in a position very similar to that of the Unfederated Malay States in the 1920s. In reality, the Constitution laid the way for major changes in the way Sarawak was administered, including more representation for members of the civil service and in its legal relationship with Britain. The invasion of the Japanese suspended Brooke rule (Vyner took up residence in Australia and Anthony returned to Britain where he joined the army) and provided opportunities for consideration of even more options for Sarawak's future.

As was their policy in peninsular Malaya, the Japanese allowed some scope for local organisations to function under Japanese rule, and several small groups representing Malays, Chinese and a Dayak Cooperative Society were able to develop in ways that had not been possible under Brooke supervision. Malays, Ibans and Chinese living near towns were eager to educate their children. They had the options of Malay-run schools (for Muslims) or schools staffed by missionaries, which were increasingly in demand by Chinese and Ibans. Many of these educated Sarawakians became leaders and people of influence in post-war Sarawak. For those who lived in the interior, isolated from the coastal centres and following more traditional lifestyles, there were still opportunities to participate in Sarawak's future. Tun Jugah, the last paramount chief of the Ibans who worked with the Brookes and the British, lived to see the Federation of Malaysia as one of the greatest leaders of his people.

Tun Jugah: an Iban experience of cession and federation

Tun Jugah was born in approximately 1903, in a traditional Iban long-house on the Kapit River, to a family famous and respected as warriors and pioneers. Although he did not have the opportunity for any formal Western education, his abilities were noticed by Brooke officials and in 1928 he was appointed as a *penghulu* which, in the system created by Charles Brooke, indicated the rank of sub-district leader and came with a salary. Within a decade he was regarded as an exceptional leader who had a flair for administration and a keen knowledge of customary law. During the Japanese Occupation he managed a subsistence life with his family and when the Australians liberated Kuching, worked with them to retake the Japanese post at Kapit, later being awarded the King George V Medal for Bravery.

During the course of the war, Bertram Brooke had officially relin-quished his title as successor to Vyner and, in November 1944, Bertram's son, Anthony, was officially nominated as the next rajah after Vyner. However, the Labour government which was elected in post-war Britain was no more keen to see Brooke rule restored to Sarawak than Vyner was to have his nephew in charge. The case was put to Vyner that the cost of rehabilitating Sarawak after the Occupa-tion was more than he could finance. In October 1945, Vyner signed a preliminary agreement with the Colonial Office as a first step in the Cession of Sarawak to Britain. The Cession was announced formally in February 1946 and immediately resisted by Anthony Brooke.

In Sarawak, news that Vyner had handed Sarawak to the British met a mixed reception. The issues surrounding the announcement of Cession to the people of Sarawak are clouded by the fact that a number of misrepresentations were made at the time, particularly by a senior assistant to Vyner who claimed that the cession had the agreement of Bertram and Anthony.

Temenggong Koh, Paramount Chief of the Upper Rejang (far left) with Malcolm MacDonald, Commissioner-General for the United Kingdom, and Penghulu (later Tun) Jugah, all in traditional Iban warrior dress, during one of MacDonald's frequent visits to confer about local issues. (Source: Straits Times Annual, 1955)

Strong opposition came from Malay leaders in the main towns who had held high positions under the Brookes and feared for their futures under outside rule. The Malay leaders believed that an influx of immigrants (such as had occurred in Malaya under the British) would totally undermine their culture as well as their influence. Some of these leaders lobbied prominent Ibans, including Tun Jugah, for their support. The protests took the form of letters to the Colonial Office and to the British press, so that the opposition to the scheme became an issue in Britain, coinciding with reactions there to the Malayan Union scheme.

Within Sarawak itself, very few ordinary Sarawakians understood the meaning, or implications, of cession. When the British Parliament

213

sent representatives to gauge local reactions they found mixed responses but believed the populace could be persuaded to accept cession. By this time, Lord Louis Mountbatten, British Supreme Commander in Southeast Asia, and his policy advisers believed it was imperative for their strategic interests in Southeast Asia, particularly in view of the revolutionary struggle in Indonesia against the Dutch, that Britain be in full control of British North Borneo and Sarawak. In May 1946, the document of cession was passed by the Council Negeri. The British commissioner-general for Southeast Asia, Malcolm MacDonald, began making frequent visits between Singapore and Sarawak, usually including weekend stays with Ibans in the Balleh/Kapit region during which he is said to have persuaded Tun Jugah and others of the benefits of British rule.

During the final quarter of 1946, Sarawakians learned that the proposals for the Malayan Union had not been accepted by peninsular Malays, and anti-Cession sentiments were strengthened. The installation of the first British governor was a tense event, with no Iban representatives present. Anti-cession feeling became so strong that, when Anthony Brooke proposed a visit in November 1946, he was refused permission by the British lest he rally even greater support against the handover. Some disaffected Malays moved to Singapore to be with Anthony, who established headquarters of the anti-Cession movement there. Some of these anti-cessionists are said to have sided later with Indonesia during the period of Confrontation in the early to late 1960s.

In December 1949, a tragic incident occurred. A group of young Malay nationalists assassinated the second British governor, Duncan Stewart. The governor was stabbed by Rosly bin Dhobie, a trainee schoolteacher, whose fellow conspirators believed he would not be hanged because of his youth. Rosly's trial was probably attended by Tun Jugah, who came with other Iban leaders to witness the results of what they regarded as an act of treason. Rosly and three others were hanged and seven Malays were given substantial prison terms. The assassination and its aftermath effectively ended the anti-cession movement within Sarawak, although the split between pro- and anti-cession groups was reflected in Sarawak politics a decade later. Rosly bin Dhobie is celebrated in Malaysia's national history as a nationalist hero, lifting him above the local and very specific causes for which he struggled.

In taking over Sarawak, the British emphasised that they were preparing its peoples for self-government and would achieve this by training them for participation in local administration. Tun Jugah was one of the local leaders who became an essential figure in this process and he introduced his people to the workings of the local council. For personal reasons, in 1949, together with a group of Iban leaders, Jugah converted to Christianity and was baptised as a Methodist. He worked with missionaries to improve the education, health and agriculture of the people in his district. In 1953 he was selected by the governor to represent the indigenous peoples of Sarawak at the coronation of Queen Elizabeth, the first Iban ever to visit England. In 1958, just over a decade after cession, the governor of Sarawak introduced the concept of an independent federation which would be composed of North Borneo, Sarawak and Brunei. Tun Jugah, like many in Sarawak, felt his people did not understand the implications and that of the trio, Sarawak was the least economically developed and might suffer as a consequence. Shortly afterwards, in 1959, Sarawakians became more interested in using political parties to express their views and one of the first to be formed was the Sarawak United People's Party (SUPP), to represent all races and to emphasise loyalty to Sarawak. Other parties were formed over the next few years, including *Party Pesaka Anak Sarawak* (PESAKA) which Tun Jugah agreed to lead in order to represent Iban interests.

While Sarawakians had been introduced officially to the concept of a federation of Borneo states only in 1958, there had been informal working parties of senior administrators from the three states since 1953. Brunei's lack of interest in a Bornean federation had stalled progress. In 1961, however, Tunku Abdul Rahman made the first public statements about the advantages of a much bigger union between Malaya, Singapore and the Borneo territories. In Sarawak there was considerable skepticism about this proposal. Borneo leaders had been working towards the independence of their own states and their first reaction was that a merger would deprive them of their independent status. Many also thought things were moving too quickly, particularly in view of the very recent practice of formal politics in Sabah and Sarawak. Tun Jugah and others felt that the Borneo territories should move closer to each other before entering a bigger federation.

Lee Kuan Yew and Tunku Abdul Rahman agreed in August 1961 that Malaya and Singapore should merge. They held talks in London to try and determine how the concept of the wider federation with the Borneo territories should be pursued. In November 1961, Sir Harold Macmillan and Tunku Abdul Rahman agreed to set up an independent commission whose terms of reference were to assess the opinions of the peoples of North Borneo and Sarawak about the merger with Malaysia. Known as the 'Cobbold Commission' (after its chair, Lord Cobbold), it came to the conclusion that the people they had interviewed represented one of three positions: pro federation, anti federation and pro if certain guarantees could be met. One political scientist has described the situation as follows: 'By and large the Islamic communities were enthusiastic in their support for Malaysia and the Chinese opposed to it. The Dayaks as a whole were ill-equipped to assess the merits of the scheme; the minority Kenyahs and Kayans were quite hostile to it.'[3] It was the eventual support of the Ibans which ensured that federation would go ahead and Tun Jugah was a key figure in winning that support.

The Cobbold Commission encouraged the case for federation: it permitted the official spread of British-inspired propaganda which emphasised the dangers of communism as a threat in Borneo (from Indonesia) and which portrayed the future of the Borneo territories separated from Malaysia as economically untenable. Local leaders, such as Tun Jugah, were influenced by these arguments but put forward a number of conditions they wanted met in the terms under which Sarawak would enter the federation. As was later pointed out, 'the Cobbold Commission can be said to have functioned as an important "cover" to legitimise the British decision to withdraw from Sarawak without having first granted self-government, as promised at the time of Cession. . .'.[4]

In the formal consultations between Kuala Lumpur and the constituent states of the proposed federation, Tun Jugah was one of the representatives from Sarawak. He is credited with achieving the inclusion of a special clause in the new federal Constitution: that the indigenous customs of the native peoples of Sarawak should be protected. In July 1963, Jugah was one of four Sarawakians to fly to London and sign the Malaysia Agreement to legally establish the Federation of Malaysia, which celebrates its anniversary as 31 August 1963.

It had been understood that the most senior appointments in the new government of Sarawak would reflect the ethnic composition of the state and represent power-sharing between Malays and Dayaks. The first chief minister was an Iban, Stephen Kalong Ningkan and so a Malay, a respected magistrate and head of the *Majlis Islam Sarawak* (Islamic Council), Tun Abang Haji Openg, was appointed as first governor. Tun Jugah was given the newly created post of federal minister for Sarawak Affairs and, because he was not literate, appointed an Iban assistant who summarised documents for him. At the regular ministerial meetings in Kuala Lumpur, he was regarded as a passionate advocate for Sarawak's interests.

North Borneo becomes Sabah

The British North Borneo Chartered Company, which had ruled since the late 19th century, officially transferred and ceded all its rights and powers to Britain on 15 July 1946. Although no record of the negotiations between the company directors and the Colonial

Office is available, it is understood that the directors worked hard to obtain the best possible financial settlement for their shareholders and that the full sum received in compensation was 1.4 million pounds sterling.

Restoring the enormous damage which war had inflicted on North Borneo had been beyond the company's resources and it now fell to the Colonial Office to devise plans for massive reconstruction work. A development loan was organised to centralise the administration, rebuild towns destroyed by bombing (after the Japanese invasion of 1942 Jesselton had been flattened), extend meagre communications infrastructure and expand education and health services. The improved road and rail services were to be used for developing the state's natural resources, particularly timber.

While Tun Jugah was working with the Ibans during the 1950s in Sarawak, another local leader was making his mark in North Borneo. Donald Stephens, born and educated in North Borneo (then under company rule), spent the war years in Singapore and returned in 1945 to work as a contractor in the Public Works Department. In 1949, he began work as a journalist and in 1953 was able to start his own paper, the *Sabah Times*. During the 1950s, he was a member of the Legislative and Executive Councils of North Borneo. A leading member of the Kadazan community, he founded the United National Kadazan Organisation in 1961. In the lead-up to federation, as Tun Jugah had for Sarawak, he played a prominent role in representing North Borneo's interests to Kuala Lumpur and with Tun Jugah went to London for the signing of the Malaysia Agreement.

Donald Stephens was appointed North Borneo's first chief minister and to mark the independence of his state renamed it Sabah and insisted that the term 'Kadazan' replace the less correct term 'Dusun', which foreigners had been using to describe Sabah's main ethnic group. When he pressed for special concessions for Sabah and more autonomy from the central government in Kuala Lumpur, he was pressured to resign as chief minister (a pattern repeated later in Sabah's relations with the centre) and demoted to another ministry. He left politics a year or so later to become Malaysia's high commissioner to Australia. Unlike Tun Jugah, he was away from Malaysia during most of the period of Confrontation with Indonesia. Donald Stephens was replaced as chief minister by Mustapha bin Harun, a Muslim descended from the Sulu peoples of the southern Philippines, with whom the Kadazans and other local Sabah groups had long and uneasy relations.

Confrontation: reactions to the Federation of Malaysia

The formation of Malaysia, despite Brunei's failure to join, signalled the first and arguably most successful merger of post-colonial entities in Southeast Asia. In the context of the early 1960s, however, the realignments necessary to create the Federation of Malaysia were opposed by the Philippines and Indonesia. This set in train a series of (largely fruitless) diplomatic meetings to find a framework for mutual cooperation which were held, on and off, through the early 1960s.

Indonesia's position

In 1961, when Tunku Abdul Rahman announced a possible federation of former British possessions, the Indonesian Communist Party (PKI) denounced the idea as a British neo-colonialist plot and by early 1963 President Sukarno himself was using the same terms to describe Malaysia. Later that year, when the signing of the Malaysia Agreement looked inevitable, the PKI used the slogan 'Crush Malaysia' (*Ganyang Malaysia*), which Sukarno also took up and popularised as the phrase which became recognised internationally as signifying Indonesia's determination to break up the federation.

Although armed forces from Indonesian Borneo (Kalimantan) probably began infiltrating Sabah and Sarawak as early as April 1963, it was only after the formal declaration of the new political entity of Malaysia on 16 September 1963 that Indonesia called for volunteers to enlist and fight to liberate their fellows across the border. In December, a serious attack by a force of 100 regular Indonesian army troops on the remote timber settlement of Kalabakan in southeast Sabah killed eight members of the Royal Malay Regiment as well as one civilian and wounded 19 army personnel and five civilians. Incursions by the Indonesian air force into Malaysian airspace were so serious that in February 1964, Kuala Lumpur placed a ban on all aircraft entering Sabah and Sarawak.

Attempts to reach a cease-fire failed and when Indonesia announced it was training millions of volunteers to crush Malaysia, Australia and New Zealand sent forces to assist their fellow member of the Commonwealth. The numbers of British personnel already operating in Malaysia (especially Gurkha battalions) were increased. There was at least one positive spin-off from the Commonwealth presence. It has been said that the military personnel greatly improved the roads and bridges in Sabah during their tour of duty. In November 1964, small groups of armed Indonesians landed at a number of sites in Johor and it became clear that the Indonesian navy was targeting the Peninsula and Singapore while the army was fighting in Sabah and Sarawak.

Within Malaysia there were a variety of responses. Well-known leaders of Malay radical nationalist movements, such as Ishak Haji Muhammad and Ahmad Boestamam (both of whom had spent lengthy periods in gaol during the Emergency), were detained again. Although there was no evidence, they were accused of plotting with Indonesia to bring down Malaysia and introduce their pre-World War II dream of a region of united Malay peoples stretching from the Philippines and southern Thailand to the Indonesian archipelago. The president of PAS, Dr Burhanuddin, was also detained on the same (and equally unproven) charge but, unlike his colleagues was not held as long because of his deteriorating health. He died in 1969.

In Sabah and Sarawak, local people enlisted for service (including Donald Stephens), or joined vigilante and civil defence units. As federal minister for Sarawak Affairs, Tun Jugah flew between Kuala Lumpur and Sarawak and regularly visited all the jungle hot spots, encouraging the forces and raising morale. In one brutal action in mid-1965, seven civilians and two police, one of them the brother of the chief minister, were killed only 18 miles (29 kilometres) south of Kuching. In Sarawak, there was evidence that the banned Sarawak Communist Organisation (SCO) was in contact with and cooperating with cells of the Indonesian Communist Party (PKI) across the border. The almost impenetrable conditions of the deep jungle required total dependence on the local knowledge of the interior Dayak tribes and, just as the *Orang Asli* had assisted as trackers and guides in the Emergency on the Peninsula, so the local people assisted during the period of Confrontation.

In October 1965, Sukarno was toppled in Indonesia and the 'New Order' was begun under General Soeharto. In late May of the following year, his foreign minister, Adam Malik, met Tun Abdul Razak, Malaysia's deputy prime minister, for peace talks in Bangkok. A Peace Agreement was signed on 11 August 1966, with one of its provisions stating that Malaysia had agreed to allow the people of Sabah and Sarawak to hold general elections to reaffirm their decision to be part of Malaysia. The general elections in 1970, in both states, were won decisively by pro-Malaysia parties.

When the hostilities were declared officially to have ended in August 1966, it is estimated that over the three and three-quarter years of fighting, 114 people had been killed fighting for Malaysia and 600 lost their lives fighting against it.

The Philippines' claim

The Philippines' objections to the formation of Malaysia were both ideological and territorial. The territorial claims concerned parts of Sabah which had been the subject of agreements between the sultan of Sulu and the Dent brothers, through their agent Baron von Overbeck.

President Macapagal claimed that the 19th century treaties were for the rental and not cession of Sulu-controlled territory in Sabah and that ownership still lay with the heirs to the Sulu sultanate, incorporated into the Philippines. When Macapagal took the claim to the International Court of Justice in The Hague, Malaysia refused to participate on the grounds that this could compromise its claims to have sovereignty over the territory of Sabah. In 1966, Marcos replaced Macapagal and diplomatic relations with Kuala Lumpur were resumed. However, two years later it was alleged that Sulu forces were being trained to infiltrate and attack Sabah and in September 1968 Marcos signed a Bill defining Sabah as part of the Philippines and relations were again suspended. However, they were resumed in December 1969.

Malaysia without Singapore

Singapore experienced great social turbulence during the 1950s, the period when James Puthucheary and others with radical socialist beliefs were active in the various trade union movements of the time. The turmoil of the period is captured graphically in an impressive three-dimensional film of Singapore's history which is screened for visitors to the Singapore History Museum. Puthucheary was just one of the Leftist group (in some accounts referred to as 'pro-Communists') within the People's Action Party (PAP) which was receiving increasing support within the party. To forestall any threat to the group around Lee Kuan Yew, in August 1957, Puthucheary and others of similar mind were detained for nearly three years. During that time, Lee Kuan Yew led the PAP to power in the 1959 elections and became chief minister then, after Independence, prime minister, a position he held until 1990. Puthucheary and seven others were released on condition they supported PAP's anti-communist position.

Prime Minister Lee's new government was faced with substantial public debt and active trade unions which were fed by considerable unemployment. When Tunku Abdul Rahman took up the idea of a Malaysia federation which would include Singapore as well as the Borneo territories, Lee already knew the advantages to Singapore of access to the Peninsula's raw materials and the potential for solving his government's unemployment problems. He indicated this in the speech he made only one week after the Tunku's statement on federation (see opening quote at beginning of this chapter). The Tunku saw the advantages of linking the Peninsula economy to that of export-oriented Singapore, but realised that demographically, the Chinese of Singapore, when added to the Chinese domiciled on the Peninsula, would outnumber the Malay population. This was a situation he knew would unsettle the Malays and lead to serious inter-ethnic tensions. However, if the Malay and non-Chinese populations of Sabah and Sarawak were added to the number of peninsular Malays, they balanced the Singapore Chinese numbers. It was therefore more important, in the Tunku's estimation, that the Borneo territories join the federation than Singapore. The terms of entry reflect this concern: Sabah and Sarawak were given generous development loans while Singapore would concede 40 per cent of its revenues to Kuala Lumpur. In return, however, Singapore was granted three large parcels of British Crown Land, now in the heart of Singapore's central district. The distribution of seats in the new federal government (House of Representatives) was also not in Singapore's favour: 40 seats to Sabah and Sarawak and 15 to Singapore. At the 1962 referendum on the proposal to merge, the PAP proposition of joining Malaysia was supported and Singapore became part of Malaysia on 16 September 1963.

Singapore's entry to Malaysia was not wholeheartedly welcomed by Chinese and Malays on the Peninsula. Some members of the Malayan Chinese Association (MCA) viewed their colleagues in the PAP as potential rivals for Chinese votes and feared Singapore competition in the Chinese business world of the Peninsula. The very conservative members of the United Malays National Organisation

Singapore's Prime Minister, Lee Kuan Yew, taking the oath on 2 November 1963
in Kuala Lumpur at the first session of the Federal Parliament of Malaysia.
(Source: National Archives of Malaysia)

(UMNO), who jealously guarded the special position of the Malays, were suspicious of the multiracial platform of the PAP. It has been said that Prime Minister Lee Kuan Yew was insufficiently sensitive to these concerns and, disregarding them, fielded PAP candidates in seats in peninsular states in the 1964 general elections. This was followed by rallies in Singapore organised by the UMNO in support of Malays in Singapore. The Malay rallies heightened ethnic feeling and led, directly or indirectly, to riots in which 21 were killed and 460 injured. More riots followed.

In the following year, May 1965, a period when Indonesian attacks in Sabah and Sarawak were increasing, the PAP announced it would form a coalition of five of the opposition parties in Malaysia, to be named the Malaysian Solidarity Convention. Despite the fact that the Solidarity Convention presented a platform of abolishing poverty wherever it existed, the ultra-conservatives in the UMNO saw this as a threat to the special position of the Malays and reacted very strongly against the new grouping. The position of the Solidarity Convention will be outlined here, because it represents a continuing theme in Malaysian political history. Similar platforms have been tried a number of times by various groups opposed to the UMNO's policies but, at the time of writing, not one has succeeded in winning government.

The Solidarity Convention deliberately used the slogan 'Malaysian Malaysia' to represent their platform of a nation for all Malaysia's citizens rather than a nation dominated by the interests of one group (the Malays). They openly argued that special privileges for the Malays were not the solution to improving their social and economic condition. What was needed, in their view, were specific economic policies which would benefit the poor and disadvantaged wherever they were and from whatever community they come from. They went further and attacked the attitudes of those in the UMNO who maintained what they termed as 'feudal' attitudes which 'protected' one group of Malaysians at the expense of others.

The position and statements of the Malaysian Solidarity Convention were unacceptable to many in the UMNO who, on the grounds that the policies were anti-Malay and threatening to racial harmony, urged Tunku Abdul Rahman to deal with the PAP and Lee Kuan Yew. Tactics to split the PAP failed and Tun Abdul Razak tried but failed to reach a compromise with the Convention. Whatever the public statements of the Convention, its strong PAP component meant that Malays viewed it as a Chinese construction and believed, therefore, that it was unable to represent Malay interests. The racial, or communal divide, proved stronger than the rational force of policies and platforms, even when they were presented in terms of helping all Malaysians.

After secret meetings with his cabinet, the Tunku publicly announced the expulsion of Singapore from the federation on 9 August 1965. This was followed by a television appearance by

Prime Minister Lee. Genuinely distressed, he explained that although he had worked all his life for a merger of Singapore and the Federation of Malaya, he had become convinced that disagreements were now so serious that to avoid future conflict and violence he believed separation was inevitable.

Singapore became, and remains, an independent republic with whom Malaysia still has altercations. These become exacerbated in times of regional economic downturn when Singapore's advanced economy appears able to weather even global downturns and to solve its internal problems more effectively than Kuala Lumpur. After his retirement as prime minister in 1990, Lee Kuan Yew was granted the title of senior minister. He has remained a strong influence on domestic as well as regional affairs.

Development and the concept of the Bumiputera

The manner of the Tunku's expulsion of Singapore, without consultation with the leaders of his Borneo states, aroused their severe criticism. The departure of Donald Stephens as chief minister of Sabah indicated the Tunku's attitude to dissension in his ranks. The chief minister of Sarawak, Stephen Kalong Ningkan, met a similar fate when he clashed with the Tunku while defending Sarawak's interests in the federation. As one analyst has written: 'East Malaysian leaders are aware that no one who is confrontational to Kuala Lumpur will last long and this has led to symbiotic relationships between the Federal Government and the East Malaysian state governments.'[5]

One of the causes of the tension between the federal and Borneo state governments has been the lower level of economic development and the late practice of formal, Western-style politics in Sabah and

Sarawak. Kuala Lumpur recognised that the central government had to inject funds into the new states in east Malaysia and when the threat of armed attacks from Indonesia ended in 1966, the First Malaysia Plan (1966–70) was implemented. Its stated aim was 'the integration of the peoples and states of Malaysia by promoting the welfare of all'. The poor economic condition of rural Malays led to the formation of a special Bank Bumiputera in 1965.

The definition of a Bumiputera ('son of the soil' or indigene) varies according to context. Following federation, Article 153 of the federal Constitution was amended to extend the special privileges reserved for Malays (but not *Orang Asli*) to the 'natives' of Sabah and Sarawak. Together with Malays throughout the federation, they became known as 'Bumiputera'. When referring exclusively to peoples of peninsular Malaysia, the term sometimes includes *Orang Asli* and sometimes does not. In reality, the special benefits available to Bumiputera in peninsular Malaysia rarely reach *Orang Asli*. The indigenous peoples of Sabah and Sarawak, however, are unambiguously covered by the term.

The development projects for Sabah and Sarawak required huge investment to provide basic infrastructure (roads, railways, public buildings) so that raw materials (particularly timber) could be transported out for export. The situation in the Borneo states during the late 1960s has been described as 'largely a matter of frontier resource development in which the extraction of timber resources led to the opening of new land for agriculture . . . and the expansion of industries closely related to the primary sector'.[6]

The situation on the Peninsula was different. Development programs had been in place since the early 1950s, when 56 per cent of the employed work force was in agriculture. The best known of these is the rural resettlement scheme organised by FELDA (Federal Land Development Authority), established in 1956 as a statutory body to assist in the eradication of rural poverty. Poor families (and over 95 per cent of those selected have been Malay) were settled on small grants of agricultural land which they brought into production and, over 15 years, repaid their government loans. After repayment of the loan, they received the title to the land. Between 1960 and 1981, 71 000 families were resettled on 308 schemes and their incomes initially improved. However, the amount of land granted was sufficient for only one family and was usually unable to provide a livelihood for adult children as well. The rate of population increase outstrips the provision of land—although 71 000 families were settled over a 20-year period. During that same period, the population increased by more than 2.5 million.

The FELDA scheme has been better than no scheme at all, but its deficiencies have been analysed. The most serious are that, first, in cost benefit terms, FELDA has made very little impact on the condition of the majority of the rural poor and second, that a large proportion of the settlers were selected in return for political or other support. It must be noted also that the clearing of land for some of the schemes encroached on the traditional lands of the *Orang Asli* and reduced the land on which they depended for their livelihood.

Kelantan: Islam and the peasantry

The northern peninsular states of Kedah, Perlis, Kelantan and Terengganu have a high percentage of Malaysia's rural poor (peasants) yet, compared with the southern states, only 17.4 per cent of the total number of FELDA settlers have been drawn from there. While there may be several factors involved in this apparent inequality of land distribution, one which is cited often concerns political affiliation. The peasants of Kelantan and Terengganu were attracted to the policies of the Islamic Party, PAS and many supported it rather than the UMNO. This was in strong contrast to the southern peninsular states where Malays voted overwhelmingly for the UMNO and also received most of the FELDA land grants. The link between politics and development grants was spelled out in a speech by Deputy Prime Minister Tun Razak at a Kelantan by-election in 1968:

> It is said that we of the Alliance Party harbour ill-will against the people of Kelantan, and that we refuse to help this state progress from its backward condition. This is not true . . . I shall be completely frank and sincere with you. We cannot help you until you turn PAS out of power in this state and elect an Alliance Party government in its place . . . We can provide projects only for those who vote for us.[7]

A detailed analysis of the relationship between local politics, class interests and Islam in Kelantan during the 1950s and 60s has been done by sociologist Clive Kessler. His classic study shows that Kelantan's long history of tension between the Malay aristocracy of Kota Bharu and the peasant settlers of the coastal plains and beyond found expression in voting choices. During the general elections of 1959, the first post-independence elections, PAS won a landslide vistory in Kelantan which shocked the UMNO, who expected to gain the majority of Malay votes. The Malay elite, nurtured by the British and transformed into leaders of the UMNO, failed to address the concerns of the Kelantan peasantry. The young leaders of PAS, although not necessarily peasants themselves, presented PAS as an Islamic grouping which stood for the ideals of Islam and offered an alternative to the leadership of the traditional Malay aristocratic elite.

The broader implications of the success of PAS among the peasant voters of Kelantan caused concern to the UMNO tacticians. As Kessler points out, the UMNO's domination of Malaysian politics depended on gaining most of the Malay vote and the support of the Malay, Chinese and Indian voters for the parties which constituted the ruling Alliance formed the basis of their success. The support of Kelantan Malays for PAS revealed that the Malay community could be split and that, although expressed in religious terms (Islam), actually reflected a class divide between elite and non-elite Malays. This was confirmed after the 1959 general elections, when some of the wealthier peasants (many with substantial landholdings) left PAS and gave their allegiance to the UMNO.

Race Riots in Kuala Lumpur: 13 May 1969

A consistent challenge for all Malaysian political parties, a challenge which the British had failed to solve before their colonial administration ended, was how to persuade Malays that sharing political power with non-Malays would not threaten their interests. When Lee Kuan Yew and others used the Solidarity Convention to try and unite Malaysians on grounds of common allegiance rather than race, the ultra-conservative members of the UMNO reacted so negatively that Singapore had to be expelled from the federation. Yet, even within its own ranks, as shown by the degree of support for the Islamic party PAS in Kelantan, the UMNO was failing to answer the needs of its poorest constituents.

The two other members of the Alliance, the MCA (Malayan Chinese Association) and the MIC (Malayan Indian Congress), were also perceived by their poorer constituents, such as Chinese and Indian workers who had come to the cities in search of employment, as failing to address their needs. In a strategy to meet those needs and provide an alternative to the MCA and the MIC, two new parties were formed: the Democratic Action Party (DAP-a direct descendant of the PAP) in 1966 and the Gerakan (*Gerakan Rakyat Malaysia* or Malaysian People's Movement) in 1968. Both new parties upheld the concept of equal rights and forged an electoral pact for the 1969 elections to avoid splitting any votes not directed to the Alliance. Astute observers recognised that the weakened support for the Alliance carried the potential for serious trouble.

At the general elections held on 10 May 1969, the UMNO and the MIC lost some of their urban seats but the MCA lost very heavily, due to a loss in support from urban Chinese voters. As a result, the non-Malay opposition parties gained more than two-thirds of the urban vote and began to celebrate enthusiastically especially when it seemed they would have victory in several states. The loss of support for the MCA, a crucial member of the ruling Alliance, threatened to undermine the inter-communal basis on which the Alliance was built.

The exuberance of the DAP and Gerakan supporters was expressed in motor cavalcades and marches through the streets of Kuala Lumpur on 11 and 12 May and prompted the UMNO to organise a counter celebration on 13 May. While the Malay marchers were assembling, a report was received that several Malays trying to join the main group had been attacked by Chinese and Indians. This inflamed the main group of Malays who armed themselves with a variety of home-made weapons and missiles and set out to hunt down non-Malays in Kuala Lumpur, focusing particularly on areas of Chinese settlement in Kuala Lumpur. The Malay groups were met by equally determined and well-armed non-Malays and extreme violence broke out causing loss of life, serious injuries and destruction of property. Through the night, 2000 military and 3600 police were rushed to the capital. The violence continued through to Thursday 15 May when a State of Emergency was declared and a National Operations Council (NOC) of eight prominent figures under the leadership of Deputy Prime Minister Tun Razak was established to direct the restoration of order. Elections in progress in Sabah and Sarawak were suspended, as was federal Parliament. The *Internal Security Act* (ISA) was invoked to detain without trial anyone considered a threat to order.

Kuala Lumpur was flooded with anxious people seeking safety and over 15 000 refugees crowded into the city's stadiums. It was a week before a sense of order was restored and isolated outbreaks of violence continued to be reported until the end of May when the worst of the rioting had passed. Official figures at the end of May were

177 killed, 340 injured and 5750 arrested, but unofficial figures were higher. Although it was announced that the Alliance had won the elections at the federal level, and although it was known that in several states the Alliance had done quite poorly, in the public's mind the need to restore order and public safety assumed top priority and far overshadowed electoral matters.

The New Economic Policy

Prime Minister Tunku Abdul Rahman's immediate response to the violence and rioting was the establishment of the NOC, under Tun Razak. In effect, this meant that the country was being led by the deputy prime minister. In early June, when some calm had been restored, there was public discussion about the future role of the MCA in the Alliance in the light of its poor electoral performance. Dr Mahathir Mohammad, a young UMNO member who had lost his seat in Kedah (to a PAS candidate), accused the prime minister of favouring the MCA at the expense of the UMNO and Malay interests. In a letter to Tunku Abdul Rahman he blamed the prime minister for losing the confidence of all the Malays and called on him to resign. Copies of the letter were circulated and many Malay teachers and students took up the call, believing that the Tunku had not pushed the adoption of Malay as the official language of the nation as he could have done. Other Malaysians spoke out against any moves to further protect Malays and insisted that Malaysia must adopt a policy of equality for all its citizens. Musa Hitam, then an assistant minister, was one of the few UMNO members who publicly supported Dr Mahathir and was removed from his post. Dr Mahathir himself was expelled from the UMNO's Central Committee and then expelled from the UMNO.

Tunku Abdul Rahman, who had been recovering from eye surgery, headed a National Good Will Committee to build interracial tolerance and embarked on a national tour to restore public confidence in the stability of the federation. Parliament was not recalled but the NOC established a National Consultative Council (NCC) in October 1969, to which representatives of a wide range of Malaysian groups—political, religious, social and economic—were appointed. The NCC was to discuss all issues which might effect the future peace and unity of Malaysia and a new Department of National Unity was set up to focus specifically on race relations. The NCC promoted a national ideology, the *Rukunegara*—which has much in common with Indonesia's Pancasila—as the basis for new programs in civics and citizenship.

Tun Razak

The individual at the centre of this strategic reorganisation of the federation after the 1969 elections was Tun Abdul Razak. Born in Pahang in 1921, his primary schooling was in Malay and then his father, one of Pahang's four great chiefs, sent him to Malay College, Kuala Kangsar, where he did exceptionally well. During the war he was an interpreter for the Japanese as well as working with the special Allied guerilla Force 136. He studied Law in London (where he met Tunku Abdul Rahman) and returned to work in the civil service, becoming state secretary for Pahang in 1952. He joined the UMNO in 1950 and the following year, when the Tunku succeeded Dato Onn as president, Razak became his deputy. In the lead-up to Independence, he prepared the multiracial education policy which was maintained into the 1970s. After Independence, he was appointed deputy prime minister, defence minister and minister of rural development. He thus came to the task of restoring stability with experience in crucial portfolios and with intimate knowledge of the Malaysian political system. In 1970, the Tunku resigned as prime minister and Tun Razak replaced him and remained prime minister until his widely mourned death from leukemia in 1976.

When the National Consultative Council reviewed the factors which had contributed to the interracial violence after the 1969 elections, they were faced with the fact that the rural development schemes had not reached the people and areas where they were most needed—rural industries, fisheries, cooperatives, agricultural education and extension work, and rural credit and marketing schemes. The ethnic group overwhelmingly involved in those areas was Malay. It also emerged that the Malays (closely followed by Indians) had the highest unemployment rates. In the investment sector the figures were perhaps even worse: Malays held only 1 per cent of investment in registered businesses. Although the most senior positions in the civil service were held by Malays, they were not well represented in lower divisions. The NCC did not mention that even though UMNO politicians held the majority of seats in Parliament they had failed to successfully represent the interests of the majority of their constituents.

As well as his official advisers, Tun Razak had gathered around him a special team of able people who believed the Tunku's policies would not deliver the changes needed to improve economic performance. Among them was James Puthucheary who, after his banning from Singapore in 1963, was living in Kuala Lumpur. Following Puthucheary's ideas on the benefits of state intervention, they argued that the most efficient way of transforming the Malaysian economy and improving the participation of the Malays was through public corporations funded by the government. Also following Puthucheary, they suggested that foreign-owned corporations in Malaysia could be restructured to benefit the Malays and raise their meagre share of participation in the investment sector. Tun Razak appointed Puthucheary to the NCC and his theories were incorporated into a new development plan which became known as the NEP (New Economic Policy).

Tun Razak chose to reform both the economy and the political system. He did so against a background of censorship suggested by the NOC. To avoid any further outbreaks of violence provoked by inter-racial conflict, the NOC embargoed public discussion of the following issues, claiming they were too sensitive and could be inflammatory: citizenship, special privileges for Malays and the native peoples of Sabah and Sarawak, the position of the Malay rulers and the role of Malay as the sole national language. The NEP, scheduled to remain in operation until 1990, aimed to reduce and eventually eradicate poverty as well as to restructure Malaysian society so that race was no longer identified with economic function. To meet these twin goals, economic strategies formulated as 'Malaysia Plans' were designed so that by the Fifth Malaysia Plan (1986–90) all the objectives of the NEP would have been achieved and by 1990, Bumiputeras would own and manage at least 30 per cent of the corporate sector.

Criticism of the NEP emphasised that economic efficiency was not always the outcome when state enterprises were in charge of businesses and that senior bureaucrats were not necessarily the best managers. Critics also predicted that plans to reduce regional disparities in economic development (as between the west and east coasts of the Peninsula and between the Peninsula and the Borneo territories) would probably not assist the distribution of income among the ethnic groups of the federation. It was the intention of the planners that national unity would result from a more equitable distribution of income and wealth across Malaysia's social and economic groups. However, economic research from elsewhere, as well as later events in Malaysia, indicates that national unity does not necessarily flow from improved economic circumstances.

A key body established to oversee the creation of a Malay industrial and commercial community leading to a greater share of the business sector was PERNAS (*Pertubuhan Nasional* or National Development Corporation). Incorporated as a public company in 1969, PERNAS moved swiftly to form seven subsidiaries in the key areas of securities, engineering, construction, trading, property and insurance. It had joint ventures in other areas such as mining, and hotels and in all of its activities the aims were to expand opportunities for the employment of Malays and other indigenous peoples (although *Orang Asli* did not benefit), to assist in the formation of businesses by Malays, and to hold in trust share capital in companies until Malays and other indigenous peoples had the capital to acquire them.

Under the NEP, the development of export-oriented industries became a national priority. There was remarkable growth during the 1970s in electrical and electronic items, textiles, manufactured rubber products, chemicals and metal products. The development of offshore oil and gas deposits discovered off the coast of Terengganu and Sarawak brought rich revenues to the state-owned Petronas Corporation, especially following the rise in world oil prices in 1973 and 1979. Foreign investment was encouraged through incentives such as Free Trade Zones, offering special industrial sites, the first of which was established in Penang in 1971. Labour for the new factories attracted young women and, by the mid-1980s, women made up just over 95 per cent of the manufacturing industry's workforce on the Peninsula. The industrialisation of Sabah and Sarawak lagged badly behind the Peninsula and when it did come was focused on the processing of natural resources, such as wood products and a natural gas plant.

Building stability: the National Front

While the NEP was designed to respond to the economic grievances of the Malays, Tun Razak also addressed the system of political parties which, in the UMNO's view, had contributed to the violent outbursts of 13 May. The electoral results at the state level had been particularly worrying for the Alliance and had shown clearly the loss of support for the MCA and the consequent gains by parties outside the Alliance. Many analysts have seen this period as the beginning of increased federal intervention in state level politics, particularly in the Borneo states.

Tun Razak believed that political campaigning based on claims which involved racial differences inflamed voters and provoked competition which might then be expressed in violent demonstrations. This could be overcome, he reasoned, by including opposition parties within the ruling coalition where they would be given representation in the cabinet, state assemblies and Parliament and would have the opportunity to fight for their interests in the party room rather than in public.

The National Front (*Barisan Nasional*) was formally registered as a new confederation of parties in June 1974, two months before a national election. By that time it included the UMNO as dominant member, the MCA and the Gerakan, both representing Chinese interests, the Islamic party PAS, the People's Progressive Party (a small party from Perak), the MIC, the Sabah alliance in Sabah and a state coalition in Sarawak. The National Front was successful in the 1974 elections and has won every national election up to the time of writing. It has been described as a coalition between a central core party, the UMNO and smaller parties who joined on the UMNO's terms: 'It was certainly not a coalition between equals.'[8] A successful coalition, however, involves compromise and falls apart if cooperation and accommodation are not practised. Although the UMNO is the dominant partner, it occasionally has to adapt its position if pressured sufficiently by the other partners.

The legacy of Tun Razak

When Parliament resumed in 1971 after the period of Emergency rule following May 13 1969, Tun Razak held the positions of prime minister, minister of defence and minister of foreign affairs. His policies as minister of foreign affairs have often been overshadowed, at least in the appraisals of Western commentators, by his economic policies but they deserve greater recognition for their lasting influence on the orientation of Malaysia's foreign policy. It was his strong support for the concept of ASEAN which ensured that it became a meaningful regional alliance during the mid-1970s and he promoted the concept of Southeast Asia as a non-aligned or neutral region. Among his other initiatives were the promotion of trade with communist nations in eastern Europe and with Russia, and the establishment of closer relations with the People's Republic of China. In 1974, he hosted the Fifth Islamic

Conference of Foreign Ministers and urged the oil-rich Islamic states to direct some of their profits to assisting the poorer Islamic nations. His recognition of the importance of international Islam remained a component of Malaysia's foreign policy after his death.

Another lasting legacy of Tun Razak's period as prime minister was the national language policy. Beginning with primary level one in English medium schools in 1970, Bahasa Melayu (Malay) became the language of instruction for primary and secondary schools in the Peninsula, with Sabah joining the conversion in 1971 and Sarawak in 1977. Chinese and Tamil primary schools were not affected by this policy and this was to arouse later criticism from some Malays. As well, a new national university was established, *Universiti Kebangsaan Malaysia*, teaching exclusively in the national language, a policy which required a massive effort to translate text books into Malay, with the assistance of the National Language and Literature Council (*Dewan Bahasa dan Pustaka*). A policy of positive discrimination in favour of Malay students was also intensified (a policy still in operation and regarded as unfair by non-Malay students) with large numbers of overseas scholarships for tertiary study awarded to Malays.

Less positively, Tun Razak's term coincided with the implementation of a number of repressive measures which were invoked in the aftermath of the violence of May 1969 but which have remained in force. The federal government actively used its powers to suspend state constitutions, to allocate federal revenues to states, and to invoke the Internal Security Act (ISA) to detain without trial any person 'with a view to preventing him from acting in a manner prejudicial to the security of Malaysia'.[9] Even a cursory examination of the list of those arrested under the ISA indicates that it has been used to silence political opposition, as much as to maintain peace and order.

By 1974, the increasing numbers of tertiary students generated a campus culture of political involvement in social issues. Students took up the cause of rural Malays and demonstrated in mass rallies against the government. The then education minister, Dr Mahathir, was stern in his condemnation and the ISA was used against some of the leaders of the protests, who included Anwar Ibrahim, a founder of the Islamic Youth Movement of Malaysia (*Angkatan Belia Islam Malaysia* or ABIM). In 1975, the government passed a Bill strengthening prohibitions against student demonstrations and involvement in national politics.

Leadership changes

After Tun Razak's death, his deputy prime minister (and brother-in-law), Hussein Onn, succeeded him as prime minister. Hussein Onn was son of the first leader of the UMNO, Dato Onn Jaafar, and had left the party in 1951, when his father did. He returned only in 1969 and Tun Razak's unexpected death, in January 1976, came before he had demonstrated his own qualities and built up his own group of supporters. At this time factionalism within the UMNO was strong—as it was during most periods of its turbulent history. Tunku Abdul Rahman was an influence within the party until his death in 1990. He remained in the public eye in many positions, but particularly through his acerbic weekly columns in the popular daily, *The Star*. Tun Razak had promoted his own group while he was in power and those not close to him saw the opportunity to gain influence under a new prime minister. They were disappointed when Hussein Onn chose Dr Mahathir Mohamad as his deputy prime minister.

The supporters of Tunku Abdul Rahman, remembering Mahathir's criticisms of his policies and style, were dismayed at his promotion. In their minds, Mahathir, Musa Hitam and Tengku Razaleigh (a Kelantan aristocrat), all supporters of Razak, were a threat to their powers and spheres of influence. Their strategy to discredit those formerly close to Tun Razak, including Hussein Onn, was a clever smear campaign. Rumours were spread that advisers close to the ruling group were secret agents of the Malayan Communist Party. Although the MCP was no longer a force in Malaysian politics, there was sufficient paranoia still evident in the mid-1970s to give credibility to the rumours. The fact that members of the so-called 'Intellectual Left', such as James Puthucheary, had contributed to some of Razak's policies, was used as a further means of discrediting some of his close colleagues.

In this context of personal rivalry within the UMNO, the minister of home affairs, Ghazalie Shafie, who harboured his own disappointment at losing the post of deputy prime minister to Mahathir, invoked the ISA to arrest two leading journalists for subversive activities linked with communism. When they made 'confessions' implicating leading figures of the UMNO, many ordinary Malays believed there had indeed been communist influence on figures close to Tun Razak.

In July 1981, citing ill-health, Dato Hussein Onn retired. The UMNO General Assembly unanimously elected Dr Mahathir as its new leader which made him automatically the prime minister. The UMNO's selection of the deputy prime minister was not as clear-cut, the candidates being the minister of education, Musa Hitam—a long-time supporter of Mahathir—and the minister of finance, Tengku Razaleigh. Musa was elected narrowly, leaving Tengku Razaleigh defeated but determined to pursue his ambitions and move higher.

10
DEVELOPING
NEW VISIONS

We Orang Asli are often taken for granted; not taken seriously. We are left without many rights although we have given much service.

We must seek rights not only for ourselves, but also for all Orang Asli, all suku-kaum *(ethnic groups), all* kampungs *(villages). Or else we will have no land later.*

Members of *Orang Asli* communities
at a public meeting, Perak 1993[1]

Under Prime Minister Dr Mahathir Mohamad, one of the longest serving political leaders in Asia, Malaysia's society and urban landscape were transformed. Economic growth was sustained until the mid-1980s when it faltered but was resumed in the late 1980s at annual growth rates of at least 7 per cent until 1997. In that year, all Asian nations were affected by an economic crisis whose global implications were substantial and ongoing. Before the crisis, however, Malaysia had already implemented restrictions on foreign borrowing and banking regulations, thus avoiding the catastrophic banking collapses which occurred in neighbouring countries. These measures contributed to Malaysia's ability to withstand the crisis better than many analysts had predicted. The Malaysian and international press chose to highlight Dr Mahathir's unorthodox policies of foreign currency and capital controls as the major factors in successfully quarantining the Malaysian economy from some of the global impacts. While economists have continued to debate the reasons behind Malaysia's upswing, the figures indicate that from mid-1999 onwards Malaysia's economy has shown signs of recovery.

Malaysia's economic management policies have created debate for some years. The New Economic Policy of the early 1970s with its positive discrimination in favour of Bumiputeras did result in greater numbers from that group becoming employed in white collar jobs. Many of them entered the professions or rose to become managers and supervisors, creating a substantial urban middle class. Many in this new, comfortable class believed they owed their rise to the generosity of the UMNO and responded with increased support for Dr Mahathir. Closer analysis of the distribution of income as a result of the NEP reveals that although the number of people on the poverty line decreased (there were fewer living in absolute poverty) the gap between rich and poor remained and was, in fact, widening.

The divide was most marked between very rich and very poor Malays, so that the possibility of serious divisions within the Malay community was very strong. The UMNO tacticians realised that any split in the Malay vote could spell disaster for the UMNO and therefore for the ruling coalition, the National Front. In the mid-1970s, when students and others demonstrated against the policies of the National Front on behalf of the very poor, their leaders were detained without trial under the Internal Security Act (some for up to seven years). One of the detainees was Anwar Ibrahim, the fiery leader of the Islamic youth movement, ABIM. Malay authors and poets composed works which, in quite dramatic terms, conveyed the tensions they perceived between the haves and have-nots from the mid-1970s onwards. As a barometer of tensions in Malay society, the best of Malay fiction is a remarkably reliable guide.

The success of the NEP was based on state intervention in the corporate business sector. The implementation of this strategy was accomplished by government ministers and senior bureaucrats in a way which made them central to the process and gave them privileged access to sources of funding. As a result, patronage and factionalism flourished. Two groups of Malaysians who felt disaffected towards the National Front's social and economic policies were the *Orang Asli*, who remained on the margins of Malaysian society, and the Kadazans and other native peoples of Sabah, who, for a brief period in the 1980s, succeeded in asserting Sabah's interests over those of the federal government in Kuala Lumpur.

The *Orang Asli*

The majority of Malaysians find it difficult to acknowledge that their 'Original Peoples' (the *Orang Asli*) are also their true indigenous people who occupied the Malay Peninsula long before other peoples. When Prime Minister Mahathir, for example, uses the phrase 'the indigenous people' in his speeches he is referring to the Malays rather than the *Orang Asli*. Theoretically, and according to the Constitution, the Malays, the *Orang Asli* and the native inhabitants of Sabah and Sarawak are all equally 'indigenous'. However, in practice, it is the Malays and some of the native peoples of Sabah and Sarawak who benefit from the special economic advantages which the NEP provides for Bumiputeras.

It was the need to win their support during the period of the Emergency which led to more sustained bureaucratic contact with various *Orang Asli* peoples. The Department of Aborigines was set up in 1950 and after Independence became known by its Malay name of JHEOA (*Jabatan Hal Ehwal Orang Asli*: Department of Orang Asli Affairs). The low status officially accorded the JHEOA is indicated by the fact that it is not a full ministry, but a department whose affiliation has changed nine times since 1955. Its director-general has always been a Malay.

Since 1961, the JHEOA has had almost total control over all matters concerning the *Orang Asli* groups who live in peninsular Malaysia. It has been responsible for matters as diverse as bureaucratic procedures (the appointment of headmen, for example), health and education services, and having the legal right to represent the *Orang Asli* and determine their interests. As might be expected, it is the JHEOA which represents the *Orang Asli* in the majority of legal cases involving claims to traditional territories, claims which are most often made by 'developers'. Most of the cases are decided without reference to the *Orang Asli* and in favour of the outside parties. The attitude of the JHEOA has united the *Orang Asli* in their criticism of its policies and practices and has led to the establishment of the Peninsular Malaysia Orang Asli Association (*Persatuan Orang Asli Semenanjung Malaysia* or POASM). By the year 2000, POASM's membership had grown to over 17 000 and membership was not restricted to *Orang Asli* but open to all Bumiputeras interested in supporting the *Orang Asli*. In broad terms, POASM concerns centre round two broad issues: attempts to assimilate the *Orang Asli* and land rights.

Assimilation

In 1997, it was estimated that the peninsular *Orang Asli* population was 106 131 or only 0.5 per cent of the national population of Malaysia. Recent surveys of all *Orang Asli* groups indicate that many now live near towns and settlements with less than half of their total population living near or in forested land. This reflects also the fact that Malaysia's jungle areas are diminishing.

The government's attitude to integration affects all *Orang Asli* because of the economic and social implications for them. For the sake of their own well-being, the government argues, the *Orang Asli* must be drawn into the economic network of the modern state. In response to this, the *Orang Asli* emphasise that they have been integrated into regional commercial networks since pre-modern times. Most *Orang Asli* living in contemporary Malaysia want to be part of modern economic life but on their own terms. They take particular exception to the official policy of social integration. The government believes that social integration is best achieved by *Orang Asli* adopting a 'Malay' lifestyle of settled living (in government-built housing) with conversion to Islam being an essential element. If this path is chosen, the government urges, the *Orang Asli* would enjoy all the benefits and privileges available to Malays. In 1990, the then director-general of the JHEOA considered the best future for the *Orang Asli* would be as an Islamised subgroup of the Malays. Some *Orang Asli* have converted to Islam but the majority have not and resent the persistent attempts (some performed by well-meaning Malays, others by political groups with less honourable motives) to convert them to Islam.

The increasing membership of the POASM has added strength and confidence to those *Orang Asli* who feel motivated to challenge government policies which affect them. As the quotations at the beginning of this chapter show, there is an emerging sense of cohesion among not only various groups of the *Orang Asli*, but also with any group disadvantaged by government land programs.

Land rights

The link between the *Orang Asli* and their traditional use of land is an essential part of their identity. Their traditional environment meets most of their economic needs and is the source of their spiritual life. Many supporters of the *Orang Asli* argue that the Malaysian government's policies for the *Orang Asli* are aimed at removing them from their traditional environments through resettlement schemes and denying them control over their traditional territories. The aim of these policies is to integrate the *Orang Asli* into mainstream Malay culture by severing their connection with their land.

Control over land in Malaysia rests with the individual member states of the Federation of Malaysia. Each has the power to designate land for the exclusive use of traditional peoples but they are not compelled to do this. The states also have the power to resume and sell land so-declared and compensate the traditional users only for any planted trees (for example, fruit and rubber). The *Orang Asli* have no rights to the title of their lands and thus no sense of security. In the past, the state governments have resumed traditional lands for a number of 'development' purposes: land schemes (for Malays), roads, plantation industries, logging, public buildings, airports, mines, golf-courses and dams. A recent judicial decision, in favour of traditional land use, has created an encouraging precedent for land rights claims made on behalf of *Orang Asli* groups.

In 1993, the Johor state government made an agreement with Singapore to build a dam to supply water to both Johor and Singapore. The Johor section of the JHEOA argued that this would not affect the Jakun people of the area because they did not depend on access to the land for their livelihood. The Jakuns (who numbered 225) complained that they were being denied access to their lands which they used as sources of income. They claimed compensation for loss of traditional rights and were offered US$147 300. The amount which Singapore paid to the Johor state government for the dam was US$84.2 million and, after learning this, the Jakuns refused the initial compensation offer and took the matter to court. A judgement was given in the High Court of Johor in late 1996 in favour of the Jakuns and granting them US$7 million in compensation for loss of income over 25 years. The judgement was appealed at both the state and federal levels, but the decision was upheld. Since the Jakuns' success, the High Court in Sabah and Sarawak has upheld the principle established in the Johor judgement, that customary rights over land are recognised by common law. It remains to be seen how the compensation payment to the Jakuns will be made and whether this will encourage further claims which may challenge the federal government's development policies and its attitude to indigenous people's land rights.

The politics of survival

Many *Orang Asli* leaders believe that full participation in Malaysian life would improve the position of their people. This is not possible, they argue, while they are administered by the JHEOA which treats them as a special category in Malaysian society and cannot provide the standard of housing, health and education services which other Malaysians enjoy. After Prime Minister Mahathir's 'Vision 2020' policy was announced in 1990, they responded with their own plan for *Orang Asli* development within that Vision. Their first concern was that the Constitution be amended so that the special privileges accorded Malays and native peoples of Sabah and Sarawak be given also to the *Orang Asli*. If this were done, if the rights to their lands were recognised and their traditional customs included as part of the national culture (as is done for the indigenous peoples of Sabah and Sarawak), many *Orang Asli* believe their people would be empowered to take their place as a respected group in the nation.

On the other hand, the government has argued that if the *Orang Asli* claims were to be recognised it would impede the 'development' of some of Malaysia's natural resources and curtail the economic benefits which have flowed to private hands from plantation, logging, mining and building on traditional lands. The contest, as the *Orang Asli* and their supporters argue, is not *only* for control of land and natural resources, but for the right of the *Orang Asli* to be recognised as a group of peoples whose culture and identity is indigenous to Malaysia but distinct from that of the Malays.

Politics on the edge: Sabah's Kadazans

In Sabah and Sarawak, unlike peninsular Malaysia, native peoples are in the majority and numerically large populations, like the Ibans, have the right to own land. Minority native peoples, such as the Rungus of

Sabah and the Penans of Sarawak, have more difficulty maintaining their rights in the face of pressure from multinational logging companies. The complexities which can arise when local, national and international interests are at stake are illustrated in the political upheavals which Sabah experienced during the 1970s and 80s.

During the 1950s, Donald Stephens and others tried to promote a sense of Kadazan identity among the non-Muslim peoples of Sabah. The Kadazans are the largest indigenous group in Sabah, are mostly Christian, and represent about 28 per cent of the total population. At the time of federation in 1963, the Kadazans insisted that Islam, the religion of Malaysia, would not apply to Sabah. When Stephens was forced to resign as first chief minister because of his frequent clashes with the federal government, he was replaced by Mustapha bin Harun. Mustapha, a Muslim descended from the Sulus of the southern Philippines, began his working life as a house boy for officers of the British North Borneo Company but during the war joined Filipino guerilla forces to resist the Japanese. During the 1950s, he was a member of the Sabah Legislative Council and, in 1961, became founder and leader of the United Sabah National Organisation (USNO). When he became chief minister he governed with a Sabah Chinese–Muslim alliance.

Mustapha's Sabah alliance was initially supported by the federal government which, following the race riots of 1969, was promoting national unity through inter-ethnic cooperation. However, Mustapha's style of government—using revenues and concessions to reward his supporters, conducting an aggressive campaign of Islamising Sabah's native peoples and declaring Islam the official religion of Sabah in 1973—resulted in attempts to force him out of office. These were stepped up when Mustapha not only gave open support to the Muslim separatists in the southern Philippines but also threatened to take Sabah out of the federation. Tun Razak, then prime minister, encouraged the formation of a new, multiethnic political party under Stephens, known as Berjaya (*Bersatu Rakyat Jelata Sabah*, Sabah United People's Party) which had

Kadazan, Malay and Chinese support. The first of Sabah's changes of government was poised to occur.

At the 1976 elections, Berjaya swept to office but Stephens and some of his cabinet were killed only three months later in a plane crash. Stephens was succeeded as chief minister by Harris Salleh, a Malay-Pakistani, who resumed many of Mustapha's policies—Islamisation and political patronage through access to revenues from natural resources. Harris's period in office coincided with the first fruits of the NEP in the form of greater participation by Bumiputeras in businesses, banks and development projects. In 1982, however, a world recession affected revenues derived from natural resources and Sabah's rural population, particularly the Kadazans and other native groups, were hard-hit. Their feeling of dissatisfaction with the corruption evident in Berjaya was exacerbated by Harris's pro-Muslim (pro-Malay) policies.

From the early 1980s there had been a Kadazan cultural revival, with educated, mainly urban Kadazans wanting to know more about their traditional culture. As part of this, they revived older ceremonies such as the annual Kadazan harvest festival. Linked with this was renewed interest in a position known as 'paramount chief of the Kadazan' and in 1984, a Catholic lawyer called Joseph Pairin Kitingan, who had entered politics to join Berjaya in the 1970s, was installed as chief. Just before the 1985 elections, a new Kadazan-based party was formed led by Kitingan. Named the PBS (*Parti Bersatu Sabah*, United Sabah Party) it attracted not only a Kadazan (Christian) following but also many Chinese and it defeated the Berjaya party.

Prime Minister Mahathir had not welcomed the formation of PBS and did not invite it to join the ruling National Front. Former Chief Minister Mustapha had not disappeared from the political scene and after the PBS victory used his vast reserves of wealth to encourage opposition to Kitingan, even assisting the entry to Sabah of thousands of Muslim migrants from the southern Philippines to boost the Muslim vote. However, when PBS was again successful in the 1986 elections, Mahathir relented and PBS was admitted to the National Front. The arrangement did not last and, in 1990, when an alternative alliance at the federal level appeared, at the eleventh hour Kitingan took PBS into an opposition coalition with an UMNO dissident, Tengku Razaleigh of Kelantan. The prime minister retaliated by withholding federal development funding from Sabah, charging Kitingan with corruption, and using the ISA to arrest his brother and several other close colleagues. Dr Mahathir also encouraged the establishment of a branch of the UMNO in Sabah, thus entering into direct competition with the existing pro-Muslim party for the Malay–Muslim vote.

During the early 1990s, tension within Sabah increased as federal pressure against Kitingan mounted. The rapid increase in migrants from the Philippines was resented by large numbers of indigenous Sabahans who regarded them as a drain on the state's welfare resources. When their numbers swelled to half a million, they were seen as a threat to the position of Sabahans in their own land. During the same period, Indonesians, particularly from eastern Indonesia, began working in Sabah as temporary migrants but most did not settle permanently with their families as the Muslims from the Philippines had done. The influx of immigrants, the majority of whom were Muslim, presented a challenge to the Sino-Kadazan National Front. In 1994, PBS won the elections narrowly but failed to govern when some of its members defected to join an UMNO-led coalition. Kitingan lost his position as chief minister and since 1994 Sabah has been ruled by an UMNO-backed alliance.

Political activity in Sabah during the 1980s highlights the special context of the Borneo territories. In Sabah and Sarawak the indigenous (Bumiputera) population contrasts with the Bumiputeras of the Peninsula because the former are not all Muslims. They may not, therefore, be attracted to the Malay-dominated policies of the UMNO. For the federal government to maintain influence in Sabah and Sarawak, it has to work with local parties to convince voters (by favourable policies or by patronage) that they should support the National Front. The federal government holds the winning card of oil and gas revenues. Although Sabah and Sarawak produce about one third of Malaysia's oil and gas, they receive back only 5 per cent of the royalties derived from those resources. Petronas, the federal government's corporation to develop and exploit oil and gas in Malaysia, takes the lion's share of profits from east Malaysia's oil and gas resources and this income has been used to finance massive projects on the Peninsula.

Religion and social change: Islamic renewal

In peninsular Malaysia the administration of Islam was conducted through a religious bureaucracy which had close links with the sultan of each Malay kingdom. By the early 20th century, British colonial policy had succeeded in restricting the sultan's official activities to those matters concerned with religion and traditional custom so that Islam became rather disconnected from mainstream political activity.

This changed in the 1950s with the formation of the Islamic party PAS. The heartlands of PAS support were the east coast states of Kelantan and Terengganu where it enjoyed considerable success in the late 1960s and 70s. However, when PAS agreed to join the ruling National Front in the mid 1970s, it lost much of its earlier momentum. Coincidentally, it was at this time that new energy was being injected into Islam by young Malays who, benefitting from the policies of the NEP, were entering senior secondary and tertiary education in far larger numbers. As well, the industrialising policies of the NEP needed thousands of workers to operate machines and to assemble components for the foreign-owned industries being encouraged by the government to establish off-shore branches in Malaysia in specially developed Free Trade Zones. Young men and women left their villages to work and study in urban centres. Some left for study outside Malaysia (in the Middle East, Europe, Australia and America), and small groups of these overseas Malay students established organisations for mutual help and support.

251

In global terms, the 1970s was a period of intensified Islamic activity, the rise of the Middle East in world politics (linked with the Arab–Israeli conflict and the rise in oil prices) and the revolution in Iran, which brought an exiled Muslim scholar, the Ayatollah Khomeini, to political power. Malay students, at home and abroad, became aware of the international profile of Islam and aware that Islam could play a much greater role in their own personal and national lives. This stimulated what became known in Malaysia as the *dakwah* movement. The Arabic word *dakwah* means 'to call' or 'invite'. In Malaysia, it became the term to describe two kinds of Muslim activity—first, encouraging individual Muslims to intensify their devotion to Islam and second, persuading non-Muslims to convert to Islam.

There has been a tendency by non-Muslims to gloss all *dakwah* activities with the term 'Islamic resurgence' or, more inaccurately as 'Islamic fundamentalism'. It is important to understand that *dakwah* activities in Malaysia were (and remain) various, not restricted to PAS, are rarely extreme in their aims and behaviour, and are usually motivated by the desire to implement Islamic ideals in daily life. A somewhat unusual example of a *dakwah* program is the JHEOA-sponsored efforts to induce *Orang Asli* to convert to Islam. The aim of these efforts had several purposes: to offer the spiritual benefits of a 'true' religion, to integrate *Orang Asli* into a Malay way of life and to bring them into the political orbit of the UMNO. Those who converted to Islam were rewarded with improved living conditions and/or cash payments. In Kelantan and Terengganu, PAS was also active in *dakwah* programs for *Orang Asli* in those states.

One of the groups best known for its efforts to expand Islamic activities is ABIM (*Angkatan Belia Islam Malaysia*, Malaysian Muslim Youth Movement), established by students of the University of Malaya (Kuala Lumpur) in 1971. The group's motto was 'toward building a society that is based on the principles of Islam' and it provided support for graduates to implement Islamic principles in the community after they left the university. It also supported a school to help educate those who could not afford to further their education and it coordinated the *dakwah* activities of a number of Muslim youth groups. One of the founders of ABIM, Anwar Ibrahim, was destined to become an international name in the 1990s.

Anwar Ibrahim

Born in 1947, Anwar studied at Malay College, Kuala Kangsar between 1960 and 1966 where he was school captain. He was studying at the University of Malaya at the time of the 1969 riots and supported the formation of ABIM because he believed in applying Islamic principles to everyday life. The members of ABIM urged Malays to see Islam as guide for life, not limited to the observance of its prescribed rituals.

Despite being urged by Prime Minister Tun Razak and others to enter politics, Anwar spent the 1970s as principal of the private school ABIM had founded and as an activist for Muslim and other youth organisations. During his period as president of ABIM he was an articulate critic of government policies and in 1974 he was arrested under the ISA and detained for two years without trial. In 1981, when Dr Mahathir became prime minister, he urged Anwar to join the UMNO and stand for election. To the surprise of many of his followers, Anwar agreed and campaigned for a seat in his home region of Penang. He was successful and entered Parliament in 1982 as a deputy minister in the Prime Minister's Department (for Islamic affairs) to be followed by rapid promotions through several ministries until, in 1993, he was both minister for finance and deputy prime minister.

Many who had followed Anwar because he was a trenchant critic of the National Front were shocked when he seemed to change sides. Some believed Dr Mahathir had wooed Anwar so that the constituency of ardent young Muslims who supported him would also join the UMNO. From the beginning of his prime ministership, Dr Mahathir had pursued a policy of identifying 'moderate' elements in the *dakwah* movement and incorporating them into government programs. In this way, the government contributed funding towards the establishment of an Islamic bank, an International Islamic University and an Islamic insurance company, supported the establishment of Islamic think-tanks and introduced compulsory courses on Islamic civilisation into university degrees. Anwar's supporters claimed that he had been instrumental in increasing the government's attention to Islam. Both Anwar and Dr Mahathir claimed that they were seeking to apply the universal values of Islam such as social justice, self-discipline, humanitarianism and ethics to all areas of government. Anwar believed that Muslims should be contributing to the shaping of a new world by reasserting the universalism of Islam, 'its values of justice, compassion and tolerance'.[2] This understanding of Islam has been termed 'moderate Islam' and is understood by both Malaysians and non-Malaysians to mean the promotion of Islamic principles which support modernisation and humanistic values, and which are tolerant of diversity and of other religions. 'Moderate Islam' has an established history in Malaysia through the writings and work of innovators such as Syed Shaykh al-Hady, in the early 20th century.

Dr Mahathir has contrasted 'moderate Islam' with 'radical Islam', that is, the expression of Islam which is more literal in its interpretation of the Qur'an and more aggressive in its desire to persuade others to its views. During the 1980s, several Muslim organisations in Malaysia tried to implement as literally as possible the injunctions of Islam (including Islamic law). They attracted considerable public attention because of their Middle-Eastern style of dress, their practice of polygamy and the fact that many of their adherents were highly educated Malays, employed in important positions. The best known of these organisations was the Darul Arqam movement founded in 1968 as a study group for Muslims wanting to deepen their knowledge of Islam. Taking its name from one of the Companions of the Prophet Muhammad, it then developed into an attempt to recreate Muslim life as it had been during his lifetime. Darul Arqam established its own villages, cooperative business ventures and independent education system, so that it, in fact, offered a real alternative to both the government and to PAS. By the early 1990s, it claimed to have over 10 000 members and business assets worth over MR$300 million. With an educated, committed, highly organised and successful membership, Darul Arqam was thriving and gaining an increasingly high profile. Dr Mahathir responded by accusing it of deviating from the fundamental principles of Islam (a very serious allegation) and in 1994 the movement was officially banned and declared an illegal organisation.

Over the years of his term in office, Dr Mahathir has labelled as 'radical' or 'extreme' Muslim groups which oppose the policies of his government. He has argued that 'radical Islam' is hostile to technological development, discriminates against non-Muslims and is a threat to Malaysia's racial harmony and the stability of the nation. On those grounds he has used the ISA to detain Muslim leaders and activists. He has specifically accused PAS of promoting 'radical Islam', of being hostile to non-Muslims and against rapid modernisation as promoted by his government.

Dr Mahathir's criticisms of PAS grew in direct proportion to its electoral successes. After the riots of 1969, PAS agreed to join the National Front to assist national unity but with the increasing profile of international Islam from the mid-1970s, some of the younger members of PAS became dissatisfied with the party's politics of accommodation. As a result, in 1978, PAS withdrew from the National Front which responded by declaring a State of Emergency in Kelantan, dismissing the elected government and calling a snap election. Employing tactics such as draconian censorship measures (including a ban on public rallies), the National Front roundly defeated PAS in its traditional heartlands and a group of PAS's younger members, most of whom had degrees from Middle Eastern universities, took over leadership positions. The best known of these 'young Turks' (as they were called) became long-term leaders of PAS: Haji Fadzil Noor, Haji Nik Abdul Aziz (Kelantan) and Haji Abdul Hadi Awang (Terengganu). In the mid-1980s, they began a campaign to present PAS as the party which fought to protect the poor and oppressed and uphold justice.

In this way, PAS aligned itself with social justice and criticised the NEP as being racially oriented and against the teachings of Islam that all are equal. Viewed by many as an attempt to win Chinese support for PAS, any gains from this policy have to be set against the criticism that PAS supports the implementation of Islamic law and the establishment of an Islamic state.

Dr Mahathir has exploited the feeling of 'threat' which many Malaysians (particularly non-Muslims but also middle-class 'moderate' Malays) feel a PAS-dominated government would pose if it were elected to take power at the federal level. In the general elections of 1999, PAS won an overwhelming majority in Kelantan and Terengganu and formed government in those states. An analysis of voting support for the UMNO revealed that it had lost half the Malay vote and, for the first time in its history, had had to rely heavily on support from Chinese and Indian voters. While commentators in Malaysia believe that the Malay desertion of the UMNO was a protest against the treatment of Anwar Ibrahim, Dr Mahathir presented the swing against him as a move towards support for 'Islamic radicalism'. He stressed that the UMNO would not embrace a more extreme form of Islam to recapture electorates lost to PAS.

The acts of terrorism conducted by extremists in the United States in September 2001 are alleged to have been perpetrated by Muslims in the name of Islam. Dr Mahathir used this as an opportunity to step-up government pressure on Muslim activists in PAS and other Malaysian organisations and to detain them under the ISA. He continued to present the UMNO's programs for Islam as the only way to foster development and prosperity in Malaysia. The leaders of PAS continued to negotiate their political agenda with various groups within the party, which range from hardliners (who insist on a literal and narrow interpretation of the Qur'an) to pious, 'ordinary' Malays, and younger, tertiary-educated and IT-literate middle-class professionals. To gain increased support, PAS would need to convince all Malaysians that their rights and beliefs would be protected and respected under a PAS-led federal government. They are far from securing that credibility and many Malaysians fear that if PAS insisted on the implementation of Islamic law it would seriously inhibit their established lifestyles.

Dr Mahathir Mohamad

Dr Mahathir's exceptionally long period in office must be ascribed in large measure to his control of power and his personal style which he has developed as a composite image of closeness to ordinary Malaysians, to high flying business entrepreneurs and to Malay nationalists. He has achieved this through a rhetoric which emphasises Malaysia's achievements and aspirations in both national and international contexts, and by projecting a public image of charm and charisma. This image gained him the respect of many Malaysians and even gave him the status to challenge the traditional authority of the Malay sultans. Dr Mahathir, it can be argued, has taken key elements from traditional ideas about 'power' in Malay society and used them in a contemporary context to maintain power for himself and the UMNO.

Mahathir Mohamad was born in Kedah in 1925, where his father was a teacher in the first government English school in 1908. His father remained with the school which later became the Sultan Hamid College, as its first headmaster. Mahathir's own schooling was interrupted by the Japanese Occupation, during which he helped run a small market stall. After the war, he completed his schooling, joined the UMNO early in its life, and moved to Singapore in the late 1940s to study Medicine. Unlike Tunku Abdul Rahman and Hussein Onn, he did not go to Britain for his tertiary education, nor was he from the traditional Malay ruling class.

By 1953, he had returned to Kedah and in 1957 established the first private medical clinic to be run by a Malay doctor. Here, he gained a reputation for his kindness and concern for poorer Malay patients and when elected to Parliament in 1964, championed the rights of Malays. Mahathir was defeated in the 1969 general elections by a PAS candidate, the well-known Muslim scholar Haji Yusof Rawa. Mahathir's criticism of Prime Minister Tunku Abdul Rahman led to his expulsion from the UMNO but, undeterred, Mahathir developed his ideas about the social and economic condition of the Malays and in 1970, published them in a book entitled *The Malay Dilemma*.

Under Tun Razak's leadership of the UMNO, Mahathir was restored to the party and in 1974 was appointed minister of education, followed in 1976 by promotion to deputy prime minister when Hussein Onn succeeded Tun Razak. In 1978, Mahathir took over the ministry of trade and industry and initiated his policies for increasing the pace and quality of Malaysia's industrialisation (as he would later promote high technology). His determination that Malaysia would have its own car, the Proton Saga, is a telling example of his philosophy. What mattered to him was not so much the vehicle but rather the technology and know-how it would bring to Malaysia and the role that would play in enriching the knowledge and experience of those involved in its production. He was also well aware of the boost to morale which a 'national car' would provide for all Malaysians.

In 1981, Mahathir succeeded Hussein Onn as prime minister and leader of the UMNO, a position he still holds at the time of writing (2002). The early years of Mahathir's national leadership were characterised by his clash with the sultans, the symbols of Malay traditional authority and a series of serious financial scandals involving key figures in his government. It was largely his personal political skills which resulted in impressive Malay support for the UMNO in the general elections of 1986 although a substantial number of Chinese voters deserted the MCA, UMNO's alliance partner, and supported the opposition parties, Gerakan and DAP.

Despite the UMNO's electoral success under Mahathir, the Kelantan politician Tengku Razaleigh, together with Musa Hitam, decided to mount a leadership challenge at the UMNO General Assembly of 1987. Although supported by members of the UMNO who were dismayed by the preceding years of scandals, cronyism and mismanagement, they lost narrowly to Dr Mahathir and all UMNO members who had been aligned with Razaleigh and Musa were excluded from positions in the next Mahathir cabinet. Malay concepts of loyalty demanded absolute support for the leader and Mahathir indicated he would not tolerate criticism or opposition in his ranks.

The internal divisions within the UMNO reflected a wider dissatisfaction with the government's performance and when social rights campaigners voiced their concerns, and Chinese protests about government interference in Chinese schools became stronger, Dr Mahathir responded by invoking the Internal Security Act. In a widespread campaign known as Operation Lalang (the name of a hardy grass species which, if unchecked, becomes difficult to eradicate) 119 people were detained, among them leading opposition politicians, academics, conservationists and Chandra Muzaffar, leader of a prominent social justice movement. While most of those arrested were released after several months' detention, some were held for well over one year. Dr Mahathir's use of the ISA was seen by critics of the government as an abuse of its powers and prompted some members of the judiciary to question the propriety of using the law in this way. Dr Mahathir responded by limiting the role of the judiciary.

Mahathir's vision for Malaysia

Dr Mahathir's political philosophy was developed in his first decade in politics (although he had begun formulating it while a medical student in the late 1940s). Two decades later, he stated that he still held to that philosophy, as set out in his two books, *The Malay Dilemma* (1970) and *The Challenge* (1976). In *The Malay Dilemma*, he claims that the Malay sense of being overtaken by non-Malays (especially in the areas of education and commerce) in 'their own land' was the root cause of their 'dilemma'. He believed that only a policy of 'constructive protection' through special state-sponsored programs would succeed in 'rehabilitating' the Malays. In *The Challenge* he is critical of those traditional values in Malay culture which discourage competition and material success and urges the strengthening of values, such as self-discipline and a thirst for knowledge, which foster economic advancement. He notes that many of those values are also promoted by Islam and these, he says, should be practised by the Malays.

In 1991, the final phase of Dr Mahathir's vision for Malaysia's future was announced in a speech to the newly-established Malaysian Business Council entitled 'Malaysia: The Way Forward'. The program he outlined became known as 'Vision 2020', a 30-year plan to replace the NEP and designed to make Malaysia a fully developed nation by the year 2020. In Vision 2020, the NEP emphasis on advancing the Bumiputeras was broadened to encompass all Malaysians. The aim was to create a united Malaysia with a 'Malaysian race' living in prosperity and harmony under a system of Malaysian democracy in a society which valued knowledge, economic success and dynamism, and which was inspired by values of tolerance and compassion.

Although Vision 2020 is a vision for all Malaysians, Dr Mahathir maintained his long-standing concern for the Malays as the definitive people of Malaysia and promoted the term 'the New Malay' (*Melayu Baru*) to describe the kind of Malay who would implement the new program. Skilled in high technology, the New Malay would be creative in business, confident in the international world and capable of leading Malaysia successfully into the 21st century. He did not describe Chinese or Indians in these terms nor did he make any reference to the *Orang Asli*.

Dr Mahathir's Vision 2020 also reaffirmed his views on Malaysia's place in world affairs which he expressed in terms which would appeal to his domestic constituency. During his early years as prime minister, he continued Tun Razak's policy of non-alignment (although Malaysia remained a member of the Commonwealth) and also continued the links established by Tun Razak with the Middle East and the Organisation of Islamic Conference, as well as with ASEAN. However, his special contribution to Malaysia's global orientation was an open admiration for the achievements of Japan and South Korea which he expressed in his 'Look East' policy of 1981. He was strident in his criticism of Britain and other developed nations for their exploitation of their former colonies and their post-colonial demands that under-developed nations should comply with policies such as environmental conservation which, he argued, hindered Third World development. Dr Mahathir's articulate and confident speeches to international audiences raised Malaysia's profile and he established a reputation as a leading spokesperson for issues concerning the Third World, not only in the ASEAN region but also for many African nations.

The limits of power: the sultans and the judiciary

In 1983, Malaysia faced a constitutional crisis which resulted from the National Front's attempts to define more strictly the limits to royal authority. In the view of Dr Mahathir's government, the concept of royal power in traditional Malay society (a supernatural force which gives the sultan unique personal powers) was not appropriate for the workings of a constitutional democracy. As well, each of the state sultans was very wealthy, maintained extravagant lifestyles and, by using their patronage, gained controlling interests in businesses and state corporations. To ensure that the power of the king of Malaysia (*Yang Dipertuan Agong*, one of the hereditary state sultans chosen every five years by his fellow sultans) would not over-ride that of the Parliament, legislation was introduced to amend the Constitution. The amendment, to have effect at both federal and state levels, stated that if the king's assent to Bills were not forthcoming the Bills would automatically become law. After consultation with his fellow rulers, whose powers at the state level were also under threat, the king refused his assent. As a result, between October and December 1983 there was a legal impasse between the king and the government and large-scale public rallies were organised in support of each side. A compromise was reached in December which saved face for all involved but Dr Mahathir's warning to the sultans was clear. The issue re-emerged in 1993, when an act of assault by one of the sultans prompted the passing of a constitutional amendment to limit legal immunity for the sultans and their power to grant pardons.

Dr Mahathir's views on the outmoded nature of feudal authority in Malay society had been expressed clearly in *The Malay Dilemma* and the legislation to curb the powers of the sultans was designed to recognise that power resided with Parliament (and the people) rather than with hereditary rulers. These actions suggested that Dr Mahathir and the National Front respected and supported the constitutional framework of the state and its mechanisms for protecting due process. In 1988, however, Dr Mahathir advised the king to suspend the head of the judiciary, who, together with two Supreme Court judges, was later dismissed. The dismissals came after several legal judgements in 1986 and 1987 which had not pleased the government. There had been earlier indications of Dr Mahathir's displeasure with the judiciary: several lawyers had been detained under Operation Lalang and in a parliamentary speech in December 1987, he had claimed that the judiciary was interpreting the law in a way which undermined the authority of Parliament.

Closely linked with Dr Mahathir's attitude to the judiciary was a challenge to the legality of the UMNO as a political party. In 1987, Dr Mahathir had been challenged as leader of the UMNO by Tengku Razaleigh. When Dr Mahathir narrowly won the leadership ballot, Tengku Razaleigh brought the legality of the election before the courts and, in February 1988, they ruled that because of certain irregularities in its structure, the UMNO was an illegal organisation which had to be dissolved. This precipitated what became known as 'the UMNO crisis'. Dr Mahathir reacted quickly and formed a new party, the New UMNO (*UMNO Baru*) and initiated a major publicity strategy known as the SEMARAK (*Setia Bersama Rakyat*, Loyalty with the People) campaign, to attract members to the party and consolidate his position as its leader.

The ruling declaring the UMNO an 'illegal' organisation (because some of its branches were not registered) was cited by the UMNO as proof of the judiciary's independence. It was also precisely the outcome needed by Dr Mahathir to prevent Tengku Razaleigh's supporters increasing their position within the old UMNO. However, there were signs that future rulings would not always be in the UMNO's interests and shortly afterwards, in March 1988, constitutional amendments were passed so that judicial power was restricted by executive control. It was the concern and the protests by individual judges which led to their eventual dismissal. The treatment of these judges was strongly criticised by the international legal community. International bodies of jurists continue to monitor the treatment of the judiciary in Malaysia. Since the dismissals there has also been international concern expressed about some judicial appointments and controversial judgements.

Patronage under pressure: the 1997 financial crisis

The SEMARAK campaign, to publicise and attract members to Dr Mahathir's New UMNO party, was executed through a series of mass public rallies, each addressed by Dr Mahathir, lavishly funded by federal and state money and symbolised by the 76-metre Semarak Tower (costing MR$1.5 million, paid for by the federal government). Civil servants were involved in organising the rallies to ensure there was a huge turn-out of admiring Malays. In his speeches, Dr Mahathir continually stressed the need for Malay unity and support for his government so that it could continue to work for the prosperity and welfare of all. As well, Dr Mahathir ensured that the press and public media gave little or no coverage to his opponents, who were refused permission to hold public rallies.

Opposition groups, including those supporting Tengku Razaleigh, could not match the huge funding which the prime minister was able to call on to run his campaign. The execution of the SEMARAK campaign could be compared with the tactics of the Malay sultans from the Srivijaya and Melaka periods. Traditional rulers relied on attracting loyal followers and needed access to resources to reward and maintain them. Similar concepts of patronage and reward lay at the heart of the UMNO (and New UMNO) system which relied on the fruits of the NEP for access to sources of wealth. As a leading political scientist has noted:

> The rapid expansion of the state's role in business also placed vastly enhanced patronage resources in the hands of the government leaders who were able to consolidate their political power through the distribution of business opportunities to political supporters . . . Established non-Malay businesspeople became increasingly dependent on government patronage while a new class of dependent Malay businesspeople was created.[3]

The National Front had ensured that the government controlled the key areas of the economy and within the cabinet different ministers had access to different state corporations and enterprises and so built their own networks of patronage. When the government was forced to curtail spending in the economic downturn of the early to mid-1980s, the slow-down flowed through to its dependent clients and some were faced with bankruptcy. The competition for linkages with successful ministers contributed to the leadership struggle within the UMNO and fuelled the UMNO crisis of 1987–88. The lavish spending of the SEMARAK campaign may have had the dual purpose of attracting mass support for the New UMNO as well as restoring confidence in the prime minister's ability to tap into major funding resources.

A decade after the UMNO crisis, the economic collapse of 1997 which began in Asia but spread globally, again placed the UMNO networks of patronage under pressure. The fall of prominent Malay tycoons and rumours about the safety of state trust funds (especially the all-important civil service pension fund) increased public concern about corruption and mismanagement by senior members of the UMNO. Competition within the UMNO for access to resources and for control of the party developed in a way which was reminiscent of 1987. Both Dr Mahathir and Anwar Ibrahim, as his deputy prime minister, announced that corruption would not be countenanced. During 1997, Anwar stood in for Dr Mahathir on several occasions and, when he called for cutbacks in government spending, it became clear that his handling of Malaysia's response to the regional economic crisis and his views on who should be rescued contrasted with those of the prime minister. Anwar was also quoted as speaking out strongly in support of human rights and his views on democracy, civil society, ethics, Islam (as a religion of tolerance) and synergies between East and West, became widely available in 1996 when his book *The Asian Renaissance* was published.

At the UMNO General Assembly in June 1998, supporters of Anwar openly criticised the corruption and nepotism they claimed existed within the UMNO and their comments were perceived as an attack against the prime minister. Soon afterwards, a campaign against Anwar was revived through poison pen letters and accusations about his morals. On the basis of these allegations, on 2 September 1998, Dr Mahathir dismissed Anwar as deputy prime minister and finance minister and he was later expelled also from the UMNO. With the Commonwealth Games opening in Kuala Lumpur, further public action against Anwar was restrained and for a few weeks he was able to travel and address mass rallies of his supporters who were angry and stunned by his treatment. In response to the increasing signs of public hostility towards Dr Mahathir, Anwar was arrested, together with a number of his leading supporters, under the ISA on 20 September and taken into detention from which he has not been released at the time of writing (2002). The Malaysian Bar Council later issued statements about their concern over the manner of Anwar's arrest, his subsequent assault while in police custody and the conduct of his trial. Many Malaysians described Anwar's treatment in terms of the traditional epic, the *Malay Annals*. They referred to the social contract between the first Malay ruler and his chief in which the chief swore loyalty to the ruler who on his part agreed never to publicly humiliate the chief or his descendants. Dr Mahathir's behaviour was seen as arbitrary and cruel and not worthy of a leader.

Many within Malaysia saw Anwar's detention under the ISA as just one in a series of repressive measures taken by the government to silence influential critics. They predicted that the wave of mass demonstrations which occurred immediately after Anwar's arrest would lead to a new public interest in the actions of the National Front and greater scrutiny of its policies and attitudes. They anticipated that the movement for reform (*Reformasi*) in Indonesia which was working for greater government transparency and accountability might be duplicated in Malaysia.

In an interview for the international weekly the *Far Eastern Economic Review* (October 24 1996) two years before the detention of Anwar, Dr Mahathir defended his use of the ISA. He is quoted as saying that the 'multiracial, multireligious, multicultural and multilingual' differences among Malaysians make open debate dangerous. He believes, 'The threat is from the inside. So we've to be armed, so to speak. Not with guns but with the necessary laws to make sure the country remains stable.' Political stability, he argued, is essential if Malaysia is to achieve the 7 per cent annual growth rate which will bring it to developed nation status by 2020. In his view, and in the view of many influential Malaysians, it is only an UMNO-led coalition which can guarantee the necessary degree of political stability for continued economic growth.

Alternative visions: Dr Wan Azizah Ismail

After the arrest of Anwar Ibrahim, his wife, Dr Wan Azizah, became a symbol of the fight for reform in Malaysian politics. Many educated Malaysians were able to identify with her because she embodied the best of the modern world and the values Malays admired such as modesty and gentleness, combined with being the mother of six children. Dr Wan Azizah, in fact, represented all the qualities the NEP had been designed to foster in Malays and her successful career as a doctor, specialising in opthalmology, made her an excellent example of Dr Mahathir's 'New Malay' (*Melayu Baru*). Since the 1980s, Malaysian women have held senior positions in the business world, civil service and the professions. Several have held cabinet rank but Wan Azizah was the first to head a political party.

Datin Seri Dr Wan Azizah Wan Ismail was born in Singapore in 1952, the daughter of Dato Wan Ismail (originally from Palembang and of Arab descent) and Datin Mariah (of Korean descent). Wan Azizah's father was a clinical psychologist who had worked during the later years of the Emergency as director of psychological warfare, and while he was studying in London, sent his daughter to stay with relatives in Kedah. Wan Azizah was educated at St Nicholas Convent in Alor Setar and an elite college in Seremban before entering the University of Malaya to study Medicine. Almost immediately she was awarded a government scholarship (as part of the NEP) to study at the Royal College of Surgeons, Dublin. After six years in Dublin, Wan Azizah completed her medical degree and was awarded the MacNaughton-Jones gold medal for Obstetrics and Gynaecology by the Royal College. She returned to Kuala Lumpur in 1978 to complete her internship at the General Hospital before joining the University Hospital in Petaling Jaya in 1980, the year she married Anwar Ibrahim. In 1984, she qualified as a specialist in Opthalmology in Dublin and worked also as a lecturer in Opthalmology at the University of Malaya. When her husband was appointed deputy prime minister in 1994, Wan Azizah retired from her professional career and, besides raising her family, played an active role as patron for a wide range of medical and humanitarian organisations.

None of her training prepared Dr Wan Azizah for the role she would play after her husband's detention. Anwar was arrested at home on 20 September 1998 by a large number of masked security officials. Exactly one week later, two new opposition coalitions, the National Front for People's Democracy (*Gagasan Demokrasi Rakyat*) led by Chua Tian Chang, and the Malaysian People's Justice Movement (*Gerakan Keadilan Rakyat Malaysia*) led by PAS President Datuk Fadzil Noor, were formed to work for reform and justice. On 10 December 1998, a third coalition, the Movement for Social Justice (*Pergerakan Keadilan Sosial*) was announced, with Dr Wan Azizah as its president. The appearance of the three new social justice coalitions, prompted by the dismissal and arrest of Anwar, represented renewed efforts to work across the ethnic divide for social and political reform. Membership of the coalitions covered a broad spectrum of middle class Malaysians and included a wide range of non-government organisations and human rights groups.

In November 1998, Anwar Ibrahim was brought to trial on four charges of obstructing the course of justice. As the trial proceeded, the judge's rulings raised grave concerns over his procedure and practice (for example, 25 days of evidence was ruled irrelevant and ten defence witnesses were excluded). In April 1999, Anwar was found guilty of all four charges and sentenced to six years imprisonment on each charge, to be served concurrently. In the same month, the Movement for Social Justice was registered as a political party called the National Justice Party (*Parti Keadilan Nasional* or *keADILan*), led by Dr Wan Azizah and with Chandra Muzaffar as Deputy.

The tenth general elections of November 1999 provided opposition parties with their first chance to challenge the UMNO-led National Front. Calling itself the Alternative Front (*Barisan Alternatif*), four parties—PAS, the Chinese Democratic Action Party (DAP), the socialist Malaysian People's Party (PRM) and the National Justice

Party—joined together to campaign for 'a just and democratic Malaysia'. Dr Mahathir's response was to play on non-Muslims' fears of the spectre of an extremist Muslim government if PAS and its partners were voted in. Dr Mahathir warned voters repeatedly that support for the Alternative Front would be votes against religious freedom. This was countered by a strong statement from Anwar in prison, read by Dr Wan Azizah, that there would be no threats of violence or religious extremism if Dr Mahathir were voted out of office.

The results of the November 1999 general elections were the worst ever for the UMNO. It lost 22 seats, nine of which had been held by ministers or deputy ministers. According to some UMNO leaders, the party may have won less than 40 per cent of the vote. The National Front only retained office because non-Malay voters remained loyal to the government. For the first time in Malaysia's history, Malay voters deserted the UMNO in large numbers and supported PAS and, to a lesser extent, the National Justice Party of Dr Wan Azizah. PAS more than doubled its number of federal seats and won a huge majority at the state level in both Kelantan and Terengganu. Dr Wan Azizah won a seat in Penang and four other members of her party were elected.

In August 2000, the verdict of Anwar's second trial, for sodomy, was delivered and he was sentenced to a further nine years in gaol, making his term a total of 15 years. International and regional legal organisations expressed criticism of Malaysia's judicial system. Within Malaysia, the government's handling of Anwar's trial and its treatment of alleged Muslim extremists lowered its credibility in the eyes of many of its citizens. Aware that the government controlled the public media, Malaysians turned to alternative sources for information on contemporary events. The official publication of PAS (*Harakah*) increased its circulation to 300 000, attracting government attention and restrictions on its publication. To avoid official censorship and restrictions, Malaysians developed hundreds of new websites, email networks and online sources of news and commentary, the most successful of which is *malaysiakini.com* which has attracted a huge response from Internet users. With at least two million Malaysians having access to the Internet, it is no longer possible for the government to control information or criticism of its policies. Alternative visions are available.

Justice for all

The ongoing movement for *Reformasi* which followed the sacking of Anwar Ibrahim proved that tens of thousands of Malaysians have strong views about how their future could and should be shaped. What is lacking are channels and networks to integrate the opinions of representatives of all Malaysia's communities. Parliament under Dr Mahathir has not always fulfilled that role. The *Orang Asli* are just one group of Malaysians who feel they are not heard there. Although each of the major political factions in Malaysia, the UMNO, PAS and *keADILan*, include the concept of 'justice' in their political platforms, they have not succeeded in achieving social justice for all their followers.

The results of the 1999 elections revealed deep fissures in the Malay community, reflected in the shift in Malay support from the UMNO to PAS and *keADILan*, and increased pressure for the UMNO to respond positively to its critics. The choices for the UMNO are not easy. If it tries to replace its networks of patronage with a merit-based and more inclusive system, it jeopardises its current base of support with Malay tycoons and the Malay upper class elite. If it continues to demonise PAS as a party of Muslim extremists, it may lose more credibility and more Malay votes. A major consequence for the UMNO of losing Malay support would be the loss of its dominant position in the ruling National Front and consequently its access to the national revenues which pay its backers and clients. It is this fear which has been behind the implementation of repressive and authoritarian measures against critics of the UMNO's policies, including Anwar, leading members of PAS, journalists and academics.

The opposition parties face their own dilemmas. The coalition which came together as the Alternative Front to fight the 1999 elections has been seriously weakened by internal dissension and the loss of many of its key *keADILan* figures who were detained under the ISA in 2001. The diverse groups meeting under the umbrella of *keADILan* remain in the process of establishing their priorities, negotiating common ground and gaining experience in the tough world of Malaysian politics. They also face difficulties accepting the views of some of the more hardline members of PAS. The major issues being debated in Malaysia as it enters the new millennium include affirmative action policies for Malays, reform of business and government practices, liberal democracy, conservative (literalist) Islam, militant (radical) Islam and moderate (tolerant) Islam. In the early 21st century each has persuasive and well-educated advocates, and even if they are subject to censorship and detention their followers can still maintain contact through various forms of information technology.

Like its regional neighbours, Malaysia is in a period of transition from a system of patronage politics to something else. Any future system will have to include at least a recognition of the values and ethics of the dominant religion, Islam, and this will have to be balanced by a more inclusive form of representation for all Malaysians. In 1996, in an article for *Time* magazine, Anwar Ibrahim wrote:

> A plural, multi-religious society is living perpetually on the brink of catastrophe. Relations between Muslims and non-Muslims must be governed by moral and ethical considerations. The seeds of militancy are everywhere and each community must ensure that they will not germinate and multiply through discontent and alienation. So, participation and social justice is fundamental in Southeast Asia in the age of the nation-state . . . The challenge to Muslims and the people of other confessions is to

effectively articulate their moral vision and intensify the search for common ethical ground.[4]

Anwar's vision suggests a move from the traditional Malay concept of power (residing in one charismatic leader) to a position where deliberation, debate and consensus are used to find solutions and resolve disputes. This is the method traditionally used by Malaysia's original peoples, the *Orang Asli*. Sadly, however, in the early 21st century their vision for their own future and that of Malaysia is rarely heard.

A sustainable future?

The policies of Dr Mahathir, in office for longer than the combined terms of his three predecessors, have committed Malaysia to an economic and social future which it will be difficult for his successors to change. His success in achieving consistently strong levels of growth has raised the expectations of the majority of Malaysians about the standard of living they can aspire to, even if that level is beyond the reach of some. As a Malaysian commentator has noted, 'One of Mahathir's signal triumphs was to have persuaded Malaysian society that "less politics" and "more economics", "less democracy" and "greater stability" were the guarantees of continued prosperity.'[5] The promised prosperity, however, has often been at the expense of the environment, sound financial practices and, last but not least, the land rights of the weakest groups in Malaysian society. The development of Sarawak provides examples of the some of the long-term effects of Dr Mahathir's emphasis on growth at all costs. It indicates also the complex links between politics and economic practices, federal–state relations and environmental degradation.

Sarawak and Sabah joined the Federation of Malaysia on the understanding that the federal government would allocate special funding to develop these two states which were behind the Peninsula in services and basic infrastructure. What happened was the reverse. In the early 1970s, both states surrendered their rights to finds of oil and gas to the federal government (through Petronas) in return for 5 per cent of the revenues derived from those resources. Since then, the revenues derived by the federal government from oil and gas have far outstripped the flow of funding from the centre to Sarawak. One of the few state-based sources of income left to Sarawak was control over land, particularly for logging and development of plantation enterprises. To achieve this, the state government amended the Sarawak Land Code in 1996 so that it became possible to convert native customary rights to land to private ownership for plantation purposes.

The new Land Code contains provisions for traditional owners to contest the conversion of title, to be granted a 30 per cent interest in a plantation company if the deal proceeds successfully, and for the land to revert to native title after 60 years, but only after complex conditions are met. In fact, it became clear that 'Most farmers had little knowledge of or control over the process followed by the companies, even though they would be substantive owners of a joint venture concern responsible for repayment of all loans and up-front expenses'.[6] Although in the short term the Sarawak state government will receive some increase in revenues, the long-term costs may be irreversible. Land clearing necessary for plantation development not only increases erosion, leading to siltation of rivers, but also destroys the bio-diversity and delicate ecosystems for which Borneo has long been famous. In the context of global markets, the monoculture which characterises plantations (especially vast plantings of oil palm) precludes the diversity which can respond to changes in world demand. The plantations may be trapped into huge investments in products for which there is declining market interest. But, like the threat to the environment, the social costs for the traditional land owners may have the most serious repercussions. Unable to use their lands for their own purposes, the majority of the traditional owners have to seek employment elsewhere and almost inevitably move to towns and cities where they are forced to adopt a totally different way of life and often this is, in every sense, on the margins.

One alternative to this pattern would be for a new federal–state agreement over the distribution of the oil and gas revenues so that a greater percentage of profits were returned to states. Militating against this possibility is the fact that the UMNO and the Office of the Prime Minister are heavily dependent on oil and gas profits flowing to them through Petronas. The patronage politics of the major political parties, especially the UMNO, have become so entrenched that loss of revenue to the central government might cause its collapse. In addition, the Bumiputera corporations supported under the NEP remain over-dependent on government support. The extent of their dependence was revealed in the wake of the 1997 regional financial crisis when some failed and others survived only because they were subsidised by the government. In 1998, when the combination of poor financial management and economic crisis drove major Bumiputera enterprises to the wall, Finance Minister Anwar Ibrahim reportedly thought that some of the weaker companies should be allowed to sink but was over-ruled by Dr Mahathir. Petronas falls under the jurisdiction of the Office of the Prime Minister and thus it was Petronas funds which he drew on to rescue the Malaysian International Shipping Corporation (a deal which involved a major purchase of tankers from a firm controlled by one of his sons), the Heavy Industries Corporation of Malaysia and the national automobile company, Proton. Petronas funds were also invested in Dr Mahathir's prestige projects of the Petronas Twin Towers and Putrajaya, the new 'smart city' and centre of government. Political life as the UMNO knows it would not be possible without income from Petronas.

During the early 1990s, Malaysia joined the ASEAN campaign to boost significantly the tourism industry in Southeast Asia. With the orang-utan as its symbol and with strong emphasis on its 'unspoilt' national parks and primal jungle, Malaysia's Tourism Promotion Board has recorded annual rates of well over seven million visitors and tourism has become the third biggest foreign exchange earner. Charter flights and special packages bring large groups to Sabah and Sarawak for 'ecotourism' and to experience the famed animals of Borneo at first hand. Some tourists are content to view indigenous crafts in 'cultural villages' close to the major cities but others want safari experiences into the interior to observe rare wildlife, their favourite creature undoubtedly being the orang-utan. The 'natural jungle' of the interior, especially areas accessible by river, has been diminished by logging, plantations and other development projects. The dilemma of developmentalism versus tourism places extra burdens of choice on the Sarawak state government and demands a rapid solution or the 'eco' part of tourism will become meaningless and the mascot of the Tourism Board, the orang-utan, will be lost.

Since Independence, two events have dominated the conduct of politics and the social fabric of Malaysia and neither is featured in the Museum of National History. The race riots of 1969 produced the New Economic Policy whose emphasis on the privileged treatment of Bumiputeras remains a dangerously emotive political issue. It has served as the excuse for harsh authoritarian action in the name of maintaining national stability. The second event was the dismissal and then public disgracing of Deputy Prime Minister Anwar Ibrahim in 1998, almost 30 years after the race riots.

The treatment of Anwar, coming after the emasculation of the judiciary, a number of political scandals and the use of public monies to bail out enterprises close to the UMNO, mobilised the greatest mass demonstrations against the government since Independence and fuelled the growing calls for reform of the political system. Dr Mahathir, as he had in 1987, used the ISA and a number of other authoritarian Ordinances and Acts to silence critics and dissidents, especially leaders of the Alternative Front parties. Since 2001, it has been increasingly difficult (although not impossible) for alternative views to be publicly aired. Malaysia faces threats not only to the future of its environment but also to the practice of Westminster-style democracy which it had claimed previously to uphold.

One of many Internet responses to the restricted opportunities for public debate is a monthly webzine for the under-35s, *SuaraAnum.com*. Supported by the Institute for Policy Research, a think-tank established by Anwar Ibrahim in the 1990s, it invites contributions from young Malaysians who believe in change and a diversity of views. This diversity, the site urges, should be accepted in 'the spirit of openness, tolerance and freedom'. Poems, short stories, sports features and social commentaries are posted on the site. The views they express all suggest that the challenges of a sustainable future are being taken seriously by the newly emerging generation. Writing in Malay, one contributor argues that Muslim religious teachers and intellectuals must struggle to develop a progressive Islam which looks at fundamental issues with openness and tolerance and that an Islamic framework need not reject ideas and concepts from other civilisations. The repetition of the words 'openness' and 'tolerance' throughout the article and the call for Muslim intellectuals to work harder to achieve these ideals suggests that many young Malaysians are disillusioned with both secular and religious leadership.

For the next generation of Malaysians, the prosperity and growth which characterised the Mahathir era may not be accepted as sufficient reason to ban peacefully expressed dissent. Alternative visions concerned with good governance, environmental conservation, human rights and 'Islamic democracy' have been formulated for some time but have had to be debated in covert rather than public ways. As the under-35s webzine *SuaraAnum.com* shows, the unstoppable process of generational change is underway and the attitudes of contributors to the site express a greater inclusiveness and tolerance than previous generations of Malaysians.

The history of Malaysia suggests that its peoples, past masters of diplomacy, alliances and adaptation will continue to participate actively in the flows of international trade and culture. And, as in the past, they will express their membership of the wider world in ways that are characteristically Malaysian. Independence came to Malaya only in 1957 and the federation with Sabah and Sarawak was achieved in 1963. This is a very young nation-state. There has been time for a mere two generations of leaders and they have presided over immense social, political and economic change. The successors to the current leadership wait in the wings and behind them are their replacements. The younger generations have had the opportunity to recognise both the benefits and the pitfalls of the New Economic Policy. Their views of Malaysia are more critical and their access to information is wider than any previous group. As the current leaders emphasise, there are great challenges ahead, but as the leadership patterns take shape for the 21st century, there are grounds for optimism that many of the mistakes of the older leaders will not be repeated.

APPENDICES

Time chart

40000 to 2500 BCE (approximately)

Palaeolithic and Hoabhinian period; currently oldest known evidence for human habitation of Borneo and Peninsula territories. Around 8000 BCE the land bridges between Borneo and the Peninsula were covered by sea and the territories separated.

2800 to 500 BCE (approximately)

Neolithic period with evidence of beginnings of expansion of Austronesian-speaking peoples through Sabah and Sarawak. Finds of earthenware pottery and possibility of horticulture.

500 BCE to 500 CE (approximately)

Metal age finds of bronze bells and drums associated with the Dongson culture of northern Vietnam as well as beads and pottery from India and China indicate active participation in international trade.

500 to 1300 CE

Iron production at Santubong (Sarawak); Bujang Valley culture (Kedah); megaliths in Sabah, Sarawak and southern parts of Peninsula; Srivijaya (southern Sumatra) as centre of extensive federation of trading networks.

1300 to 1511

Singapore and then Melaka follow Srivijaya as major entrepôts for international trade through Straits of Melaka.

1511

Portuguese occupy Melaka and Malay elite move south to continue. their trading activities from islands south of Singapore and from sites on the Johor River.

278

1550s to 1630s
Aceh (north Sumatra) becomes leading trade and cultural centre in the Melaka Straits. Acehnese carry off large numbers of people from the Peninsula to work in Aceh.

From the early 17th century
Increasing migrations from Minangkabau areas of Sumatra and from Sumatra's east coast into the river valleys south of Melaka in the region now known as Negeri Sembilan.

1641
The former court of Melaka, re-established in the Johor region, joins with Dutch forces from Batavia to dislodge the Portuguese from Melaka, which the Dutch then occupy.

1720s to 1780s
Migrations of Bugis from south Sulawesi into the territories of Johor including the Riau islands where they dislodge a Minangkabau pretender to the Johor sultanate and obtain permanent positions at the Johor court, one of their number becoming under king.

1766   First sultan of Selangor, a relative of the Bugis in Johor.

1786   Francis Light takes possession of Penang in the name of George III.

1794   Melaka held by British in trust for the Netherlands.

1819   Raffles signs treaty with Sultan Husain of Riau-Johor for rights to Singapore.

1821   Thais attack Kedah whose sultan takes refuge in Penang.

1824   Anglo-Dutch Treaty of London divides Malayo-Indonesian world into British and Dutch spheres.

1826   Penang, Melaka and Singapore administered by the British as the Straits Settlements.

1826   Agreement (not ratified) of Bangkok defines Thai and British spheres of influence on the Peninsula.

1838   Civil war in Kelantan.

1840s to 1886

Sultan Muhammad II establishes centralised government in Kelantan.

1839   Baginda Omar becomes sultan of Terengganu.

1842   James Brooke made rajah of Kuching and surrounding districts by sultan of Brunei.

1860s   *Temenggung* moves from Singapore to nearby Johor and builds a new capital, the beginning of Johor Bahru; in Perak, serious disturbances in tin mining areas provoked by Chinese secret societies.

1863   Charles Brooke succeeds his uncle as rajah of Sarawak.

1874   Pangkor Treaty between Perak ministers and governor of Straits Settlements for appointment of British resident to Perak.

1875   Birch, first British resident of Perak, assassinated.

1877   Sultan of Brunei leases parts of Sabah to the Dent brothers.

1881   North Borneo Chartered Company established in Sabah.

1885   Temenggung Abu Bakar assumes title of sultan of Johor.

1896   Perak, Selangor, Negeri Sembilan and Pahang rulers agree to become the Federated Malay States under a British resident-general in Kuala Lumpur.

1906   British resident in Brunei which becomes a British Protectorate.

1909   Anglo–Siamese Treaty recognises transfer of Siam's authority over Kedah, Perlis, Kelantan and Terengganu to British.

1917   Charles Brooke succeeded by son Vyner Brooke.

1921   Official census figures show that together, Chinese and Indians outnumber Malays causing Malay leaders concern about their future in 'their own' land.

1930   Effects of the Great Depression hit Malaya and mass unemployment results in labour unrest through the 1930s.

1941   Japanese land on Malay Peninsula.

1942 to 1945

Japanese Occupation of Malay territories during World War II.

1945 September to 1946 March

British Military Administration of Malaya.

1946 to 1948

Malayan Union.

1946 Formation of the UMNO.

Sarawak and British North Borneo become Crown Colonies.

1948 Federation of Malaya replaces Malayan Union scheme.

State of Emergency declared in response to violence of MCP.

1950 Briggs Plan of New Villages to quarantine Chinese settlers from MCP terrorists initiated.

1953 Administration of *Orang Asli* moved from state to federal control.

1955 First elections for local rule and Alliance coalition wins 51 of 52 seats.

1957 Independence declared on 31 August.

1960 End of Emergency.

1963 16 September, Federation of Malaysia (Sabah, Sarawak, Malay Peninsula and Singapore).

Indonesia calls for volunteers to crush Malaysia and 'liberate' the peoples in Sabah and Sarawak thus beginning 'Confrontation'.

1965 9 August, Singapore is expelled from the Federation.

1966 11 August, Confrontation ends with signing of Malaysia–Indonesia peace agreement.

1969 13 May race riots, emergency rule declared, Parliament suspended for 21 months and NOC established.

1970 Tun Abdul Razak succeeds Tunku Abdul Rahman as prime minister.

1972 NEP adopted; Constitution amended to control freedom of expression and ensure political dominance of Malays.

1974	Alliance government enlarged to include more parties and renamed National Front.
1976	Death of Tun Razak, succeeded by Dato Hussein Onn.
1981	Dato Onn retires; succeeded by his deputy, Dr Mahathir Mohamad.

1984 to 1986

Rise of non-Muslim Kadazan party in Sabah, success of Joseph Kitingan and loss of Sabah to National Front.

1987	Internal factions within the UMNO challenge Dr Mahathir; ISA used against critics of National Front.
1988	Chief justice suspended and two senior judges sacked.
1991	Vision 2020 and NDP publicised and promoted.
1993	Anwar Ibrahim deputy PM.
1995	General elections return the UMNO with highest ever vote.
1997	Asian economic crisis.
1998	September, Anwar Ibrahim dismissed from office then arrested under ISA.
	Reformasi (Reform) movement gains momentum and opposition coalitions formed.
1999	National Justice Party (keADILan) registered with Dr Wan Azizah as leader, joins an opposition coalition with PAS and others, called the Alternative Front.
1999	Anwar found guilty of obstructing justice and sentenced to six years imprisonment; general elections show major losses to the UMNO and gains to PAS.
2000	Anwar found guilty of sodomy and sentenced to a further nine years in gaol.
2001	11 September, terrorist attacks in USA; in following months Mahathir cracks down on 'Islamic extremists' including leaders of PAS.

Fact File

Alliance Party, 1957–69: the first coalition of political parties in Malaya, consisting of the **UMNO** and the Malayan Chinese Association (**MCA**) which successfully contested the municipal elections in Kuala Lumpur in 1952. Joined by the Malayan Indian Congress (**MIC**), it had a spectacular win in the first general elections of 1955 and formed the first government after Independence in 1957. It remained in power until the 1969 race riots. Succeeded by a more inclusive coalition known as the **National Front (Barisan Nasional)**.

Bajau Laut: sea-based peoples from the southern Philippines and eastern coasts of Sabah.

British North Borneo: the name given to the area administered by a chartered company from 1881. In 1888, it was granted Protectorate status under the British government and by 1901 included most of modern Sabah. It became a British colony in 1946 and joined the Federation of Malaysia in 1963.

Bumiputera: the term literally means 'sons of the soil' and theoretically applies to all indigenous peoples of Malaysia. Since Federation (1963) it is used in political contexts to mean the Malays and the native peoples of Sabah and Sarawak, all of whom are eligible for special affirmative action policies. The *Orang Asli* of peninsular Malaya, although also indigenous people, are rarely eligible for the same policies.

Communist Emergency: refers to the State of Emergency proclaimed by the British government of Malaya in 1948 in response to an armed uprising by the Malayan Communist Party (MCP) which soon went underground. Although the State of Emergency was lifted in 1960, an estimated 900 to 1200 members of the MCP crossed the border into southern Thailand and remained there until agreeing to end their struggle in 1989.

Confrontation: President Sukarno responded to the formation of the Federation of Malaysia by declaring a State of Confrontation between Indonesia and Malaysia, claiming the Borneo territories had been forced into federation against their will. There were numerous border incursions by Indonesian forces and suspension of diplomatic relations but under President Soeharto peace was restored in 1966.

Constituent states: 13 states and two federal territories (Kuala Lumpur and Labuan).

Currency: the Malaysian ringgit (RM) is based mainly on the US dollar. Before the 1970s it was pegged at RM3: US$1. During the 1970s with the move to flexible exchange rates, it ranged between RM2.4 to 2.7: US$1. Since 1997, it has been fixed at RM3.80: US$1.

Dongson: Bronze-Age culture characterised by large bronze artefacts (bells and drums) named after a site in North Vietnam where finds date back to 500 BCE

Federated Malay States (FMS): between 1874 and 1888, the Malay states of Perak, Selangor and Negeri Sembilan accepted a British resident and were British protectorates. In 1896, they were federated with Kuala Lumpur as capital.

Federation of Malaya 1948–57: consisted of nine Malay states plus Penang and Melaka. Singapore was a separate Crown Colony.

Federation of Malaysia: 16 September 1963: all states of the Federation of Malaya with Sarawak, British North Borneo thereafter called Sabah, and Singapore. Singapore left the federation in 1965.

Governor: until 1942, the head of the British administration of Malaya, located in Singapore held the position of governor of the Straits Settlements and was also high commissioner for the Federated Malay States.

High commissioner: See **Governor**

Hoabinhian: Term to describe Stone Age culture which was practised throughout Southeast Asia 14 000 to 4000 years ago and named after a site in North Vietnam, Hoa Binh.

Independence: 1957 for Federation of Malaya.

Land mass: 329 758 sq. km (peninsular Malaysia: 131 582 km; Sabah: 73 709 sq. km Sarawak: 124 445 sq. km).

Languages: Bahasa Malaysia (Malay—closely related to Indonesian) is the national language. Most tertiary-educated Malaysians speak English. A number of Chinese dialects are also spoken and many Indians speak Tamil. At the local level there are numerous dialects of Malay, and each ethnic group in Sabah and Sarawak has its own language. The languages of the *Orang Asli* have been divided into broad categories of Northern, Central and Southern Aslian.

Location: 1 to 7 degrees north of the Equator.

Malayan Union: the brief (1945–46) administrative reorganisation of the Peninsula by the British after World War II into a unitary state whereby the FMS and UMS with Penang and Melaka were merged. Sovereignty was to be transferred from the sultans to the British Crown (through a governor) and all citizens, whatever their origin, would have equal rights. Public protest was so great that in 1948 the Union was superseded by the Federation of Malaya.

MCA: Malayan Chinese Association led by Tan Cheng Lock which in 1952 joined with the **UMNO** led by Tunku Abdul Rahman to form a coalition known as the **Alliance**.

Merdeka: Independence (Malay).

MIC: Malay(si)an Indian Congress, founded in 1932, joined the **Alliance** before the general elections of 1955. It has remained a junior partner in the ruling coalition.

National Day: 31 August 1957 when Independence was officially declared.

National Front (*Barisan Nasional*): the coalition of political parties established in 1974 to include opposition parties and

285

restore confidence after the 1969 race riots. It is this alliance (without some of its original members, e.g. PAS) which has dominated Malaysian politics and won all general elections up to the time of writing.

New Development Policy (NDP): 1990–2020 economic program which succeeded the NEP and is designed to bring Malaysia to fully developed status by 2020 through growth of high technology industries and major new building projects (e.g. the Kuala Lumpur International Airport).

New Economic Policy (NEP): 1970–90 program to foster national unity by reducing poverty and discriminating positively in favour of increased development for Bumiputeras through education, state intervention in the business sector to restructure wealth ownership in favour of Bumiputeras. In 1990 the NEP was replaced by the **New Development Policy** (NDP).

Orang Asli: Original Peoples, (largely) non-Muslim indigenous peoples of the Peninsula who have chosen to remain unassimilated with Malay culture and on the basis of ethno-linguistic and socio-cultural criteria are divided into 19 subgroups.

Orang Suku Laut: Sea Peoples, Austronesian groups who specialise in collecting marine products and work the seas and islands of the Melaka Straits and the southerly parts of the South China Sea. A few groups of *Orang Suku Laut* still maintain parts of their traditional lifestyle but are under pressure from authorities in Indonesia, Singapore and Malaysia to settle permanently in one location.

PAS: *Persatuan Islam SaTanah Melayu* or Pan Malay(si)an Islamic Party (PMIP). Until the 1970s it was referred to often by its official English translation, PMIP, but thereafter its Malay acronym, PAS, was preferred. In 1973 the full Malay name was changed to *Parti Islam Se Malaysia* but PAS remained the acronym. PAS began in 1951 as a breakaway from the UMNO and has established its main following in the northern peninsular states of Kelantan, Terengganu and Kedah.

Political system: parliamentary democracy with nine of the states having a hereditary ruler (see *Yang Dipertuan Agong* below).

Population: 23 260 000 (as at 2000) with the official breakdown given as 61.9 per cent Bumiputera, 29.5 per cent Chinese, 8.6 per cent Indian.

Religions: Malays are Muslims, Chinese practise Confucianism, Taoism and Buddhism with some converts to Christianity and Indians are Hindus, Sikhs or Christians. The native peoples of the Peninsula and Sabah and Sarawak may follow indigenous religions and in the case of Sabah and Sarawak have been influenced by Christianity.

Rukunegara: (the Five Pillars of the Nation) Malaysia's national ideology based on Belief in God; Loyalty to Ruler and Nation; the Constitution; the Sovereignty of Law; Respect and Moral behaviour and adopted after the 1969 race riots to promote national unity and good citizenship.

Shari'ah/**Syari'a(h)**: the revealed or canonical law of Islam.

Straits Settlements: the British settlements of Penang, and the small strip of territory opposite called Province Wellesley, Melaka and Singapore. They were brought together for administrative purposes in 1826 with Singapore being named their administrative centre in 1832. In 1846, the sultan of Brunei ceded Labuan Island to Britain and it was administered as part of the Straits Settlements.

UMNO: established in March 1946 in response to British plans for a Malayan Union. First president was Dato' Onn who was succeeded by Tunku Abdul Rahman. Under his leadership the UMNO established a coalition with the Chinese party the **MCA** and then with the Indian **MIC** to form the **Alliance Party**. The UMNO remains the dominant partner in the current ruling coalition, the **National Front**, but lost considerable Malay support at the general elections of 1999.

Unfederated Malay States (UMS): Between 1909 and 1914, the states of Johor, Kedah, Perlis, Kelantan and Terengganu became Protectorates but did not join the Federated States.

Yang Dipertuan Agong: king or paramount ruler of Malaysia, a rotating position whereby one of the nine state rulers is elected by his fellows (the Council of Rulers) to serve for a five-year period as constitutional sovereign of Malaysia.

GLOSSARY

Adat   custom and customary law (in contrast to Islamic or *shari'ah* law)

Austroasiatic   in the context of language groups refers to languages of the Southeast Asian mainland such as Mon-Khmer, in contrast to Austronesian languages

Austronesian   in the context of language groups refers to the very large language family which spread through island Southeast Asia over two thousand years ago, and includes Malay

Baba/Nyonya   (also known as *Peranakan Cina*), locally born men and women of Chinese descent (particularly in Penang, Melaka and Singapore) who have adopted some aspects of Malay culture and now have a distinctive cuisine and style of traditional dress

Bajau Laut   sea-based peoples from the southern Philippines and eastern coasts of Sabah

Batin   title of local chief or headman especially in the southern parts of the Malay peninsula and nearby islands

Belacan   pungent paste made from dried and fermented prawns and an essential ingredient in many Malay dishes

Bendahara   the most important position in a traditional Malay kingdom after the ruler. The Bendahara usually controlled the treasury, was closely related to the ruler, and was the ruler's chief adviser

Bumiputera   literally 'Sons of the Soil' and theoretically applies to all indigenous peoples of Malaysia. In political contexts it usually refers to the Malays and the native peoples of Sabah and Sarawak, all of whom are eligible for special affirmative action policies

Candi   small Buddhist or Hindu stone monument

Chettiar   money lender from South India

Dakwah   (from Arabic **da'a**, to call or summon) refers to organised activities to encourage Muslims to intensify their devotion to Islam, also to persuade non-Muslims to convert to Islam

Dato   title bestowed by state and federal governments to recognise outstanding public service

Daulat   the supernatural power of sovereignty which is invested in Malay rulers at the time of their coronation

Derhaka   disloyalty to, or betrayal of, a traditional Malay ruler and still used to describe acts of treachery

Desa   a rural settlement or village

Durbar   an official meeting of Malay rulers and colonial governors (from British India usage)

Entrepôt   a port where goods are assembled, traded and stored for transhipment

Gambier   *uncaria gambir*, a shrub whose leaves and twigs contain tannins used for tanning leather and dyeing

Gunung   mountain (Malay)

Gutta percha   the sap of trees in the *Sapotaceae* family used in medicine, for gum and for insulating electric wires

Hajj   (Arabic *hajj*) to make the pilgrimage to Mecca (one of the five pillars of Islam enjoined on Muslims if they can afford it)

Hijrah   (Hejira, Hegira) the Muslim era based on the year of the flight (*hijrah*) of the Prophet Muhammad from Mecca to Medina in 622 CE

Istana   royal residence or palace (Malay)

Junk   a sea-going vessel originating in China with characteristic high stern, flat base and square sails

Kampung   village; in urban context a quarter or suburb

Kangchu   'river lords', Chinese leaders who were granted contracts to develop land and services (especially along rivers in Johor)

Laksamana   one of the highest officials at a traditional Malay court whose duties included organising and leading the ruler's fleet

Laukeh ('old guest', Chinese), in 19th century usage Chinese labourers who had been working for some time in the Malaysian territories (in contrast to 'sinkeh' or 'new guests')

Madrasah Islamic schools which offer a combination of religious and secular subjects, first established in the Malay territories in the early 20th century to spread modern interpretations of Islam

Malay any inhabitant of the Malaysian territories who meets the Constitutional definition of speaking the Malay language, professing Islam and following Malay customs

Malaya in general refers to the Malay peninsula up to the declaration of Independence in 1957

Malayan the term used to describe Indian and Chinese inhabitants of Malaya before the Federation of Malaysia in 1963 after which all citizens were called 'Malaysians'

Malaysia the Federation of Malaysia formed in 1963

Melaka/Malacca Melaka (Malay) is used in preference to the anglicised form of the place name

Merdeka Independence (Malay)

Mestizo a person of mixed blood

Myanmar Burma

Penghulu district chief or headman (Malay)

Primus inter pares (Latin) first among equals

Pondok 'hut' (Malay) but in context of education refers to traditional-style of Islamic schooling where pupils live in groups of huts near the residence of their religious teacher

Punkahwallah a servant who operates a large ceiling fan (punkah)

Reformasi (from English 'reform') the grassroots movement in Malaysia which demonstrated publicly in Malaysia after the dismissal of Anwar Ibrahim (1998) and demanded reform of public institutions

Shahbandar (harbourmaster, Persian) an official appointed by the ruler of a traditional Malay court to supervise foreign trade. Each foreign community could have its own Shahbandar

Shari'ah   (also Syariah) the revealed or canonical law of Islam

Siamese   see Thai below

Sinkeh   literally 'new guest', referring to Chinese indentured labourers who were brought to the Malaysian territories in large numbers during the 19th century (in contrast to the 'laukeh', see above)

Sungai   river (Malay)

Swidden   method of preparing land for agriculture by felling and then burning overgrowth before planting

Syce   an attendant for horses and also a driver

Temenggung   office at a traditional Malay court, second only to the Bendahara and responsible for the internal security of the kingdom

Thai/Siamese   the word Thai is the preferred name for the people of Thailand whose country was known as Siam before 1939

Tuan   a term of respect for males and formerly for females (Sir, or Lady)

Tuan Besar   Great Lord (Malay), or if a European, the head of an office

Tuan Muda   Junior Lord (Malay)

Tunku   Malay title for male, non-reigning royalty (roughly equivalent to 'prince')

NOTES

Chapter 1   Malaysia as history

1. *Guide to the Museums of Melaka*, 1990s, The Melaka Museums Corporation, *Kompleks Warisan Melaka*, Jalan Kota, 75000 Melaka, Malaysia, n.d.

Chapter 2   Peopling Malaysia

1. Rehman Rashid, *A Malaysian Journey*, 5th printing, Academe Art and Printing Services, Selangor, 1997, p. 14.
2. David Bulbeck, 'Holocene Biological Evolution of the Malay Peninsula Aborigines (*Orang Asli*)', *Perspectives in Human Biology*, vol. 2, 1996, p. 59.
3. Crawford, *History of the Indian Archipelago*, Archibald Constable & Co., Edinburgh, 1820, vol. 1, p. 2.

Chapter 3   Networks of power and exchange

1. O.W. Wolters, 'A few and miscellaneous *pi-chi* jottings on early Indonesia', *Indonesia*, no. 36, 1983, p. 55. The *P'ing-chou K'o-t'an* is an early 12th century historical notebook written by the Chinese scholar Chu Yü.
2. Peter Bellwood, 'Southeast Asia before History', *Cambridge History of Southeast Asia*, vol. 1, part 1, Nicholas Tarling (ed.), Cambridge University Press, Cambridge, 1999, p. 110.
3. Jan Wisseman Christie, 'State formation in early maritime Southeast Asia: a consideration of the data', *Bijdragen tot de taal-, land- en volkenkunde*, 1995, vol. 151, no. 2, p. 247.

4. Cheah Boon Keng, 'Is this what Kedah looked like one thousand years ago?' in *Lembah Bujang Entrepôt Terbilang*, Abdul Manaf bin Saad (ed.), *Persatuan Sejarah Malaysia*, Kedah Branch, 1980, p. 28.
5. Wisseman Christie, 'State formation in early maritime Southeast Asia . . .', p. 269.
6. A.C. Milner, *Kerajaan: Malay Political Culture on the Eve of Colonial Rule*, University of Arizona Press, Tucson, Arizona, 1982, p. 28.
7. A.C. Milner, *Kerajaan . . .*, p. 28.
8. Anthony Diller, 'Sriwijaya and the First Zeros', *JMBRAS*, vol. 68, no. 1, 1995, pp. 53–66.

Chapter 4   Melaka: a traditional Malay kingdom

1. Dr Mahathir Mohamad, *The Way Forward*, Weidenfeld & Nicolson, London, 1998, p. 109.
2. A. Cortesao, *The Suma Oriental of Tome Pires*, Hakluyt Society, London, 1944, vol. II, p. 287.
3. A.C. Milner, 'Islam and the Muslim state', *Islam in Southeast Asia*, MB Hooker (ed.), EJ Brill, Leiden, 1983, p. 44.
4. Leonard Y. Andaya, 'Interaction with the outside world and adaptation in Southeast Asian Society 1500–1800', *Cambridge History of Southeast Asia*, Nicholas Tarling (ed.), Cambridge University Press, Cambridge, 1999, part 1, vol. 2. p. 41.

Chapter 5   Johor and Kedah: contracts and alliances

1. Leonard Y. Andaya, *The Kingdom of Johor: 1641–1728*, Oxford University Press, Kuala Lumpur, 975, p. 326.
2. Jane Drakard, *A Kingdom of Words: Language and Power in Sumatra*, Oxford University Press, Selangor, 1999, p. 49.
3. Drakard, p. 49.

Chapter 6   Pressures for change

1. A.H. Hill, *The Hikayat Abdullah: Abdullah bin Abdul Kadir: An annotated translation*, Oxford University Press, Kuala Lumpur, 1970, p. 310.
2. A.H. Hill, *The Hikayat Abdullah . . .*, p. 159.
3. James Low, 'An account of the origins and progress of the British colonies in the Straits of Malacca', *Journal of the Indian Archipelago and Eastern Asia*, pt. 1, 1850, pp. 110–11.
4. Clive Kessler, *Islam and Politics in a Malay State: Kelantan, 1838–1960*, Cornell University Press, Singapore, 1978, p. 42.

Chapter 7   Responses to colonialism

1. Syed Shaykh al-Hady, 'Menuntut Ketinggian akan Anak-anak Negeri', *al-Imam*, II, (1), 12 July 1907, translated in *The Real Cry of Syed Shaykh al-Hady*, Alijah Gordon (ed.), Malaysian Sociological Research Institute, Kuala, 1999, p. 181.
2. Milton Osborne, *Southeast Asia: an introductory history*, seventh edition, Allen & Unwin, Sydney, 1997, p. 63.
3. C.M. Turnbull, *The Straits Settlements 1826–67: Indian presidency to Crown Colony*, Athlone Press, University of London, 1972, p. 1.
4. Clifford Sather, *The Bajau Laut: adaptation, history and fate in a maritime fishing society of south-eastern Sabah*, Oxford University Press, Kuala Lumpur, 1997, p. 54.
5. Margaret Clark Roff, *The Politics of Belonging: political change in Sabah and Sarawak*, Oxford University Press, Kuala Lumpur, 1974, p. 38.
6. R.H.W. Reece, *The Name of Brooke: the end of White Rajah rule in Sarawak*, Oxford University Press, Kuala Lumpur, 1982, p. 12.
7. Robert Pringle, *Rajahs and Rebels: the Ibans of Sarawak under Brooke rule 1841–1941*, Cornell University Press, Ithaca, 1970, p. 304.

8. Kernial Singh Sandhu, *Indians in Malaya: some aspects of their immigration and settlement 1786–1895*, Cambridge University Press, Cambridge, 1969, p. 139.
9. William R. Roff, *The Origins of Malay Nationalism*, 2nd edn, Oxford University Press, Kuala Lumpur, 1994, p. 37.

Chapter 8   Transition to Independence

1. Tunku Abdul Rahman Putra, *Political Awakening*, Pelanduk Publications, Selangor, 1986, p. 58.
2. Khoo Kay Kim, 'The Great Depression: the Malaysian context', *The History of Southeast Asia, South and East Asia: essays and documents*, Khoo Kay Kim (ed.), Oxford University Press, Kuala Lumpur, pp. 78–94.
3. Chin Kee Onn, *Malay Upside Down*, 3rd edn, Federal Publications, Singapore, 1976, p. 25.
4. T.N. Harper, *The End of Empire and the Making of Malaya*, Cambridge University Press, Cambridge, 1999, p. 35.
5. Cheah Boon Kheng, 'Preface' to Sybil Kathigasu, *No Dram of Mercy*, Oxford University Press, Singapore, 1983, p. vii.
6. J.M. Gullick, 'Prelude to Merdeka: public administration in Malaya, 1945–57', *South-East Asia Research*, vol. 5, (2), July 1997, p. 157.
7. Anthony Short, *The Communist Insurrection in Malaya 1948–1960*, Frederick Muller Ltd, London, 1975, pp. 314–19.
8. Short, *The Communist Insurrection . . .*, p. 443.
9. Dominic Puthucheary and K.S. Jomo (eds), 'No cowardly past: James J. Puthucheary: Writings, poems, commentaries', *INSAN*, Vinlin Press, Kuala Lumpur, 1998, p. 3.
10. Puthucheary and Jomo, 'No cowardly past . . .', p. 7.
11. Puthucheary and Jomo, 'No cowardly past . . .', p. 9.
12. R.K. Vasil, *Politics in a Plural Society: a study of non-communal political parties in west Malaysia*, Oxford University Press, Kuala Lumpur, 1971, p. 80.

13. T.N. Harper, *The End of Empire and the Making of Malaya*, Cambridge University Press, Cambridge, 1999, p. 355.

Chapter 9   Malaysia is born

1. Lee Kuan Yew, quoted in James P. Ongkili, *Nation-building in Malaysia: 1946–1974*, Oxford University Press, Singapore, 1985, p. 159.
2. Quoted in R.H.W. Reece, *The Name of Brooke: the end of White Rajah rule in Sarawak*, Oxford University Press, Kuala Lumpur, 1982, p. 72.
3. Michael B. Leigh, *The Rising Moon: Political Change in Sarawak*, Sydney University Press, Sydney, 1974, p. 40.
4. Leigh, *The Rising Moon*, p. 41.
5. Amarjit Kaur, *Economic Change in East Malaysia: Sabah and Sarawak since 1850*, Macmillan Press and St Martin's Press, London and New York, 1998, p. 170.
6. George Cho, *The Malaysian Economy: spatial perspectives*, Routledge, London, 1990, p. 68.
7. Clive Kessler, *Islam and Politics in a Malay State: Kelantan, 1838–1960*, Cornell University Press, Ithaca, 1978, p. 224.
8. Harold Crouch, *Government and Society in Malaysia*, Allen & Unwin, Sydney, 1996, p. 34.
9. Crouch, *Government and Society in Malaysia*, p. 79.

Chapter 10   Developing new visions

1. Colin Nicholas, *The Orang Asli and the Contest for Resources: indigenous politics, development and identity in peninsular Malaysia*, International Working Group for Indigenous Affairs for Orang Asli Concerns, Copenhagen, 2000, pp. 172–3.
2. Anwar Ibrahim, *The Asian Renaissance*, Times Books International, Singapore, 1996, p. 124.
3. Harold Crouch, *Government and Society in Malaysia*, Allen & Unwin, Sydney, 1996, p. 203.

4. The article was reprinted in Anwar Ibrahim, *The Asian Renaissance*, Time Books, Singapore, 1996, p. 123.

5. Khoo Boo Teik, 'Politics after Mahathir', in Colin Barlow (ed.), *Modern Malaysia in the Global Economy*, Edward Elgar, Cheltenham UK, Northampton MA, 2001, p. 143.

6. Michael Leigh, 'New Realities for Sarawak', in Colin Barlow (ed.), *Modern Malaysia in the Global Economy*, p. 127.

BIBLIOGRAPHIC ESSAY

This brief essay lists sources for the study of Malaysian history and acknowledges the work of specialist authors whose detailed research has provided crucial material for this book. Some of that research is available only in academic journals where it comes to the notice of relatively few readers so it is a privilege to be able to include it in a more general work and thus make it accessible to a broader audience. The essay also highlights sources which extend material presented in each chapter of the book.

Chapter 1   Malaysia as history

The Museums of Malaysia are an exciting way to begin a study of Malaysian history. The National Museum in Kuala Lumpur, Jalan Damansara, 50566 Kuala Lumpur (Fax: 03-2827294) has details of all other museums. The Malaysia Tourism Promotion Board (Tourism Malaysia) has many overseas offices (see also website *http://tourism.gov.my*) and provides useful information about historical sites and tours.

Standard general reference histories for Malaysia are Bellwood (1997) (for prehistory), Andaya and Andaya (2001), and relevant essays in *The Cambridge History of Southeast Asia* (Tarling 1992, 1999). Kaur's *Historical Dictionary* (1993) is a little dated but useful for an overview. Osborne (2001) sets Malaysia in the context of regional history. *The Encyclopedia of Malaysia* (Sham Sani 1998) presents up-to-date research in a number of volumes focusing on a specific subject: Early History, The Environment, Architecture, Plants and so on.

John Gullick has written prolifically on many aspects of Malaysia's history and any of his books are recommended reading for those interested in more detailed information about Malaysia's past. Of particular interest to the traveller is his edited collection of traveller's accounts (1993). There are now many outstanding coffee-table books on Malaysia. One which remains a classic is *Vanishing World: the Ibans of Borneo* (Wright et al. 1972).

Two highly recommended introductions to contemporary Malaysia are the reflective and lively writings of Rehman Rashid (1997) and Karim Raslan (for example, Raslan 1996).

Chapter 2   Peopling Malaysia

Bellwood (1997, 1999) are essential reading for serious studies of Malaysia's prehistory. Benjamin in Benjamin and Chou (2002) provides the most comprehensive account of the socioreligious patterns of the *Orang Asli* and peninsular Malays and is used as the basis for descriptions in this chapter. Sather (1995) and Dentan et al. (1997) are rich sources for further information on the lifestyles and environment of *Orang Asli* groups and sea nomads.

An unusual overview rich with insights into the human occupation of peninsular Malaya is R.D. Hill (1979).

Chapter 3   Networks of power and exchange

The most attractively presented, up-to-date and easy-to-read survey of the complex pre-14th century history of Malaysia is Volume 4 of the *Encyclopedia of Malaysia*, entitled *Early History* (Sham Sani 1998). Its beautifully illustrated essays refer to current theories and debates about Malaysia's distant past and expand on information presented in this chapter. Frank (1998) provides a wide-ranging account of the development of global trade with particular attention to the commercial interaction between East and West.

Benjamin has pioneered an inter-disciplinary approach to early Peninsula history (see Benjamin 1986, 1997). Detailed accounts of local archaeological research include Bellwood and Omar (1980), Bulbeck (1998), Adi (1993), and Nik Hassan Shuhaimi et al. (1993). Wisseman Christie (1995) provides an excellent overview and evaluation of research into the pre-Melakan history of Southeast Asia with particular emphasis on Srivijaya.

Wolters (1967, 1970, 1986) are the basic works for any study of Srivijaya and Diller (1995) establishes the case for the earliest appearance of the graphic representation of the zero with its current function.

Maier (1988) and Milner (1982) use indigenous Malay texts in association with colonial records to describe the nature of traditional Malay authority and its misapprehension by many Europeans. Maier provides extensive material for the early history of Kedah while Milner focuses on other parts of the Peninsula and east Sumatra.

Chapter 4   Melaka: a traditional Malay kingdom

Malay royal courts from the 16th century onwards commissioned their own dynastic records, not all of which have been translated into English. However, two of the best known, *Malay Annals* and *The Precious Gift*, are available and give vivid accounts of the workings and intrigues of traditional Malay court life; see Brown (1970) and Raja Ali Haji ibn Ahmad (1982). A further primary source is the collection of laws originating from the Melaka kingdom which are rich in descriptions of formal and daily life; see Khasnor Johan (1999). Wade (1997) uses Chinese records to establish the nature of early Chinese contact with Melaka.

Detailed analyses of traditional Malay court culture are given in Milner (1982) and Muhammad Yusoff Hashim (1992). Reid (1988, 1993) draws on the earliest European accounts to give a picture of two centuries of indigenous commercial life beginning from the late 15th century. A vivid picture of the slave trade centred in the southern Philippines is given by Warren (1981).

There is a range of writing about the Islamisation of the Malay world. The essays, particularly those of Milner and of Hooker, in M.B. Hooker (1983), although slightly dated, provide a strong introduction. Riddell (2001) is a reliable general survey with an expansive bibliography.

Chapter 5 Johor and Kedah: contracts and alliances

Leonard Andaya's study of 17th century Johor Andaya (1975), brings together indigenous and European accounts of that kingdom and Bonney (1971) is the basic study of Kedah for this period. Drakard (1999) offers new insights into the relationships between Malay rulers and the foreigners who strove to do business with their courts.

Chapter 6 Pressures for change

Published material about local and colonial personalities from the 19th century is relatively plentiful. Extensive bibliographies are included in two recent books about Sir James Brooke and Sir Frank Swettenham respectively (Walker 2002; Barlow 1995). A detailed history of Selangor can be found in Gullick (1998) and an overview of the history and societies of Negeri Sembilan appears in M.B. Hooker (1972).

The basic reference for relations between the local peoples of Sarawak and the Brookes is Pringle (1970), now supplemented by Walker (2002). Detailed information about the Illanun pirates is given in Warren (2001) while Milner (1982) presents a detailed analysis of the internal politics of several of the late 19th century Malay sultanates, particularly that of Pahang. Kessler (1978) is unsurpassed for descriptions of the complex sociopolitical situation in Kelantan from the late 19th century until the 1960s.

Further information about Abdullah bin Abdul Kadir and his contemporaries is given in Carroll (1999) and Milner (1995). The latter has a comprehensive bibliography of other material, particularly written by Malays, from this period. Late 19th century photographs of Singapore and Malaya, with concise notes, are presented in Falconer (1987).

Chapter 7   Responses to colonialism

Roff (1994) and Milner (1995) are key sources and each indicates the breadth of contact between local and colonial societies. Details of Malay responses at both the administrative and social levels are described with engaging examples in Gullick (1992, 1987) while Khasnor (1984) analyses how the British created a class of Malay administrators. Butcher (1979) describes life for the British expatriate communities in Malaya from the late 19th century until the outbreak of World War II.

For the Borneo territories, Pringle (1970), Black (1983) and Clark Roff (1974) provide good background reading. Sather (1997) is a fascinating study of the Bajau peoples of northern Borneo who seized all opportunities to extend their style of maritime commerce. Gullick (2000) is a mine of information on the establishment and growth of

Kuala Lumpur with vignettes of the many individuals who contributed to its development.

A fascinating account of the rise of a Chinese family in both Malaya and southern Thailand is Cushman (1991) and Jackson (1967), who describes the career of Pickering, first Protector of the Chinese. Khoo (1998) provides an overview of immigration patterns while Sandhu (1969) and Ramachandran (1994) focus on Indian settlers in Malaysia. Drabble (1973) describes the origins and early development of the rubber industry.

Details of *Orang Asli* history during this period are found in Dentan et al. (1997) and Nicholas (2000). The development of Johor is covered in Trocki (1979), Sharom Ahmat (1984) is an excellent source for Kedah, while Shaharil Talib (1984) and Sutherland (1978) are recognised as excellent starting points for Terengganu history. A rich selection of material on Syed Shaykh al-Hady has been assembled in Gordon (1999).

Chapter 8   Transition to Independence

An introduction to the expression of Malay opinions about society and politics between the 1920s and 1980s is Virginia Hooker (2000). Harper (1999) gives a very detailed picture of conditions in Malaya during the 1930s and 1940s and Khoo (1977) is also useful for the effects of the Great Depression. Studies of the hardships experienced by Indian and Chinese labouring communities are Ramachandaran (1994) and Loh (1988).

The fall of Singapore and the Japanese occupation of the Malay territories have been described extensively by participants and historians. Kratoska (1998) is one of the most recent and has an extensive bibliography. Chapman (1949) describes the guerrilla movement which operated throughout the occupation but gives little information about the Malay members of Force 136 who also made major contributions to anti-Japanese operations. Reece (1998) provides firsthand accounts of the occupation of the Borneo territories.

Stockwell (1979) provides an excellent basis for understanding the Malayan Union and the reasons for its failure. The 'classic' account of the Communist Emergency is Short (1975), ably supplemented by Cheah (1983). Background to the formation of early political groups is given in Funston (1980), Firdaus Haji Abdullah (1985) and Christie (2001). Means (1970) gives a concise but comprehensive overview of Malaysian politics from 1945 to 1963, written from the perspective of the late 1960s, to which Vasil (1971) is an excellent adjunct.

Further details about individuals described in this chapter are given in Roff (1978) for Abdul Majid, Yeo (1990) for Tan Cheng Lock, Puthucheary and Jomo (1998) for James Puthucheary and Ramakrishna (2000) for C.C. Too.

Chapter 9   Malaysia is born

The final years of Brooke administration are traced in Reece (1982) while Clark Roff (1974) and Leigh (1974) are pathbreaking accounts of political development in Sabah and Sarawak in the 1950s and 60s. A valuable personal memoir of life in Sarawak during the same period is Morrison (1993).

Mackie (1974) is the benchmark account of the 'Confrontation' between Malaysia and Indonesia. The political history of federation is described in Milne and Ratnam (1974) and the stormy relationship between Malaya and Singapore is outlined in Milne and Mauzy (1990) and in more detail in Lau (1998). Ongkili (1972, 1985) describes the early years of federation from the perspective of East Malaysia and Kaur (1998) gives further details about economic development in the two Borneo states, particularly after federation. Tun Jugah's life and achievements are documented in Sutlive (1992).

The political development of Malaysia after Independence is covered by Crouch (1996). Ishak Shari (1994), Cho (1990) and Drabble (2000) describe the effects of economic development.

Kessler (1978) combines local knowledge with astute analysis to describe the success of the Islamic party PAS in Kelantan. An excellent discussion of Islam and Malay politics in general is given in Hussein (1989). Shamsul (1997) considers the relationship between Islamic revivalism and Malay identity particularly during the 1970s and 80s.

Chapter 10   Developing new visions

The most comprehensive information on indigenous peoples in the Malaysian territories is to be found in Nicholas (2000), Dentan et al. (1997), and Benjamin (2002). Hooker (2001) provides the legal reasoning behind recent decisions on claims for native title.

Useful general overviews of Malaysia in the late 1990s and early years of the new millennium, which update material in Crouch (1996), are Funston (2001) and Loh and Khoo Boo Teik (2002). Jomo (2001) presents a careful analysis of the effects of the 1997 financial crisis by a team of regional experts.

Analyses of the contributions and influence of Dr Mahathir to the economic and social transformation of modern Malaysia are Khoo Boo Teik (1995, 2002), and Milne and Mauzy (1999). Shamsul (1997) is still one of the best introductions to the various Islamic groups and their agendas.

A history of the status of women in Malay society is Wazir (1992) and Manderson (1980) analyses the contribution of the women's wing of the UMNO to Malay political life. Maznah Mohamad (2002) provides a wide-ranging survey of women's groups and highlights the relationship between Malaysia's feminist movements and efforts to advance democratisation.

Kaur and Metcalfe (1999) and Barlow (2001) provide a strong selection of articles on all aspects of contemporary Malaysia, including the environment. The chapters by Kaplan in Kaur and Metcalfe, and Michael Leigh in Barlow deserve special attention. Cooke (1999) is a specialist analysis of Malaysia's policies for forest conservation. Two detailed studies of the effects of the NEP on Malaysians are Shamsul (1986) and Sloane (1999). A beautifully presented and well-researched art book on contemporary Malaysian crafts is Barbara Leigh (2000).

There are many excellent websites set up by Malaysians, the majority of which are in English, with up-to-date information about most aspects of contemporary Malaysia.

BIBLIOGRAPHY

List of abbreviations
JMBRAS: Journal of the Malaysian Branch of the Royal Asiatic Society
BKI: Bijdragen tot de taal-, Land- en Volkenkunde van het Koninklijk Instituut
MBRAS: Malaysian Branch Royal Asiatic Society
INSAN: Institute of Social Analysis

Adi Haji Taha. 1993, 'Recent archaelogical discoveries in Peninsular Malaysia (1991–1993)' *JMBRAS* vol. LXVI, no. 1, pp. 67–84

Ammarell, Gene. 1999, *Bugis Navigation*, Southeast Asia Studies Program, no. 48, Yale University Press, New Haven

Andaya, Barbara Watson. 1997, 'Recreating a vision: *Daratan* and *Kepulauan* in historical context' *BKI* vol. 153, no. 4, pp. 483–508

Andaya, Barbara Watson and Andaya, Leonard Y. 2001, *A History of Malaysia* 2nd edn, Palgrave, Basingstoke

Andaya, Leonard Y. 1975, *The Kingdom of Johor 1641–1728*, Oxford University Press, Kuala Lumpur

— 1999, 'Interactions with the outside world and adaptation in Southeast Asian society 1500–1800' in *The Cambridge History of Southeast Asia*, part 1, vol. 2, Nicholas Tarling (ed.), Cambridge University Press, Cambridge

Anwar Ibrahim. 1996, *The Asian Renaissance*, Times Books International, Singapore

Barlow, Colin (ed.). 2001, *Modern Malaysia in the Global Economy: Political and Social Change into the 21st Century*, Edward Elgar, Cheltenham, UK, Northanmpton, MA USA

Barlow, H.S. 1995, *Swettenham*, Southdene Sdn Bhd, Kuala Lumpur

Bedlington, Stanley S. 1978, *Malaysia and Singapore: The Building of New States*, Ithaca, New York

Bellwood, Peter. 1992, 1999, 'Southeast Asia before history' in *The Cambridge History of Southeast Asia*, part 2, vol. 1, Nicholas Tarling (ed.), Cambridge University Press, Cambridge

— 1997, *The Prehistory of the Indo-Malaysian Archipelago*, revised edn, University of Hawaii Press, Honolulu

Bellwood, Peter and Matussin Omar. 1980, 'Trade patterns and political developments in Brunei and adjacent areas, AD 700–1500' *Brunei Museum Journal*, vol. 4, no. 4, pp. 155–179

Benjamin, Geoffrey. 1985, 'In the long term: three themes in Malayan cultural ecology', *Cultural Values and Human Ecology in Southeast Asia*. Karl L. Hutterer, A. Terry Rambo and George Lovelace (eds), Ann Arbor, MI, Center for South and Southeast Asian Studies, University of Michigan

Benjamin, Geoffrey. 1986, 'Between isthmus and islands: reflections on Malayan palaeo-sociology' Working Paper no. 71, Department of Sociology, National University of Singapore

— 1997, 'Issues in the ethnohistory of Pahang', in *Pembangunan Arkeologi Pelancongan Negeri Pahang*, Nik Hassan Shuhaimi et al. (eds), Muzium Pahang, Pekan, pp. 82–121

Benjamin, Geoffrey & Cynthia Chou (eds). 2002, *Tribal Communities in the Malay World: Historical, Social and Cultural Perspectives*, Curzon Press for IIAS, London, ISEAS, Singapore

Black, Ian. 1983, *A Gambling Style of Government: The Establishment of the Chartered Rule in Sabah, 1878–1915*, Oxford University Press, Kuala Lumpur

Bonney, R. 1971, *Kedah 1771–1821: The Search for Security and Independence*, Oxford University Press, Kuala Lumpur

Brown, C.C. 1970, *Sejarah Melayu, or Malay Annals*, Oxford University Press, Kuala Lumpur

Bulbeck, David, 1996. 'Holocene biological evolution of the Malay Peninsula Aborigines (*Orang Asli*)' *Perspectives in Human Biology*, vol. 2, pp. 37–61

Bulbeck, David. 1998, 'Origins of civilisation in West Malaysia and the Orang Asli' *Jurnal Arkeologi Malaysia*, vol. 2, pp. 95–9

Butcher, John G. 1979, *The British in Malaya 1880–1941: The Social History of a European Community in Colonial South-East Asia*, Oxford University Press, Kuala Lumpur

Carroll, Diana. 1999, 'The contribution of the Malacca missionaries and the Hikayat Abdullah to the birth of a Malay concept of Malay studies' in *Malaysian Studies I: Rethinking Malaysia*, Jomo K.S. (ed.), Malaysian Social Science Association, Asia 2000 Ltd, Hong Kong

Chapman, F. Spencer. 1949, *The Jungle is Neutral*, Chatto and Windu, London

Cheah Boon Kheng. 1980, 'Is this what Kedah looked like one thousand years ago?' in *Lembah Bujang Entrepôt Kedah Terbilang*, Abdul Manaf bin Saad (ed.), Persatuan Sejarah Malaysia, Kedah Branch

— 1983, *Red Star Over Malaya: Resistance and Social Conflict During and After the Japanese Occupation, 1941–1946*, Singapore University Press, Singapore

Chin Kee Onn. 1976, *Malay Upside Down*, 3rd edition, Federal Publications, Singapore

Cho, George. 1990, *The Malaysian Economy: Spatial Perspectives*, Routledge, London, New York

Christie, Clive J. 2001, *Ideology and Revolution in Southeast Asia: Political Ideas of the Anti-Colonial Era, 1900–1980*, Curzon Press, Richmond, Surrey

Cooke, Fadzilah Majid. 1999, *The Challenge of Sustainable Forests: Forest Resource Policy in Malaysia, 1970–1995*, Allen & Unwin, University of Hawai'i Press, Sydney and Hawai'i

Coope, A.E. (trans.). 1967, *The Voyage of Abdullah, Kesah Pelayaran Abdullah*, Oxford University Press, Kuala Lumpur

Cortesao, A. 1944, *The Suma Oriental of Tome Pires*, 2 volumes, Hakluyt Society, London

Crawfurd, John. 1820, *History of the Indian Archipelago*, Archibald Constable and Co., Edinburgh, 3 vols

Crisswell, Colin N. 1978. *Rajah Charles Brooke: Monarch of All He Surveyed*, Oxford University Press, Kuala Lumpur

Crouch, Harold. 1996, *Government and Society in Malaysia*, Cornell University Press, Allen & Unwin, Sydney

Cushman, Jennifer W. (ed. Craig J. Reynolds). 1991, *Family and State: The Formation of a Sino-Thai Tin-mining Dynasty 1797–1932*, Oxford University Press, Singapore

Dentan, Robert Knox, Endicott, Kirk, Gomes, Alberto G., Hooker, M.B. 1997, *Malaysia and the 'Original People': A Case Study of the Impact of Development on Indigenous Peoples*, Allyn and Bacon, Boston

Dentan, Robert Knox. 2000, 'Ceremonies of innocence and the lineaments of ungratified desire: an analysis of a syncretic Southeast Asian taboo complex' *BKI*, vol. 156, part 2, pp. 193–232

Diller, Anthony. 1995, 'Sriwijaya and the first zeros' *JMBRAS*, vol. 68, no. 1, pp. 53–66

Drabble, John H. 1973, *Rubber in Malaya 1876–1922: The Genesis of the Industry*, Oxford University Press, Kuala Lumpur

— 2000, *An Economic History of Malaysia, c.1800–1990; the Transition to Modern Economic Growth*, Macmillan Press Ltd, Great Britain, St Martin's Press, LLC, USA

Drakard, Jane. 1999, *A Kingdom of Words: Language and Power in Sumatra*, Oxford University Press, Selangor

Endicott, K.1983, 'The effects of slave raiding on the Aborigines of the Malay Peninsula', in *Slavery, Bondage and Dependency in Southeast Asia*, (ed.) Anthony Reid, University of Queensland Press, St Lucia

Falconer, John. 1987, *A Vision of the Past: A History of Early Photography in Singapore and Malaya, The photographs of G.R. Lambert & Co., 1880–1910*, Times Editions, Singapore

Firdaus Haji Abdullah. 1985, *Radical Malay Politics: Its Origins and Early Development*, Pelanduk Publications, Petaling Jaya

Frank, Andre Gunder. 1998, *ReOrient: Global Economy in the Asian Age*, University of California Press, Berkeley/Los Angeles/London

Funston, NJ. 1975, 'Writings on May 13', *Akademika 6*

— 1980, *Malay Politics in Malaysia: A Study of the United Malays National Organisation and Party Islam*, Heinemann, Kuala Lumpur

— 2001, 'Malaysia developmental state challenged', in *Government and Politics in Southeast Asia*, John Funston (ed.), ISEAS, Singapore, Zed Books Ltd, London

Gagliano, F.V. 1970, *Communal Violence in Malaysia 1969: The Political Aftermath*, Ohio University Centre for International Studies, Athens, Ohio

Goh Cheng Teik. 1971, *The May Thirteenth Incident and Democracy in Malaysia*, Oxford University Press, Kuala Lumpur

Gordon, Alijah (ed.). 1999, *The Real Cry of Syed Shaykh al-Hady*, Malaysian Sociological Reseach Institute, Kuala Lumpur

Gullick, J.M. 1987, *Malay Society in the Late Nineteenth Century: The Beginnings of Change*, Oxford University Press, Singapore

— 1992, *Rulers and Residents: Influence and Power in the Malay States, 1870–1920*, Oxford University Press, Singapore

— 1993, *They Came to Malaya: A Traveller's Anthology*, compiled by J.M. Gullick, Oxford University Press, Singapore

— 1997, 'Prelude to Merdeka: public administration in Malaya, 1945–57', *South-East Asia Research*, vol 5, no. 2, July

— 1998, *A History of Selangor (1766–1939)*, MBRAS Monograph, no. 28, Vinlin Press, Kuala Lumpur

— 2000, *A History of Kuala Lumpur (1856–1939)*, MBRAS Monograph no. 29, Academe Art & Printing Services Sdn. Bhd., Selangor

Harper, T.N. 1999, *The End of Empire and the Making of Malaya*, Cambridge University Press, Cambridge

Hill, A.H. 1970, *The Hikayat Abdullah: Abdullah bin Abdul Kadir: An Annotated Translation*, Oxford University Press, Kuala Lumpur

Hill, R.D. 1977, *Rice in Malaya: A Study in Historical Geography*, Oxford University Press, Kuala Lumpur

Hooker, M.B. 1972, *Adat Laws in Modern Malaya: Land Tenure, Traditional Government and Religion*, Oxford University Press, Kuala Lumpur

— (ed.). 1983, *Islam in South-east Asia*, Brill, Leiden

— 1983, 'The Translation of Islam into South-east Asia', in *Islam in Southeast Asia*, M.B. Hooker (ed.), Brill, Leiden

— 2001, '"Native Title" in Malaysia: Adong's Case' *The Australian Journal of Asian Law*, vol. 3

Hooker, M.B. and Villiers, John. 1988, 'The laws of Portugal and Spain', in *The Laws of Southeast Asia*, vol. II, M.B. Hooker (ed.), Butterworth and Co., Singapore, pp. 27–142

Hooker, Virginia Matheson. 2000, *Writing a New Society: Social Change Through the Novel in Malay*, Allen & Unwin, Sydney

Hussein Mutalib. 1989, *Islam and Ethnicity in Malay Politics*, Oxford University Press, Singapore

Ishak Shari. 1994, 'Rural development and rural poverty in Malaysia: the experience during the New Economic Policy (1971–1990) Period', in *Poverty Amidst Plenty: Research Findings and the Gender Dimension in Malaysia*, Jamilah Ariffin (ed.), Pelanduk, Petaling Jaya

Jackson, R.N. 1967, 'Grasping the nettle: first successes in the struggle to govern the Chinese in Malaya' *JMBRAS*, vol. 40, Part 1

Jomo, K.S.(ed.). 2001, *Malaysian Eclipse: Economic Crisis and Recovery*, Zed Books Ltd, London & New York

Kahn, Joel S. and Francis Loh Kok Wah (eds). 1992, *Fragmented Vision: Culture and Politics in Contemporary Malaysia*, Allen & Unwin, Sydney

Kathigasu, Sybil. 1983, *No Dram of Mercy*, Oxford University Press, Singapore

Kathirithamby-Wells, J. and Villiers, John (eds). 1990, *The Southeast Asian Port and Polity: Rise and Demise*, Singapore University Press, Singapore

Kaur, Amarjit. 1998, *Economic Change in East Malaysia: Sabah and Sarawak since 1850*, Macmillan Press and St Martin's Press, London and New York

Kaur, Amarjit. 1993, *Historical Dictionary of Malaysia*, Scarecrow Press, New Jersey

Kaur, Amarjit and Metcalfe, Ian (eds). 1999, *The Shaping of Malaysia*, Macmillan Press and St Martin's Press, London and New York

Kessler, Clive. 1978, *Islam and Politics in a Malay State: Kelantan, 1838–1960*, Cornell University Press, Ithaca

Khasnor Johan. 1984, *The Emergence of the Modern Malay Aministrative Elite*, Oxford University Press, Singapore

— 1999, 'The Undang-Undang Melaka: reflections on Malay society in fifteenth century Melaka' *JMBRAS*, vol. LXXII, no. 2

Khoo Boo Teik. 1995, *Paradoxes of Mahathirism: An Intellectual Biography of Mahathir Mohamad*, Oxford University Press, Kuala Lumpur and New York

— 2001, 'Politics after Mahathir', in *Modern Malaysia in the Global Economy: Political and Social Change into the 21st Century*, Colin Barlow (ed.), Edward Elgar, Cheltenham UK, Northampton MA

Khoo Kay Kim. 1977, 'The Great Depression: The Malaysian Context' *The History of Southeast, South and East Asia: Essays and Documents*, Khoo Kay Kim (ed.), Oxford University Press, Kuala Lumpur, pp. 78–94

— 1998, 'Malaysian Immigration' *JMBRAS*, vol. LXX1, no.1, pp.1–26

Kratoska, Paul H. 1998, *The Japanese Occupation of Malaya: A Social and Economic History*, Hurst and Co., London

Lau, Albert. 1998, *A Moment of Anguish: Singapore in Malaysia and the Politics of Disengagement*, Times Academic Press, Singapore

Leigh, Michael B. 1974, *The Rising Moon: Political Change in Sarawak*, Sydney University Press, Sydney

— 2001, 'The new realities for Sarawak', in *Modern Malaysia in the Global Economy: Political and Social Change into the 21st Century*, Colin Barlow (ed.), Edward Elgar, Cheltenham UK, Northampton MA

Leigh, Barbara. 2000, *The Changing Face of Malaysian Crafts: Identity, Industry, and Ingenuity*, Oxford University Press, Selangor Darul Ehsan, Malaysia

Leong Sau Heng. 1993, 'Ancient trading centres in the Malay Peninsula' *Jurnal Arkeologi Malaysia*, 6, pp. 1–9

Lewis, Diane. 1995, *Jan Campagnie in the Straits of Malacca 1641–1795*, Ohio University Centre for International Studies, Athens, Ohio

Leyden, John. 2001, *John Leyden's Malay Annals, With An Introductory Essay by Virginia Matheson Hooker and M.B. Hooker*, MBRAS, Reprint 20, Academe Art and Printing, Selangor

Loh, Kok Wah Francis. 1988, *Beyond the Tin Mines: Coolies, Squatters and the New Villages in the Kinta Valley, Malaysia, c.1880–1980*, Oxford University Press, Singapore

— 1992, 'Modernisation, cultural revival and counter-hegemony: the Kadazans of Sabah in the 1980s', in *Fragmented Vision*, Kahn and Loh Kok Wah (eds).

Loh, Kok Wah Francis & Khoo Boo Teik (eds). 2002, *Democracy in Malaysia: Discourses and Practices*, Nordic Institute of Asian Studies Democracy in Asia Series, Curzon Press, Richmond, Surrey

Low, James. 1850, 'An account of the origins and progress of the British colonies in the Straits of Malacca' *Journal of the Indian Archipelago and Eastern Asia*, vol. IV, pt 1, pp. 106–18.

Mackie, J.A.C. 1974, *Konfrontasi: The Indonesia Malaysia Dispute 1963–1966*, for the Australian Institute of International Affairs, Oxford University Press, Kuala Lumpur

Mahathir Mohammad. 1970, *The Malay Dilemma*, Donald Moore, Singapore

— 1986, *The Challenge*, Pelanduk Publications, Petaling Jaya

— 1998, *The Way Forward*, Weidenfeld and Nicolson, London

Maier, Hendrik M.J. 1988, *In the Centre of Authority: The Malay Hikayat Merong Mahawangsa*, Southeast Asia Program, Cornell University, Ithaca and New York

Manderson, Lenore. 1980, *Women, Politics, and Change: The Kaum Ibu UMNO, Malaysia, 1945–1972*, Oxford University Press, Kuala Lumpur

Manguin, P. 1993, 'Palembang and Sriwijaya: an early Malay harbour-city revisited' *JMBRAS* vol. 66, no. 1

Maznah Mohamad. 2002, 'At the centre and the periphery: the contribution of women's movements to democratization', in *Democracy in Malaysia*, Loh and Khoo (eds), 2002

Means, Gordon P. 1970, *Malaysian Politics*, University of London Press Ltd, London

— 1991, *Malaysian Politics: The Second Generation*, Oxford University Press, Singapore

Milne, R.S. and Mauzy, Diane K. 1990, *Singapore: The Legacy of Lee Kuan Yew*, Westview Press, Boulder, San Francisco and Oxford

— 1999, *Malaysian Politics under Mahathir*, Routledge, London and New York

Milne, R.S. and Ratnam, K.J. 1974, *Malaysia: New States in a New Nation: The Political Development of Sarawak and Sabah in Malaysia*, Frank Cass and Co., London and Oregon

Milner, A.C. 1982, *Kerajaan: Malay Political Culture on the Eve of Colonial Rule*, University of Arizona Press, Tucson, Arizona

— 1983, 'Islam and the Muslim State' *Islam in Southeast Asia*, M.B. Hooker (ed.), E.J. Brill, Leiden

— 1992, '"Malayness" Confrontation, innovation and discourse', in V.J.H. Houben, H.M.J. Maier and W. van der Molen (eds), *Looking in Odd Mirrors: The Java Sea*, Rijksuniversiteit, Leiden, pp. 43–59

— 1995, *The Invention of Politics in Colonial Malay: Contesting Nationalism and the Expansion of the Public Sphere*, Cambridge University Press, Cambridge

Morrison, Alastair. 1993, *Fair Land Sarawak: Some Recollections of an Expatriate Official*, Studies on Southeast Asia, no. 13, Southeast Asia Program, Cornell

Muhammad Yusoff Hashim. 1992, *The Malay Sultanate of Malacca*, Dewan Bahasa dan Pustaka, Kuala Lumpur

Nicholas, Colin. 2000, *The Orang Asli and the Contest for Resources: Indigenous Politics, Development and Identity in Peninsular Malaysia*, International Working Group for Indigenous Affairs and Centre for Orang Asli Concerns, Copenhagen

Nik Hassan Shuhaimi bin Nik Abdul Rahman and Kammaruddin bin Zakaria. 1993, 'Recent Archaeological Discoveries in Sungai Mas, Kuala Muda, Kedah' *JMBRAS*, vol. LXVI, part 2

Nonini, Donald M. 1992, *British Colonial Rule and the Resistance of the Malay Peasantry,1900–1957*, Monograph Series 38, Yale Center for International and Area Studies, Yale University Southeast Asia Studies, New Haven

Ongkili, James P. 1972, *Modernisation in East Malaysia 1960–1970*, Oxford University Press, Kuala Lumpur

— 1985, *Nation-Building in Malaysia 1946–1974*, Oxford University Press, Singapore

Osborne, Milton. 2001, *Southeast Asia: An Introductory History*, eighth edition, Allen & Unwin, Sydney

Pringle, Robert. 1970, *Rajahs and Rebels: The Ibans of Sarawak under Brooke Rule 1841–1941*, Cornell University Press, Ithaca

Proudfoot, Ian and Hooker, Virginia. 1996, 'Mediating time and space: the Malay writing tradition', in *Illuminations*, Ann Kumar and John H. McGlynn (eds), Weatherhill Inc., New York and Tokyo

Puthucheary, Dominic and Jomo K.S. (eds). 1998, *No Cowardly Past: James J. Puthucheary: Writings, Poems, Commentaries*, INSAN, Vinlin Press, Kuala Lumpur

Raja Ali Haji ibn Ahmad. 1982, *The Precious Gift: Tuhfat al-Nafis*, annotated translation by Virginia Matheson and Barbara Watson Andaya, Oxford University Press, Kuala Lumpur

Ramachandran, Selvakumaran. 1994, *Indian Plantation Labour in Malaysia*, S. Abdul Majeed & Co., Kuala Lumpur

Ramakrishna, Kumar. 2000, 'The making of a Malayan propagandist: the Communists, the British and C.C. Too' *JMBRAS*, vol. 73, no. 1

Rashid, Rehman. 1997, *A Malaysian Journey*, 5th Printing, Academe Art and Printing Services, Selangor

Raslan, Karim. 1996. *Ceritalah: Malaysia in Transition*, Times books International, Singapore, Kuala Lumpur

Reece, R.H.W. 1982, *The Name of Brooke: The End of White Rajah Rule in Sarawak*, Oxford University Press, Kuala Lumpur

— 1998, *Masa Jepun: Sarawak Under the Japanese 1941–1945*, Sarawak Literary Society, Ampang Press, Kuala Lumpur

Reid, Anthony. 1988, *Southeast Asia in the Age of Commerce 1450–1680: The Lands Below the Winds*, vol. 1, Yale University Press, New Haven and London

— 1993, *Southeast Asia in the Age of Commerce 1450–1680: Expansion and Crisis*, vol. 2, Yale University Press, New Haven and London

Riddell, Peter G. 2001, *Islam and the Malay-Indonesian World: Transmission and Responses*, Hurst & Company, London

Roff, Margaret Clark. 1974, *The Politics of Belonging: Political Change in Sabah and Sarawak*, Oxford University Press, Kuala Lumpur

Roff, William R. 1970, 'Southeast Asian Islam in the nineteenth century', in *The Cambridge History of Islam*, P.M. Holt et al. (ed.), vol. 2, Cambridge University Press, Cambridge, pp. 155–81

— 1978, *The Wandering Thoughts of a Dying Man: The Life and Times of Haji Abdul Majid Bin Zainuddin*, Oxford University Press, Kuala Lumpur

— 1994. *The Origins of Malay Nationalism* 2nd edn, Oxford University Press, Kuala Lumpur

Sadka, Emily. 1968, *The Protected Malay States 1874–1895*, University of Malaya Press, Kuala Lumpur and Singapore

Sandhu, Kernial Singh. 1969, *Indians in Malaya: Some Aspects of Their Immigration and Settlement 1786–1957*, Cambridge University Press, Cambridge

Sandhu, Kernial Singh and Wheatley, Paul (eds). 1983, *Melaka: The Transformation of a Malay Capital c.1400–1980*, Oxford University Press, Kuala Lumpur

Sather, Clifford. 1995, 'Sea nomads and rainforest hunter-gatherers: foraging adaptations in the Indo-Malaysian Archipelago', in *The Austronesians: Historical and Comparative Perspectives*, Peter Bellwood, James J. Fox and Darrell Tryon (eds), Department of Anthropology, Research School of Pacific and Asian Studies, Australian National University, Canberra, pp. 229–68

— 1997, *The Bajau Laut, Adaptation, History, and Fate in a Maritime Fishing Society of South-eastern Sabah*, Oxford University Press, Kuala Lumpur

— 1999, *The Orang Laut*, Academy of Social Sciences, Universiti Sains Malaysia, Occasional Paper No. 5 in cooperation with the Royal Netherlands Government

Searle, Peter. 1983, *Politics in Sarawak 1970–1976: The Iban Perspective*, Oxford University Press, Kuala Lumpur

— 1999, *The Riddle of Malaysian Capitalism: Rent Seekers or Real Capitalists?*, Allen & Unwin, Sydney

Sham Sani. 1998, *The Encyclopedia of Malaysia*, 5 vols, Archipelago Press, Singapore

Shaharil Talib. 1984, *After its Own Image: The Terengganu Experience 1881–1941*, Oxford University Press, Singapore

— 1995, *History of Kelantan*, MBRAS, Monograph No. 21, Kuala Lumpur

Shamsul A.B. 1988, *From British to Bumiputera Rule: Local Politics and Rural Development in Peninsular Malaysia*, Institute of Southeast Asian Studies, Singapore

— 1997, 'Identity construction, nation formation and Islamic revivalism in Malaysia', in *Islam in an Era of Nation States*, Robert W. Hefner and Patricia Horvatich (eds), University of Hawai'i Press, Honolulu

Sharom Ahmat. 1984, *Tradition and Change in a Malay State: A Study of the Economic and Political Development of Kedah 1878–1923*, MBRAS, Monograph No. 12, Art Printing Works, Kuala Lumpur

Short, Anthony. 1975, *The Communist Insurrection in Malaya 1948–1960*, Frederick Muller Ltd, London

Skinner, C. 1964, 'A Kedah letter of 1839', in *Malayan and Indonesian Studies*, John Bastin and R. Roolvink (eds), Clarendon Press, Oxford, pp. 156–65

— 1966, 'Abdullah's voyage to the East Coast, seen through contemporary eyes' *JMBRAS*, vol. 39, pt 2, pp. 23–32

Sloane, Patricia. 1999, *Islam, Modernity and Entrepreneurship Among the Malays*, Macmillan Press, Basingstoke and London

Southeast Asian Affairs 2001, ISEAS, Singapore

Sponsel, Leslie E. (ed.). 2000, *Endangered Peoples of Southeast Asia: Struggles to Survive and Thrive*, The Greenwood Press, Westport, Connecticut, London

Stenson, Michael. 1980, *Class, Race and Colonialism in West Malaysia: The Indian Case*, University of British Columbia Press, Vancouver

Stockwell, A.J. 1979, *British Policy and Malay Politics During the Malayan Union Experiment 1945–1948*, MBRAS, Monograph no. 8, Art Printing Works, Kuala Lumpur

Sullivan, Anwar and Cecilia Leong (eds). 1981, *A Commemorative History of Sabah 1881–1981*, Sabah State Government Centenary Publications Committee, Nanyang Muda Sdn. Bhd., Kuala Lumpur

Sutherland, Heather. 1978, 'The taming of the Terengganu elite', in *Southeast Asian Transitions: Approaches Through Social History*, Ruth T. McVey (ed.), Yale University Press, New Haven and London

Sutlive, Vinson H, Jr. 1992, *Tun Jugah of Sarawak: Colonialism and the Iban Response*, Sarawak Literary Society and Penerbit Fajar Bakti, Kuala Lumpur

Tarling, Nicholas. 1992, 1999. *The Cambridge History of Southeast Asia*, two volumes, Cambridge University Press, Cambridge

Trocki, Carl. 1979, *Prince of Pirates: The Temenggongs and the Development of Johor and Singapore 1784–1885*, Singapore University Press, Singapore

Tunku Abdul Rahman Putra. 1986, *Political Awakening*, Pelanduk Publications, Selangor

Turnbull, C.M. 1972, *The Straits Settlements 1826–67: Indian Presidency to Crown Colony*, The Athlone Press, University of London

— 1989, *A History of Malaysia, Singapore and Brunei* revised edn., Allen and Unwin, Sydney

Vasil, R.K. 1971, *Politics in a Plural Society: A Study of Non-Communal Political Parties in West Malaysia*, Oxford University Press, Kuala Lumpur

Wade, Geoff. 1997, 'Melaka in Ming Dynasty texts' *JMBRAS*, vol. LXX, no. 1 pp. 31–70

Walker, J.H. 2002, *Power and Prowess: The Origins of Brooke Kingship in Sarawak*, Allen & Unwin, Sydney

Warren, James Francis. 1981, *The Sulu Zone 1768–1898: The Dynamics of External Trade, Slavery and Ethnicity in the Transformation of a Southeast Asian Maritime State*, Singapore University Press, Singapore

— 2001, 'Savagism and civilisation: the Iranun, globalisation and the literature of Joseph Conrad' *JMBRAS*, vol. 74, no. 1, pp. 43–69

Wazir Jahan Karim. 1992, *Women and Culture: Between Malay Adat and Islam*, Westview, Boulder CO

Wisseman Christie, 1995, 'State formation in early maritime Southeast Asia: a Consideration of the theories and the data' *BKI* vol. 151, no. 2, January

Wolters, O.W. 1951, 'Emerging resettlement and community development in Malaya' *Community Development Bulletin*, vol. III, no. 1, January

— 1967, *Early Indonesian Commerce: A Study of the Origins of Srivijaya*, Ithaca and New York

— 1970, *The Fall of Sriwijaya in Malay History*, Oxford University Press, Kuala Lumpur

— 1983, 'A few miscellaneous *pi-chi* jottings on early Indonesia' *Indonesia 36*, October

— 1986, 'Restudying some Chinese writings on Sriwijaya' *Indonesia* no. 42, October, pp. 1–41

— 1999, *History, Culture and Region in Southeast Asian Perspectives* rev. edn., Southeast Asia Program Publications, Cornell University in cooperation with the Institute of Southeast Asian Studies, Singapore

Wrigglesworth, Dato' H.L. (Mike). 1991, *The Japanese Invasion of Kelantan in 1941*, Academe Art & Printing Services Sdn. Bhd., Kuala Lumpur

Wright, Leigh, Morrison, Hedda and K.F. Wong. 1972, *Vanishing World: The Ibans of Borneo*, Weatherhill, New York, Tokyo and Hong Kong

Yeo Siew Siang. 1990, *Tan Cheng Lock: The Straits Legislator and Chinese Leader*, Pelanduk Publications, Petaling Jaya

Zainah Anwar. 1987, *Islamic Revivalism in Malaysia: Dakwah Among the Students*, Pelanduk Publications, Selangor

INDEX